Preaching

FRED B. CRADDOCK

Abingdon Press

Nashville

PREACHING

Copyright © 1985 by Abingdon Press
Thirteenth Printing 1992
All rights reserved.

This book is printed on recycled acid-free paper

Library of Congress Cataloging in Publication Data

CRADDOCK, FRED B.
  Preaching.
  Bibliography: p.
  1. Preaching. I. Title.
BV4211.2.C755   1985   251   85-3606

ISBN 0-687-33648-1
Formerly published under
ISBN 0-687-33636-8

MANUFACTURED IN THE UNITED STATES OF AMERICA

Preface

Since I first began writing in the area of preaching, with the publication of *As One Without Authority* in 1971, colleagues, pastors, and seminarians have encouraged me to write a textbook. I took that to mean a book that would walk the reader through the process of preaching, from the selection of a text to the delivery of a sermon.

This volume is a response to that encouragement. Although the writing was done in a cottage in the Blue Ridge Mountains of North Georgia, I was never far from my students. By "my students" I refer to the seminarians and parish ministers who have joined me through the years in the study of the disciplines of preaching. Each morning as I sat down to write I tried to fix them in my mind, to see their faces, anticipating questions, listening to suggested alternative methods, responding to voices mellow with experience and voices quaking with the anxiety with which one approaches the pulpit for the first time.

To all those with whom I have studied and taught I am indebted. I wish also to acknowledge my respect and gratitude for all those who through book and lecture have stimulated me, especially those who remained faithful to the task during those years when the pulpit wandered through dry and waterless places.

I wish also to take this occasion to thank Dean Jim Waits of Candler School of Theology for granting me a leave from teaching duties in order to write and to Janet Gary for typing the manuscript while guarding the door of my needed privacy.

FRED B. CRADDOCK
Candler School of Theology
Emory University

Contents

PART I
Preaching: An Overview

PART II
Preaching: Having Something to Say

PART III
Preaching: Shaping the Message into a Sermon

PART I

Preaching: An Overview

_____ *one* _____

Introduction

Purpose and Format

This volume is offered to the reader as a textbook in preaching. In the opinion of some observers, such a work comes too late because the day of textbooks is now past, in this and every other discipline. This judgment is supported in part by the now familiar argument that knowledge explosions render textbooks obsolete upon publication. More particularly in the case of preaching, however, it has been contended that no useful textbook can be written as long as the field of communication remains in a state of flux due to experimentation with new technology. But these observations speak just as persuasively that a textbook in preaching would at the present be too soon rather than too late. Such a conclusion is not without support. After a generation of walking alone, the object of general ridicule and preoccupied in self-flagellation, preaching is again making new friends among other disciplines and renewing old acquaintances with biblical studies, literary criticism, and communication theory. The consumer posture is being abandoned and the discipline is again a producer. It is a fruitful time. Articles, essays, dissertations, and books on preaching and directly related subjects constitute a very respectable bibliography. Maybe this germinal time should not be interrupted with attempts to freeze the products in a textbook. Maybe textbooks should wait until the fruit has ripened fully and has been culled by more critical reflection and debate. This line of thought makes some kind of sense.

However, the teaching and learning of preaching goes on, in

season and out of season. Tools to aid the process need continually to be devised, shaped not only by the new ideas refreshing the discipline, but also by the capacities and sensibilities of preachers who are themselves products of a culture sending and receiving messages in new ways. But let us not be uncritically enamored of the new. Some older volumes on preaching could profitably be reissued, not as a sentimental return to old paths but as a confession that part of the malaise in the discipline is due not to a stubborn refusal to move beyond tradition but to a thoughtless failure to listen carefully to that tradition. One becomes a concert pianist not by abandoning the scales but by mastering and repeating that most basic exercise. Who could say, after all the centuries, that reading Aristotle's *Rhetoric* and *Poetics* or Augustine's instructions on preaching is no longer of benefit to the preacher? There are fundamentals to good writing and speaking and preaching that abide, and it is the burden of a textbook to gather and to offer these, *especially* in a time of fascination with experimentation. Granted, textbooks in this or any other field will not likely enjoy the long life as have some in the past, but length of life is not decided by anyone in particular, certainly not the writer. In fact, a book designed to serve the discipline for years to come would probably serve poorly in the present.

This volume, then, is offered as a textbook in preaching to those for whom all our research and writing is done: those who preach. It is the regular preaching in and by the church that determines finally whether homileticians are vindicated in their work or whether they have only been engaged in intramurals with colleagues.

To say that a volume is designed as a text is to say something about the readers for whom it is intended and the format in which its contents are arranged. As for intended readers, they are the men and women for whom preaching is or will be a regular responsibility in ministry. They are those who have the grace and courage to be vulnerable enough to listen, to discover, to improve. Some are in seminary; others are involved in continuing education, privately or in a structured program. Of course, the seminarian and the practicing preacher bring to their study two very different perspectives: one is in rehearsal while the other is reflecting upon experience. There is no need to debate here which is the better teaching moment; both have advantages and disadvantages as is the case in any class of students some of whom already are preaching and some of whom are not. Where experience is lacking, openness to entertaining various approaches is not. Where experience is not lacking, its advantage is often shortened by a tendency to protect and defend one's repertoire of methods and messages.

The question is, Can one's text serve both groups? The answer is yes, if two conditions are met. In the first place, the pedagogical approach must be based on recognition rather than recall. Most of us have extremely poor recall but superb powers of recognition. Learning by recognition is simply being enabled to see how much we already know about a subject which we did not know we knew and about which we had no clear terms or categories. Those taking their initial course work in preaching can be taught by this method; it is not reserved solely for those in refresher courses who recognize material covered in seminary. A child first entering the world of grammar or mathematics can learn effectively by recognition. In fact, the recognition of what one already knows is so liberating and such a builder of confidence that one's appetite and capacity for that portion of learning that demands recall is usually increased sharply. On the other hand, when the primary pedagogical approach is based on recall of names, terms, vocabulary, dates, and places, one feels ignorant and overwhelmed, not to mention confused by a mass of information with questionable bearing upon the task at hand, learning to preach effectively. Needless to say, this book seeks to make maximum use of recognition as the primary path to learning.

Second, one book can serve both the preacher and the preacher-to-be if the format provides the reader with both a clear walk through the entire process of sermon preparation and delivery and clear markers along the way for the benefit of those who might wish to review or refresh themselves on one particular phase of the process. The structure of this book is an attempt to answer the question, How do I prepare and deliver a sermon? It is hoped that the division of the answer into well-marked stages and steps will not make the process seem mechanical and rote. The risk of that criticism is taken, however, in order to provide ease of location for anyone wishing to attend to a particular point of interest or need.

Throughout the book examples and exercises are provided both to clarify the point under discussion and to invite the reader to engage in the process. Such participation enables the student to face early the anxieties and inhibitions about preaching with which we all contend during our lifetime. In addition, there comes with this participation the pleasure of one's own insights, the discovery of one's own particular gifts, and the gradual transfer of ownership and responsibility for preaching from textbook writers and teachers to the student. Most of these examples will be drawn from or directly related to biblical texts. The decision to do this was neither casual nor due to the writer's natural gravitation toward his own field of specialization. The choice is rather due to a conviction and an experience: the conviction that preaching should be nourished, informed, disciplined, and authorized by Scripture, and the experience of being taught by Scripture that there is no single form of speech which qualifies as a sermon. Both Old and New Testaments amply testify to the rich variety of shapes the proclamation may take. Whoever goes to the Bible in search of *what* to preach but does not linger long enough to learn *how* to preach has left its pages much too soon. The Bible will serve, then, as the companion to this text, and its frequent use will enable us not only to talk about what we are doing but also to do what we are talking about.

Basic Assumptions About Learning to Preach

The discussion of preaching in the chapters that follow proceeds on two basic assumptions. The first is that learning to preach is difficult, and the difficulty is not greatly relieved by having a skilled instructor or by the discovery that one seems to be naturally a "good talker." The fact is, preaching itself is a very complex activity. So many are the variables that even arriving at a satisfactory definition of preaching is a continuing task. One can attempt to be comprehensive and include in the definition the message, the messenger, the recipients, and the method and still sense immediately that other factors should have been included. For example: imagine that you are approached by a student who has just come from a seminary class. This student describes the session that day by saying the professor lectured for forty minutes and then preached the last ten minutes of the period. With no further description, how do you understand the shift from lecturing to preaching? What was the difference? The professor departed from prepared notes? The delivery was more lively and animated? The content was more personal in terms of both the lecturer's and the students' involvement in the material? Did the professor become less descriptive and more hortatory, maybe even warning or scolding a bit? Did the students continue to take notes, take more notes, or cease writing during that ten minutes? Once you have said to yourself what was involved in a move from lecturing to preaching, share the hypothetical situation with another. Is that person's response the same as yours? We all know and yet none of us seems to know what preaching is.

In order to state the complexity of preaching, "both . . . and" expressions are more suitable than the simpler "either . . . or." Preaching is the concerted engagement of one's faculties of body, mind, and spirit. It is, then, skilled activity. But preaching has to do with a particular content, a certain message conveyed. As eating is not merely chewing, but chewing food, so is preaching necessarily defined not only by speaking but also by what is spoken. And since the basic content is not a creation of, but a gift to, the speaker, preaching is both learned and given. However, hardly anyone would accept the sum of activity plus content as an adequate description, for the active presence of the Spirit of God transforms the occasion into what biblical scholars have referred to as an "event." Preachers and listeners hold and articulate doctrines of the Spirit with wide differences, but the absence of the power of God reduces the delivery of the sermon to a sad repeat of the futile efforts of the seven sons of Sceva described in Acts 19:11-16. The evil spirit over whom they imitated Paul's words and gestures turned on them with the words, "Jesus I know, and Paul I know; but who are you?" (verse 15).

Preaching is both description and address. The old debate among New Testament scholars as to whether the gospel consists of the presentation of the life, ministry, death, and resurrection of Jesus as in the Gospels, or the word of the cross with which Paul addressed his hearers has not been and should not be resolved as either . . . or. Not only are both ingredient to the biblical witness but each needs the other. Properly understood, any narration of the story of Jesus

17

must carry an implied if not expressed word of address to the listeners in order to qualify as preaching. Speaking that is "about" God or Jesus or related themes but is not "to" the hearers may be interesting and may even be followed by a cordial discussion, but it is not preaching. Preaching is to the listeners intentionally and, therefore, even the indicative mood carries the imperative in its bosom. Similarly, speaking that "addresses" the hearers but does not have the content of the faith is not preaching but empty intensity, hollow exhortation.

Preaching is both private and public. It is private in that the process of preparation, unless noticeably aborted, creates in the preacher a strong sense of ownership, a profound embrace of the message. This is not to say that one preaches only what has been practiced (a slender menu, even from the saintliest among us) or that the efficacy of preaching is totally contingent upon the faith and life of the one who preaches. But it is to say that the prayer, research, study, and reflection in which a sermon is forged tend to bury that message deep in one's values, thoughts, and passions, and generate in the preacher a strong conviction that this message is important, can make a difference, and will not be delivered as though nothing were at stake. But anyone who has spoken on a subject of immense personal significance knows that the heart lies a great distance from the tongue. Therefore, on such matters one does not speak easily, especially to an audience that includes the stranger and the casual passerby. However, preaching is also social and public. The sermon is not one person's self-disclosure any more than theology is taking one's own pulse to see how one feels about a matter. Rather, the preacher voices the message of the community of faith, articulates it to that community and from that community to the world. "For God so loved the world" is the expression which sets the sermon in its proper context. True, introverted persons often draw their breath in pain to proclaim to any and all who will hear, but the pain must not be allowed to win. Otherwise only a comfortable few will receive the Good News and that which they hear will probably be a subjective distortion of the gospel.

Preaching is both words and the Word. To deny any relationship between one's own words and the Word of God, whether due to one's notion of proper humility or to an abdication of the authority

18

and responsibility of ministry, is to rob preaching of its place and purpose. From such a perspective, a silent pulpit would be the logical and honest conclusion. On the other hand, to identify one's own words with the Word of God is to assume for ourselves God's role in preaching. Neither one's own strong convictions on a matter nor the scaffolding of many verses of Scripture can justify the claim. Nor is it the case that a changed tone of voice provides the flag by which the Word of God can be identified among many human words. Rather, the preacher takes the words provided by culture and tradition, selects from among them those that have the qualities of clarity, vitality, and appropriateness, arranges them so as to convey the truth and evoke interest, pronounces them according to the best accepted usage, and offers them to God in the sermon. It is God who fashions words into the Word.

Perhaps nothing further need be said in the service of the first basic assumption. When these attempts at description are converted into experience, the point will be more than clear. And the complexities of preaching are experienced quite early in the learning process. Even the first-year student begins to ask, Are sermons supposed to translate ideals into standards? If so, is not something vital lost? A thousand-dollar bill can be changed into quarters and dimes, but even if the change is exactly correct in value, the experience of that value has changed radically. Does the obligation to clarify always involve compromise? If our task is to evoke response in others, what happens to integrity which insists that the first obligation is honest expression of oneself? Must every bright idea pass through the fire of intense study? Careful investigation never seems to lose its power to intimidate and threaten. And on and on. Learning to preach is difficult because preaching is difficult.

The other basic assumption upon which the subsequent discussion proceeds is that while learning to preach is difficult, it can be done. There has been much discussion of whether or not preaching can be taught, given the fact that the preaching moment occurs at the intersection of tradition, Scripture, the experience of the preacher, the needs of a particular group of listeners, and the condition of the world as it bears upon that time and place. It is a good question, even if unanswerable. But the more appropriate question, Can preaching be *learned?* is answerable, and in the affirmative. Granted, the one who learns cannot name all the ones who have been teachers because learning involves listening to many voices. One listens to the voice of emerging abilities, gifts of the God who calls one to preach. One listens to the voice of one's background in family, among friends, and with other significant persons along the way. Anyone's past, regardless of how privileged or deprived, blessed or painful, can be reinterpreted and reclaimed with great gain for preaching whether or not one ever recalls that past from the pulpit. The voices of teachers in other disciplines need to be heard both for the worth of the subject matter and for its bearing upon preaching. It is a common fault of young ministers that theology, church history, biblical studies, and sociology of religion are not permitted adequately to inform and discipline preaching. Any subject that bears upon life bears upon preaching.

It goes without saying that a person desirous of learning to preach will take advantage of opportunities to hear other communicators, especially good ones, regardless of their areas of interest and expertise. Politicians, coaches, comedians, actors, children, singers, local storytellers, all can teach us if we listen. There is no one, educated or uneducated, from whom we cannot learn if we have the grace to receive. Of course, listening to other preachers is very important, and far exceeds in value the reading of their sermons. Since sermons are spoken, hearing is better than reading. Besides that, most of the preachers from whom we can learn never have sermons in print. However, let us keep in mind that learning does not mean imitating. Imitation may be the sincerest form of flattery, but it produces caricatures in the pulpit. We learn from preachers poor, fair, good, and excellent, but not one of them is to be copied. David cannot fight in Saul's armor.

Perhaps this is the point to urge the development of oral skills. The moment persons set out on the path leading to the pulpit, they need to give attention to increasing their capacities for "oralizing." In mind here are not only speech classes, although those can be invaluable for improving voice range and projection as well as organization of thoughts, but also the informal opportunities that need to be seized. One on one, in small groups, in various organizations, and in classrooms one can vastly improve one's ability to explain, to describe, to quote, to narrate, to debate, to explore aloud. No day passes without an opportunity to tell a story, talk with children, converse with the elderly, discuss with friends, tell a joke, give directions to a traveler, describe a scene, or share feelings. Some suggestions for improvement in these areas are sketched in the section of this book devoted to sermon delivery, but it might be wise to look ahead now to that discussion and begin some exercises. After all, attending to oral skills only in a preaching class or when in the pulpit is too little, too late. Perhaps taking initiative in this area more than any other marks the difference between those "taking preaching" and those who earnestly desire to preach. Student initiative is stressed here because of two facts.

The first is that many colleges and universities do not require, and some do not even offer, courses in speech communication. Few seminaries are prepared to make up the lack and even fewer students have the appetite for "remedial work."

The second fact is that much of the educational process today is silent. From grade school through college, students listen to instructors, read, write, take notes, write term papers, sit for exams, and graduate. Many students with excellent records enter seminary with sixteen years of silent education, now preparing for a vocation that will demand oral presentations every week for the remainder of their lives. And in many cases, an excessively large amount of seminary education will consist of listening to lectures, reading, taking notes, writing papers, and sitting for exams, all in silence.

In support of the thesis that preaching can be learned, nothing has been said about the contribution of classes in preaching. This is not to minimize them by neglect; most of those who work through this book will probably do so within a class framework and can, therefore, assess for themselves what benefits can be derived from such classes. But it should be said that even those homiletics professors who, after years of serious attempts, still wonder if preaching can be taught, gratefully recognize that a number of their students indeed have learned. Their learning owes much to classes in preaching which direct the student toward good bibliographies, provide feedback on presentations, offer support during periods of severe self-criticism, grant permission to develop new methods, and stake out basic guidelines within which creativity can germinate. There is, of course, no one way everyone is to preach. In fact, each preacher will not only differ from others but will vary the movement and mood of sermons in the pursuit of different purposes. Putting all sermons in the same form cannot be justified by any reasonable canon of judgment, even if some of us know of preachers of repute who did just that. As we get older our preaching changes, not simply because we grow wiser but because there are messages and methods appropriate to age that would on the lips of the young be borrowed and theatrical. And vice versa.

One final word about learning to preach. Some ministers may arrive at the painful conclusion that they cannot preach; at least, not very well. If that conclusion is supported by knowing and caring friends and peers, some form of ministry without pulpit should be sought. Such a person is no less a minister, and the church should say so clearly. As important as preaching is, neither the pulpit nor the church is served by the view that only those who preach are really ministers. That attitude has kept some too long in the pulpit and caused others whose abilities lay elsewhere to abandon the ministry altogether.

Fundamental Convictions About Preaching

Those who enter into conversation with this book have a right to know what convictions nourish and support the views on preaching expressed here. The following are basic, and while, like outcroppings of stone, they may rise to the surface of the discussion only here and there, they are in fact foundational to all that is said. These convictions are offered not for agreement or disagreement but in the service of clarity and honesty. If they prompt the reader to articulate his or her own, a vital step toward consistently strong preaching will have been taken. It does not take long for listeners to discern if sermons do not have firm support. Some less attentive may think the preacher needs to learn to "project the voice," but careful observers can identify the cause of the uncertain sound, the avoiding eye, and the gesture that contradicts the word.

The Preacher. The person of the preacher is a vital element in effective preaching. This is not said in an attempt to resurrect the old debate between Augustine and Donatus as to whether the efficacy of preaching is contingent upon the faith and morals of the minister. Nor is it to take the "minister as model" position over against those insisting that the clergy, like other professionals, should be evaluated on proficiency and not on personal behavior. Rather, this conviction about the preacher is based on two general observations.

One is that the minister works within an unusual network of trust and intimacy that makes the separation of character from performance impossible. Lawyers and physicians who deal with clients often find themselves in relationships of trust which generate high expectations quite apart from their capacities at law or medicine. How much more so is this true with ministers who do not have clients but congregations with whom they share in sermon, prayer, funeral, wedding, baptism, counseling, and other moments of quivering vulnerability, matters of ultimate significance. Whatever one's theology of ministry and whatever may be one's preferences, this condition pertaining to the preacher and preaching remains an inescapable fact.

The second observation is that all preaching is to some extent self-disclosure by the preacher. This is not offered as a comment on the practice in some quarters of making the pulpit a confessional and "a funny thing happened to me on the way to church" the subject of every sermon. It is simply a truth about communication. With the advent of Freudian psychology there arose in literary criticism an approach called biographical. To understand a literary piece one studies the life of the writer. In a rather negative acknowledgment, D. H. Lawrence said a writer "sheds his sickness" in his writing. While a homiletical evaluation of self-disclosure will be reserved until a later chapter, this realization of one's revelation of self should be with us from the outset, as a matter not to be feared, disguised, or embraced, but understood. And the realization that in preaching one says more than what is said, or less, might discipline truant resolutions concerning one's own life of prayer and faith. Pertaining to the minister's own faith journey, it is the reflection of many who have spent a lifetime in ministry that of all the exercises for keeping athletically fit one's Christian values, perspectives, and faith none excels that of preparing and delivering sermons. Those whose service is not in the pulpit take other paths to sustain and nourish the person of the minister. But the one who preaches cannot attend

23

enough retreats or retire to the chapel with sufficient frequency to recover the loss suffered by the spirit that neglects the study and reflection requisite to preaching. No stronger argument against the habit of preaching the sermons of others has ever been mounted. If preaching discloses self even when we are preaching Christ and not ourselves, then let the one revealed be that growing self which, week after week, probes Scripture, tradition, experience, and the human condition and shapes for the listeners an appropriate word. But a word of warning: if the dimension of self-disclosure moves center stage in the preacher's mind, preaching will wither under the spotlight on self, and instead listeners will be treated to those familiar dramas of disguise in which the preacher boasts of weaknesses and humbly confesses strengths.

Stated summarily, the preacher is expected to be a person of faith, passion, authority, and grace. *Faith* makes one believable, and if the messenger is not believable, neither is the message. The absence of faith is almost impossible to disguise for any period of time. No one can increase the volume in the pulpit to such a level as to muffle the echo of lost convictions. *Passion* makes one persuasive. This is not to conjure up the images of fiery fanatics whose heartless demands victimize and violate, but it is simply to state that there is a passion appropriate to the importance of the subject matter. To preach as though nothing were at stake is an immense contradiction. There are values derived from the gospel that make the preacher a center of meaning, power and influence, even when eloquence is lacking. Such a person makes a difference in a community. In many ways this is a frightening prospect, and once experienced, when a sermon has left a huddle of yes and a huddle of no on either side of the pulpit, the preacher will thereafter have to deal not only with the desire to be effective but also with the temptation to be ineffective. *Authority* is that which gives one the right to speak. Authority in ministry is most complex. It is ecclesiastical by reason of ordination; it is charismatic by reason of a call; it is personal by reason of talent and education; it is democratic by reason of the willingness of the listeners to give their attention. Authority is all this and more, but the paradoxical truth is that the servant of God is a leader, and the abdication of leadership, however blessed with proper texts, is a contradiction of one's ordination. And finally, *grace* is that which keeps the speaker a listener. Preaching, like singing, begins in the ear, and the one who has heard the word of God's grace can pronounce it properly. Grace is not an embarrassed tolerance that smiles at evil or stares at the ground before injustice. Grace is the presence of a God who sends rain upon the good and evil and who is kind even to the ungrateful and selfish. The true work of grace in us is to make us gracious also.

The Listeners. In what has been said about the preacher much has been implied about the listeners, but the conviction needs to be directly stated that listeners are active participants in preaching, whether vocal or silent in that participation. Whether one's theology of preaching locates the Word of God at the speaker's mouth or the listener's ear, the fact is, it takes two to communicate. Preaching is not simply a matter of speaking on Christian subjects; preaching is itself to be a Christian act. This means, among other things, that the one preaching does not put down, insult, violate, or ignore those whose investment in the message is no less than that of the speaker. To say that listeners are participants is to make at least three statements about the nature of preaching. First, the message is appropriate to the listeners. There is a sense, of course, in which all of us are more alike than different and, therefore, sermons can have a general fitness for a range of times and places and groups. However, sermons are not speeches for all occasions but are rather addresses prepared for one group at one particular time and place. Such sermons require a thorough knowledge of, a great deal of listening to, the congregation. In other words, the listeners participate in the sermon before it is born. The listeners speak to the preacher before the preacher speaks to them; the minister listens before saying anything. Otherwise, the sermon is without a point of contact, whatever may be the general truth of its content. The achievement of this appropriateness does not require a structured time each week when representatives of the congregation talk with the minister about the next sermon. This method, apparently productive in some situations, can be counterproductive in others, and only those involved can know for sure.

The second statement which listener participation makes about preaching is that sermons should proceed or move in such a way as to give the listener something to think, feel, decide, and do during the preaching. It is a poor division of labor that assigns the sermon totally to the preacher and the post-sermon "go and do" to the listener. Generations of tradition in some places limit the hearer's response to preferential language at the sanctuary door: "I liked your sermon," or, if not, silence or a diversionary comment. Granted, not all listeners are anxious to accept responsibility for thinking, feeling, and deciding as a sermon unfolds, but some apparent resistance is really lack of practice or skill or maybe even trust. Is this a new homiletical gimmick our pastor has picked up somewhere? The preacher who genuinely believes preaching is the activity of the whole congregation will not only develop the skills for a style of preaching which makes that possible but will also be patient while the listeners overcome years of quiet submission to someone else's conclusions. As to the skills, subsequent discussion on shaping the sermon may be helpful; as to the patience, that grows out of a pastor's understanding.

The third and final statement about preaching generated by the conviction that listeners are vital contributors is that sermons should speak *for* as well as *to* the congregation. The Bible is the church's book, not the minister's alone, and therefore a proclamation of its affirmations is the church's word to itself and to the world. Of course, there are occasions aplenty when the preacher confronts the congregation, having it hear the ringing judgment of its own confession and tradition, as Jesus did in the synagogue at Nazareth (Luke 4:16-30). However, the power of the sermon of Jesus that day lay in the fact that he read and interpreted for his listeners their very own Scriptures. Several times in the chapters that follow we will have occasion to discuss the effective force of the shock of recognition and the learning and growing which can occur when we hear what we already know. Young preachers who go backpacking to the dark side of Nahum in search of a text no predecessor has ever used or who rely on novelty to gain and keep attention ("This will get them!") are overlooking the treasury of the familiar. No one builds a church by leaping off the pinnacle of the temple every Sunday. This is in no way even a suggestion that one is to preach what people want to *hear* but rather a declaration that occasionally one should preach what people want to *say*. If a minister takes seriously the role of listeners in preaching, there will be sermons expressing for the whole church, and with God as the primary audience, the faith, the doubt, the fear, the anger, the love, the joy, the gratitude that is in all of us. The listeners say, "Yes, that is my message; that is what I have wanted to say." All of us recognize here a dynamic that has long been operative in many black churches but which has been absent in traditions in which preachers only speak to but not in and for the faithful community. We will talk of this again.

The Scriptures. Preaching brings the Scriptures forward as a living voice in the congregation. Biblical texts have a future as well as a past, and preaching seeks to fulfill that future by continuing the conversation of the text into the present. This continuum between text and sermon is necessary for preaching for several reasons.

First, the Scriptures are normative in the life of the church. To sever preaching from that norm either by neglect or intent would be to cut the church off from its primary source of nourishment and discipline. Sermons not informed and inspired by Scripture are objects dislodged, orphans in the world, without mother or father.

Second, the Scriptures, by keeping sentinel watch over the life and faith of the church, blow the whistle on lengthy exercises in self-analysis and self-saving, move the chairs out of the small circle, and scatter moods of self-pity or self-congratulation. Sermons that are self-serving are called into question by the very texts which had been selected to authenticate the message.

And finally, the Scriptures continually remind pulpit and pew not only what but how to preach. The rich variety of its passages constantly objects to the boredom of imported outlines that ill fit the contours of the text and creates a stir among preachers and listeners who had settled for monotony as somehow the way it is. Just like grandmother's view of medicine, "If it doesn't taste bad it won't help you," so it has been supposed that if it is not dull it is not a sermon. A stirring text well read creates an expectation in listeners which the sermon should not disappoint.

However, preaching that brings Scripture forward as a living voice in the church is far easier to desire than to achieve. Preaching which passively acquiesces to the text tends merely to quote the texts hoping that they will work. Such an effort at an uncritical transfer is irresponsible even if sincere. On the other hand, only to nod in the direction of the text in the rush to be current and immediate is equally irresponsible. We will spend some time later dealing with the problems involved and the methods available for negotiating the distance between the text and the present, but the beginning point is accepting the fact of that distance. The Bible is not only Scripture and therefore a word for the present, but the Bible is also an ancient book and its word is not easy to hear.

When these documents were canonized and therefore made authoritative, interpretation became an essential ingredient in all preaching. For example, when Philippians was a letter from Paul to the church at Philippi, it was read to that congregation. When Paul said, "I entreat Euodia and I entreat Syntyche to agree in the Lord" (4:2), his meaning was evident without comment, not only to the two women but to the whole assembly. However, when that letter was canonized as Scripture, it was and is now read in Christian assemblies everywhere. How are Christians in Rome or Bangkok or Little Rock to hear meaningfully the reading of the day: "I entreat Euodia and I entreat Syntyche to agree in the Lord"? It is a primary obligation of the preacher to interpret Scripture.

Perhaps it should be said now well in advance of discussions of interpretation and sermon formation that no great investment will be made in naming and identifying sermons in terms of their relation to biblical texts. The traditional categories of exegetical, textual, expository, thematic, and topical have had value in homiletical pedagogy, but in these pages such tags will receive only minimal attention. However, maximum attention will be devoted to the persistent and repeated questions, Does the sermon say and do what the biblical text says and does? This question functions as the canon for ascertaining if a sermon brings the text forward as a living voice in the church much better than the number of texts cited or biblical words repeated. It is possible that a sermon that buries itself in the text, moves through it phrase by phrase, and never comes up for air may prove to be "unbiblical" in the sense that it fails to achieve what the text achieves. On the other hand, a sermon may appear to be walking alongside rather than through a text, or may seem to pause now and then to look up at the lofty peak of a text so extraordinary as to defy the skills of the most experienced preacher, and yet be quite "biblical" in the sense of releasing that text to do its work among the listeners. Whoever spends hours every week exploring, investigating, and sometimes sauntering through the Scriptures will know if the text was a living voice in the congregation.

The Holy Spirit. To be so bold as to talk of preaching as bringing Scripture forward as a living voice in the church obligates one to make a comment about the Holy Spirit. It is, however, quite easy to say both too little and too much on this subject. To express the conviction that the Spirit is everywhere is too little, for "everywhere" is often an acceptable way of saying "nowhere." Yet it is too much to guarantee the Spirit's presence, as though we had an effective technology in matters of the Spirit, creating the conditions that assure the Spirit's arrival among us. The church is forever warned by the attempt of Simon the magician to purchase the power of the Spirit to freshen up his act (Acts 8:9-13). "The wind blows where it wills" (John 3:8). The Spirit is *of God* and not contingent upon our willing or doing. The truth is, and by this the church sometimes feels embarrassed, there is no agreement among Christians as to the canons for ascertaining the Spirit's absence or presence at the time of an event. Afterward, of course, the evidences of love, hope, trust, truth, and justice can be read clearly as footprints that say, "Yes, the Spirit was here." In fact, we do not know where to look for the Spirit's presence in preaching, even though many voices are saying, "Lo, here," or "Lo, there." Is it in the hours of study, slow and difficult and often unexciting? Yes; that is, the one studying certainly hopes so. Is it in the delivery? Yes; that is, the one preaching certainly hopes so. Is it in the listeners? Yes; that is, those hearing certainly hope so. To express the conviction this way is not an acknowledged lack of faith but is rather a hesitation to walk too far on a path where certainty shades into blasphemy. There are some areas of experience that come as gifts of God but about which no one is qualified to give expert commentary.

What can be affirmed is that we claim the promise of God's presence in preaching as surely as we do in worship and in mission. The power that transformed a supper in Emmaus into a sacrament (Luke 24:28-35) can transform our words into the Word of God. In this conviction and in this trust every sentence of this book is formed and released to the reader. However, the reader will not be reminded of this on every page, as though saying it often will make it more true. It is the writer's confidence that the readers of this book are those who are serious about the ministry of preaching and who, therefore, trust that the God who calls us to preach does not leave us alone in the world armed only with our rhetoric. All of us know it is God who wakens the ear and loosens the tongue.

Having expressed that conviction, it is important to say clearly that on the practical level, the task of preaching cannot be divided into the Spirit's work and our work. That is, believing in the Spirit does not cut our work in half. God's activity in the world does not reduce ours one iota. Any doctrine of the Holy Spirit that relieves me of my work and its responsibility is plainly false.

two

The Sermon in Context

A sermon, to be properly understood and to have its purpose fulfilled, has to be experienced in its context, or rather in its several contexts. Such a statement could, of course, be aptly made regarding most events, but when it is made about a sermon, it is especially true in one respect. A sermon is a communication and therefore is to be located as much among a particular group of listeners as with a particular speaker. A knowledge of those to whom it is addressed would contribute as much or more to its understanding as would knowing the person who delivered it. And yet one seldom hears the inquiry, Who heard this sermon? Almost always the question is, Who preached this sermon? in spite of the fact that a sermon has many ears but only one mouth.

The reason a knowledge of context is essential to understanding sermons lies even deeper. Preaching is not only communication; it is oral communication. True, some sermons are written and published in books and journals or otherwise made available to the public. In fact, some published sermons are written for the press and are never preached. It is also true that many ministers write and then deliver their sermons, perhaps by reading them aloud. However, none of this alters the fact that preaching is by its nature an acoustical event, having its home in orality not textuality. Effective preachers who write their sermons have worked hard to achieve in writing an oral style. What, then, does its oral nature say about the context of the sermon? It says that the sermon as spoken word is socially owned, having its life at a particular time and place among a group of participants who are not only influenced by the nature and purpose of the occasion but who also bring to their hearing personal and social factors which are ingredient to the experience of the sermon. The actual preaching of a sermon is a non-repeatable, non-portable event. If a sermon happens to enjoy an afterlife in print, its readers' experience is far different from its hearers' experience. Some ministers make available to the parishioners copies of their sermons. Those who read these sermons after hearing them participate in ways unavailable to those who read instead of hearing.

Writers of novels and short stories have to bear almost all the burden of communication because they do not know the persons who will read their work or the contexts in which it will be read. The same novel is read during an office lunch break, in bed late at night, on a park bench, in a library, on a plane. But a sermon is oral communication and the preacher expects both the context and the listeners to bear some of the burden of the process. This is not to say that all preachers prepare with this in mind; some obviously carry all the freight, own the whole sermon, and deliver it completely finished and wrapped, hoping someone is present to receive it. Admittedly, this is the easiest method, less filled with the anxiety which attends reliance on contexts and listeners to cooperate. But whatever the method of preparation and delivery, however resolute the preacher is not to be influenced by Sunday morning variables and contingencies, the fact remains, a sermon is but a gathering of paragraphs until placed in its several contexts. It has a context of history and tradition affecting how it is delivered (we all have many teachers) and how it is heard (we all have many predecessors). A sermon has a pastoral context, for all the ways the minister interacts with and relates to the parishioners heavily influence what is said and what is heard. In addition, most sermons are prepared for and delivered in a liturgical context, spoken and heard in an assembly gathered for prayer and praise. And finally, a sermon has a theological context, cut out of the fabric of the minister's own beliefs, delivered as a part of an ongoing theological conversation with the congregation, and heard by persons whose own values and convictions, shaped by experiences and reflections that far exceed all recollection, mix with the preacher's words to create the real sermon.

The Historical Context

It may seem no more than paying dues to the academy to begin with the sermon's historical context. After all, few if any preachers enter the pulpit thinking about the history of preaching. This may be true especially of those who attended seminary during the late sixties or early seventies when homiletics was hanging by its fingernails on the edge of the curriculum and history was mocked as a hiding place. The reader may relax; there will be no rehearsal of the past here. Such histories, both abridged and multi-volumed, are readily available. We will, however, look briefly at the two levels on which historical context affects the preaching and the hearing of the sermon.

On one level there is the history which lies within the personal memories of both preacher and listener. For the preacher there are those who have by their influence provided an informal and yet working definition of what it is to preach. Pastors from one's youth, guest speakers of unusual abilities who left their mark, retreat and conference preachers, campus ministers, seminary chapel speakers, theological professors: some or all of these come to mind when one says "preacher." One is remembered and we say, "If only I could preach like that"; another prompts us to say, "I certainly will never be that kind of preacher," but in both cases we have been influenced. Their effect on us may be subtle: a small gesture, a tone of voice, a way of standing. But it may also be profound, not so much evidenced in direct imitation as in the thought now and then, *Would he approve of the way I am handling this? How would she bring this to conclusion?* All of us have significant persons, living and dead, who sit in our balconies and we hope they are pleased with our preaching. It is healthy to know this about ourselves and to talk of it with others. Peer groups can have very enjoyable as well as helpful sessions on reflecting on the persons who have contributed to disciplines of preparation and styles of preaching. One's own unique gifts are not at all minimized nor is one embarrassed about them. On the contrary,

33

someone evoked and stirred up those gifts. Such recollections both humble and gratify.

To the listeners of our preaching the situation is hardly any different. It is a rare preacher who is the first and only pulpit voice a listener has known. Most parishioners hear a sermon as it is filtered through many sermons and attend to a pulpit that is still partially occupied by prior tenants. This is not to say that games of comparison and contrast are consciously going on all over the sanctuary. Some do that, of course, and all of us know their names; they have been doing it since Jesus was unfavorably compared to John the Baptist, and Paul to Apollos. It is rather to say that what we think we delivered as the sermon may not be what the listeners heard as the sermon, because the Scripture reading, the prayers, the anthem, phrases in the sermon evoked memories of other times, other occasions, other voices. A suggestion: sometime have an evening with parishioners and ask each of them to respond to the question, Where did you get your ears? In other words, where were the churches and who were the preachers who affected the way you now listen to sermons? The time will yield more than anecdotes that are sometimes humorous, sometimes sad, sometimes bitter. If grace is present, patience and understanding will increase, and the next Sunday, the church will have one improved preacher and several improved listeners.

Above all, a preacher should not try to compete with predecessors or devise ways to erase the memory of other ministers known and loved by the parishioners. It is a defensive and overactive ego which assumes that the memories of the listeners are a negative factor reducing the effectiveness of one's own endeavors. The fact is, those recollections not only enrich the faith life of the congregation, but also contribute to sermons so as to make them better than they otherwise would have been. For example, a minister preaches on a certain text or subject, the treatment of which sets in motion in a listener not only recognition but a flood of recollection of another sermon which ministered effectively at a critical time in life. Without consciously deciding to do so, the listener hears in a new way, attributing to the present sermon qualities that are really positive resonances of an earlier sermon. Of course, the reverse will sometimes be the case, but why assume it always is? When we preach, listeners do not hear a sermon; they hear sermons, and the benefits of the phenomenon far outweigh the negative effects. The memory of the church is a treasury, making us all the richer.

However, the memory of the church extends farther and deeper than the personal recollections of its members, and hence, the historical context of preaching lies at another level in addition to the one just discussed. All of us are influenced by traditions that exist not only prior to but also apart from our conscious appropriation of them. Centuries after the events, Jews gather at Passover to remember the Exodus, Christians gather at the eucharistic table to remember Jesus, and Americans gather on July Fourth to remember the Declaration of Independence. This is a very meaningful activity because memory belongs to institutions and to communities as well as to individuals.

In the same sense the pulpit has a memory, participating in a tradition reaching back across the centuries. That tradition includes the poetic Isaiah singing, "How beautiful upon the mountains are the feet of him who brings good tidings" (52:7), and the tempestuous Jonah thundering, "Yet forty days, and Nineveh shall be overthrown!" (3:4). The tradition continued in John the Baptist, who dressed like yesterday but who spoke like tomorrow, "preaching a baptism of repentance for the forgiveness of sins" (Mark 1:4). And, of course, Jesus came preaching. In fact, when he read from Isaiah 61, "The Spirit of the Lord is upon me, because he has anointed me to preach good news to the poor. . . ." Luke says Jesus announced, "Today this scripture has been fulfilled in your hearing" (4:21). The twelve apostles belong to the history of the pulpit. Of them Luke wrote: "And every day in the temple and at home they did not cease teaching and preaching Jesus as the Christ" (Acts 5:42). Paul, likewise, is located in this tradition, not so much by the testimony of others as by his own: "For Christ did not send me to baptize but to preach the gospel" (I Cor. 1:17). In fact, the New Testament witnesses to the centrality of preaching in the Christian communities. The Gospels contain portions of the oral tradition of preaching, Acts is heavily sprinkled with sermons and sermon fragments, and the Epistle to the Hebrews is really a sermon in a form that flourishes even to this day. And the tradition continues to include Origen, whose exegetical homilies earned for him the title

"Father of the Christian Sermon," and Augustine, who joined Christian preaching and Greek rhetoric in the first ever textbook on the science and art of preaching.

This very brief sketch need go no further; the point is clear. The pulpit in every church is set in a long and rich tradition and whoever enters the pulpit not only continues that tradition but is also influenced by it as a part of the Christian community's memory. It has already been stated that we are influenced by traditions even when we have not consciously appropriated them. However, there are also clear and important benefits which are the gain of the preacher who makes the effort to become aware of and knowledgeable in the historical context of preaching. Three of those benefits need to be mentioned at this point in our discussion.

First, a knowledge of the historical context of preaching can encourage and sustain the preacher when the soul is wandering in waterless places. Such periods come to every preacher, when public criticism of the pulpit moves into the sanctuary and even into the mind of the preacher. Self-doubt erodes power and then finds itself confirmed in the apparent lack of effectiveness. The weekly opportunity becomes a chore, logic insists that a task of little significance requires little preparation, and the stereotype replaces the preacher. Where does one find support, encouragement, and a refreshing sense of the significance of the pulpit when it seems to be words, words, words? A sure source, without gimmicks or shallow pep talks, is the tradition of preaching. One has but to recall a few names from that tradition to return to the pulpit with reclaimed call and renewed spirit.

Second, a knowledge of the history of preaching helps one develop a constructive self-critical faculty. One can easily settle into a comfortable pattern of preparation and style of preaching that encounters no critical assessment, entertains no alternatives. In fact, preaching can, in time, come to be identified with one particular style of delivery, one form of sermon construction, even though that form or style may be inappropriate on some occasions, or may even be the residue of a mode of communication no longer effective. A study of the history of preaching reveals that forms and modes and styles are relative to times and places and audiences. The gospel is the gospel, but in its movement across time and cultures its

36

witnesses have listened to the counsel of rhetoric, communication theory, literary criticism, and skilled communicators in every field. A style or method can outlive its usefulness, but abandoning it is not easy. To change may be experienced as "not preaching anymore." Some preachers who modify their styles confess to feelings of having betrayed an old homiletics professor, long since deceased. All change is difficult, especially if it involves activity that is significant, but the discovery that all methods and forms of preaching are historically relative is quite liberating. A knowledge of history sets us free from history, enabling us to develop methods congenial to the gospel without magnifying them beyond their merits as servants of the message.

And third, as a corollary of what has just been said, the history of preaching can provide a rich resource for finding and developing ways to construct sermons and styles of delivery. We do not have to rethink everything as though wisdom were born with us. The tradition of preaching includes efforts at communicating that failed for good reason. Some forms of communication are either not congenial to the nature of the gospel or are poorly fitted to the human ear. For example, there are reasons why a parable can convey the gospel while a riddle cannot. Other methods have been suggested but not used sufficiently to be evaluated properly. For example, the apostrophe has been rarely used and even more rarely examined as an appropriate and effective mode for proclamation. And, of course, woven through the fabric of preaching's historical context are discussions and examples of methods that have never become dated because at their base are solid principles which continue to characterize effective communication. Such is the quality of Augustine's discussion of preaching as an appeal to mind, heart, and will *(On Christian Doctrine)*. Preaching without knowledge of the tradition of the discipline can be done, of course, just as one can pick up pretty stones while walking over a diamond mine. The analogy may be exaggerated, but the truth is in it.

The Pastoral Context

Except in the cases of itinerants and those whose ministry is via radio and television, preaching takes place in a pastoral context.

Actually it would be more correct to say that preaching not only occurs in a pastoral context but is itself pastoral activity. From the perspective of the one who preaches, pastoral functions and relationships influence what is said in the sermon and how it is expressed. From the perspective of the listener, the way his or her life has been touched by the pastor profoundly affects what is heard in the sermon.

In the vast majority of cases the preacher and the pastor are the same person. Because of multiple demands and the pressures of time, many ministers feel the tension between the two and occasionally wish they could be one or the other. However, others have felt the tension to be due not only to time but also to radical differences in the two functions. In other words, are preaching and pastoring contradictory and any combination of the two erosive of the effectiveness of both? There are those who are persuaded that the same person cannot wield the two-edged sword of the Word of God and also tend the flock. This sharp and irreconcilable division of labor certainly does not spring from biblical beginnings. God can both "roar from Zion" (Amos 1:2) and also "feed his flock like a shepherd" and "gather the lambs in his arms" (Isa. 40:11). Jesus was a preacher of repentance and of the approach of the kingdom (Mark 1:14-15); and he also fulfilled Isaiah's vision of the Servant of the Lord: careful not to break a bruised reed or quench a dimly burning wick (Isa. 42:1-3; Matt. 12:17-21). Even the off and running Paul, whose one thing to do was to preach the gospel (I Cor. 1:17), related to the churches as a father to children (I Cor. 4:14-15), as a woman in the pains of childbirth (Gal. 4:19), gentle as a nurse (I Thess. 2:7). It is nearer the truth to say that the distance between preaching and pastoring has been manufactured out of exaggerated descriptions and caricatured portraits of both. On the one hand, the preacher was sketched as a drone, full of authoritarian harangues, moralistic scoldings, sectarian loyalties, and promotional trivia. On the other hand, the pastor was cartooned as a passive pseudo-psychologist, relishing the intimate details of parishioners' private lives.

The past tense was used in the sentences above because preaching and pastoring now enjoy a healthier relationship of mutual enrichment. This is not to say the debate has ended. The field of homiletics continues to be nourished by two streams which carry a preacher-pastor tension. The Protestant tradition as it continues to prevail in Europe, although with some modifications here and there, not only places preaching at the center of the church, in the host's chair entertaining other forms of ministry, but also warns against allowing the listeners too large a place in the sermon. The congregation is recipient, not source in preaching. In America, that tradition has undergone a great deal of change, at least in practice. The American pulpit has sought in many ways to make the congregation more ingredient to preaching. Think of the attempts that have mildly flourished in recent times: a question or suggestion box inviting parishioners to put items on the pulpit agenda; small groups working with pastors on sermons; talk-back sessions following worship; dialogue preaching; life-situation sermons; press conference sermons in which a brief affirmation is followed by questions and answers; rearranged furniture so that the pulpit is located among the people. Books and articles aplenty champion every position on the spectrum from lofty and distant pulpit to the pastor's chair in a circle of conversation.

The issues are many and complex, but for our present discussion, one observation is essential: preaching occurs in a pastoral context and is in many significant ways influenced by that context. In fact, at every stage from conception to delivery and beyond, pastoral functions and relationships enter into the preaching ministry. Study and preparation involve careful listening to the congregation as well as to the text. The interpretation of the parishioners in their personal, domestic, political, and economic contexts does not replace but joins the interpretation of Scripture in its context to create the message. The form and movement of the sermons represent a conscious effort to implement the doctrine of the priesthood of all believers; that is, listeners are given room to accept the responsibility for their own believing and doing. Preaching that unfolds in this way is respectful of listeners and far more pastoral than tossing into biblical and doctrinal efforts a few life-situation illustrations to provide relief. Such movement in sermons can reveal more pastoral concern than heavy injections of autobiographical anecdotes, even if the anecdotes are confessional and lay bare the weak and vulnerable soul of the preacher. Identification between speaker and listener can be extremely effective in communication, as we shall discuss later, but without critical distance it can emotionally consume both. At that point, helpfulness is immobilized and dissolves into a pool of pity.

When sermons are pastoral in the sense described, both in content and movement, it is almost guaranteed that they will be delivered in a style appropriate to their nature. Only in cases of exhaustion, personal crisis, or less than adequate preparation will grace and freedom be absent from the delivery of the sermon.

In closing, a word needs to be addressed to the criticism that the number and nature of pastoral duties make it impossible to justify the time consumed in preparing to preach week after week. The question is a proper one for the minister sensitive to the obligation to be a good steward of time. As a preliminary response, it could be argued that preaching weekly is less time consuming than preaching infrequently because of the momentum and continuity that reduce the dissipation of time and energy in fruitless motions. The preparation process is kept trim and in good working order. And in addition, the accumulation of knowledge in the subject matter of preaching reduces preparation time eventually. In a subsequent chapter we will discuss study patterns which save time quantitatively and multiply time qualitatively.

However, the criticism that multiple pastoral duties make sermon preparation every week an unwise investment of time evokes three comments. One, preaching is a vital part of pastoral work in that it permits both preacher and parishioners to weigh, submit to theological examination, integrate, bring to clarity, and express issues that are scattered through the many pastoral contacts and activities. In this sense, preaching can bring to completion and closure matters that otherwise would remain fragmented and dangling.

Two, preaching is of a piece with the total ministry of the church and therefore cannot be isolated as an event that occupies a certain number of hours. A pastor cannot really answer the question, How much time is spent in sermon preparation? The inability to answer with certainty is due not to lack of a disciplined study life but rather to the interwoven and interrelated nature of acts of ministry.

And three, preaching continues in the conversation of the Christian community and hence enjoys a life beyond the pulpit. It would be difficult, to be sure, to justify using many hours to prepare a sermon that is delivered in twenty minutes and then allowed to evaporate into forgotten silence. Nor should the preacher leave it to the parishioners to continue to discuss the sermon. Some messages would never get to the parking lot, much less beyond it. But if the minister is prepared as a student of life and Scripture, knows his or her subject and believes it is important, then portions of that sermon should be introduced appropriately in meetings, in conversations, in teaching, and in other acts of pastoral care. It can be done without arrogance or offense. To do so can be an act of grace, an extension of the pulpit. To fail to do so can be poor stewardship of one's time and efforts and a surrender to the popular notion that a minister is a preacher for only a few minutes one day a week.

The Liturgical Context

Every minister is invited now and then to preach in non-worship settings. The baccalaureate service in the high school gymnasium or the civic club Thanksgiving banquet in a dining room only a curtain away from the restaurant noise will be the occasion on which a sermon is expected. Sensitive hosts will do what they can. "The Battle Hymn of the Republic" by a glee club or a few bars of "Blessed Assurance" on a semi-retired upright piano may be all the liturgy available. But these invitations are accepted gratefully. However, the preacher prepares for the bare stage, knowing that the sermon must carry the entire freight in placing these listeners in the presence of God. This will require, among other things, a longer introduction in order to create the occasion, structure a sanctuary, and cultivate the soil of the minds to receive the Word. The task is a demanding challenge and worthy of one's best efforts.

Having noted these exceptions, we now turn to the rule: preaching in the context of worship. An assembly of believers gathers to worship; that is, to narrate in word, act, and song the community's memories and hopes, glorifying the God who redeems, enables, and sanctifies. These have come to renew their vision, to hear and to speak the grand metaphors about how life and the world should be, and to do so with such trust in God that past tenses will be used as though these things were already true. And in this time and place of prayer and praise we will preach.

The liturgical setting is vital for the health of preaching. Apart from the movement of worship, sermons can fall victim to assorted illnesses. Some turn in upon themselves in emotional indulgence; others rush off on a mind trip, touring a new topic of interest; and others just stand and scream, filling the air with ought, must, and should in endless scolding. Apart from worship, the preacher's sermons can also become arrogant and boastful, as if to say, "These people came to see and hear me." But a well-conceived and well-ordered service of worship expects more from a sermon, and usually gets it.

The liturgical setting is also vital for the freedom of preaching. Worship is characterized by an order; its structures, patterns, and repetitions provide the worshiper an orientation, a sense of being at home in the sanctuary and in the world. Some priests in late Judaism while serving at the altar wore robes decorated with sun, moon, and stars to express the belief that the altar was the center of the universe and in worship chaos became cosmos. Worship gives order and place to those who present themselves before God, and in so doing satisfies a fundamental need. An ancient name for God, "The Place," expresses clearly both the human hunger and its satisfaction. And because the liturgy is not full of surprises, novelties, and gimmicks, the sermon is set free by this order to be unsettling and disorienting, as conditions and the gospel warrant. The liturgy and the sermon give the twin provisions, order and variation.

This is not to say that the service of worship is unalterable or that the sermon must always be disturbing. There may be occasions when their roles are reversed. The point is, freedom is possible in a context of order. When a minister decides that all order is a violation of freedom and treats the parish to a wildly experimental liturgy in which is placed an experimental sermon, the congregation has experienced confusion and catastrophe, instead of the prophetic presence. As we shall note below, the powerfully prophetic word can be uttered effectively in the context of structured familiarity. Replace the structure with disorientation and the sermon which was intended to be disorienting is wasted in the turbulence, the participants having been overwhelmed rather than confronted. It is the altar which makes possible preaching and listening.

Having considered the service of worship as the context for the sermon, it remains to be said that preaching is not simply in a setting of worship but is itself an act of worship. Much has been written on Word and Sacrament, relating sermon and eucharist, joining sight, taste, smell, touch, motion, and sound in the communication of the gospel. However, let us add to that discussion the relationship of the sermon to two other acts of worship, Scripture reading and prayer.

The sermon's kinship to the Scripture reading is because it is based on the biblical texts, and because both speak a word *to* the worshipers from outside themselves. In both, it addresses the congregation rather than speaking its own word of praise or confession. This truth, that the sermon is *to* and not *from* the church is dramatized vividly in those churches that hold regular worship services whether or not anyone attends. Sometimes the only persons present are the organist, the liturgist, and the preacher. When asked why they continue when there is no congregation, their reply is straightforward: we have been called to witness to the sovereignty and the grace of God in the world. Some practical heads may say it makes no sense, but there is a respect in which it makes all kinds of sense. There is a non-contingent, unconditional quality to the word we preach; it does not wait for a favorable response in order to be the true and proper word. We have other experiences which are of such size and significance as to exist totally apart from our approval or disapproval, or even our presence. No symphony conductor ever says, "I think we have enough people here to begin; we have waited twenty minutes." No; the back is turned, the baton is raised, and the magic begins. Why? Not because *we* have finally arrived, but because it is eight o'clock, the orchestra has its commitment, and they are musicians. It is a joy to attend events that will take place whether or not we are present. It is an even greater joy to hear Scripture read and the sermon preached in such freedom and authority that one is confident it would have occurred even if the congregation had not arrived. After all, these are witnesses to the sovereignty and grace of God in the world.

According to Luke 10:1-16, Jesus instructs seventy and sends them out two by two. According to Jesus' instructions, the word to those who received the messengers was, "The kingdom of God has come near." To those who rejected the messengers, the word was, "The kingdom of God has come near." There is a "regardless of the response" integrity to the message; one does not wait to check the climate of the audience in order to discover what to say. The word we speak does not wait upon visceral authentication to be true. And as inflexible as it may sound, hearts and minds yearn for a word that is from beyond ourselves. Many are weary of self-centeredness, weary of being consumers of good sermons. The desire is not to find but to be found, not to know but to be known.

Having looked at the way in which the sermon is similar to the Scripture reading in that it brings to the congregation a word from outside themselves, let us reverse our position and notice how the sermon is also very much akin to the prayers of the congregation in that it speaks to God for the people. Several statements have already been made to the effect that preaching is not only *to* but *for* the people. The matter warrants further reflection. Preaching is like prayer not only in the sense that God is the audience, but also in the sense that the message is the church's; it did not arrive in town with the pastor but was already there. Unspoken at times, yes; confused and inchoate at times, yes; but there, as surely as the Bible was there, as faith was there, as need was there, as hope was there, as a sense of mission in the world was there.

When the pastor stands among them to preach, the parishioners who have said, "Pray for us; we do not know how to pray as we ought," just as eagerly say, "Preach for us; we do not know how to speak as we ought." And when the pastor does so, the people say in their hearts, "Yes, that is it; that is our message; that is our faith." In many black churches, this response would not be in the heart but from the heart and on the lips. The dynamic of the preacher giving voice to the congregation's message is a major contributing factor in the high level of participation in preaching in the worship of black churches. Such congregations are able to recognize the sermon as their own much more than in those churches in which the sermon is the minister's own possession, before which the congregation sits silently waiting to see what the preacher has brought to them today.

To say that in many black churches the sermon is recognized as their own is to say they are familiar with it. Therein lies a problem for many. There is a fiction abroad among preachers that the familiar is without interest, without power, and without prophetic edge. Because this is believed to be the case, some very good sermons are never preached a second time, or if they are, the preacher feels guilty and knows that all the homiletical brows in all the seminaries of the world have been lowered in dark disapproval. The assumption apparently is that the interest and effectiveness of a sermon rest in its newness, in the preacher bringing to the congregation something different. Is that really true? Consider its opposite by means of a situation which we will imagine but which is not unfamiliar. A minister is invited to preach in a series of services for a small church in a neighboring town. The engagement is fulfilled by driving the forty miles each evening and delivering several of the sermons that had been well received when preached earlier at home. On the third evening, just prior to the sermon, nine faithful members of the minister's flock enter the small sanctuary, having driven over to hear and to support their pastor. Upon seeing them, the preacher immediately realizes those nine heard this sermon not over three months ago. Anxiety replaces calm as the next five minutes are occupied with altering the sermon so it won't be recognized. An easily remembered story is deleted, the introduction and conclusion are garbled, and the movement is reversed. Needless to say, the minister suffered through it, the host church thought it the poorest of the series, and the nine supporters agreed that their pastor preached much better in the home pulpit. The painful evening was the result of a preacher's ego, perhaps some old advice about never repeating a sermon, and the false notion that a message recognized is no message at all.

Let us think further on this matter, but not to justify repeating old sermons and to promote laziness in preparation. The lazy and undisciplined need no permission for indolence; they have already found the shortcuts and the countless ways to avoid the study in that flurry of high visibility which some parishioners will bless as "pastoral fervor." Of course, preachers spend a lifetime in study and preparation. Of course, some sermons should not be preached a second time, but usually for the simple reason they should not have been preached the first time. What we are discussing is the power of recognition, which is also the experience of claiming as our own that which is familiar, which is also the process of growing by learning what we already know. Very likely, those nine from the pastor's own flock would have gotten more from hearing the sermon (as they had heard it before) than anyone else in attendance. All of us know that those who have prepared get more from a classroom lecture. And what preacher has not observed children becoming more attentive when the sermon moves across a Bible story that had been their Sunday school lesson that very morning. Their attention is now that of those who know and own what is being said; the sermon does not belong to the preacher alone. The congregation recognizes itself, its pain and joy, its sin and forgiveness, its fear and hope, in the pastor's prayer for the people. Why not recognize its faith in the sermon?

A preacher can learn a great deal about recognition and familiarity by visiting a record shop. Young people come in, listen to a tape several times, and then buy it. Why purchase a song one has already heard? Or attend a concert and notice the loudest cheers are prompted by the most familiar music. If requests are taken by the performer, no one asks for a song that has not been heard dozens of times.

But again the question, Is this not simply an exercise in comfort and nostalgia, without prophetic edge? As at least a partial answer, recall Luke's account of Jesus preaching in his home synagogue (4:16-30). His sermon that day was so prophetic as to stir the congregation to such anger that they made an attempt on Jesus' life. What was done or said to arouse such hostility? There was nothing new or unusual. Jesus was in his hometown, among relatives and neighbors. It was the sabbath and Jesus was regular in synagogue worship. There was nothing different about his participation. He read from Isaiah 61, a very familiar passage. He told two stories, both familiar favorites: one about Elijah and the widow of Sidon, the other about Elisha and the leper of Syria. What could be more familiar? Every person in the synagogue could have told those stories. And that is exactly the point; they were indicted for their anti-Gentile prejudice by their own tradition, by their own Scripture, by their own relative and neighbor. Were Jesus' words new, strange, imported from another source, the people could easily have dismissed them and also him. But it is the familiar, what is already known that stabs and indicts, and when that is so, the preacher can be removed, even crucified, but the words remain, inescapable and true, in their hearts and on their lips. Jesus preached to them their own sermon.

The sermon in the worship service is very much like the prayers in that it gives voice to what the people feel and know and believe. But it can be shattering if what is often heard is finally heard.

The Theological Context

We have considered the historical, pastoral, and liturgical contexts for preaching, and we have seen that the sermon is not an entity apart from those contexts as an egg apart from the nest. Rather, preaching participates in those contexts. Preaching is not only set in tradition but is itself an act of traditioning, not only done in a pastoral context but is itself a pastoral act, not only located within a liturgy but is itself a liturgical act. Now we shall see that preaching not only has a theological context but is itself a theological act.

Preaching both proclaims an event and participates in that event, both reports on revelation and participates in that revelation, bringing it home to the listeners not only in honest reporting but with the immediacy of a living voice addressed to these gathered here and now. The preacher, then, is a theologian. Not all accept that statement as true, however. Hands are raised in protest not only among the laity but among some clergy as well. The reasons are many. For some people theology is a negative word, a term for all that is vague, abstract, antiquarian, lifeless, irrelevant, and humanly devised in religion. It is often contrasted with revelation and Scripture, the smoke screen activity of good minds gone wrong, a sophisticated hiding place for those whose own faith is suspect. There are ministers who speak disparagingly of theology, some in order to increase their popularity by feeding anti-intellectualism, and others because their seminary experience of theology was not one of learning to think theologically but one of spending two terms in the fourth century.

To be sure, failing to think through clearly the relation of theology to preaching can be harmful to the pulpit. The theological enterprise can take over the language of preaching, replacing the imagery, the graphic and concrete speech, the vocabulary of sights and sounds, of touch and taste with the abstract, conceptual terms essential for theological reflection. The immediacy of sermons that reflect life gives way to reflections about life. A theological system can become imperialistic, forcing even the Scriptures to submit to its formulations, thereby losing the rich variety and the occasional nature of many of the biblical writings. Not unlike institutions, theological constructions tend to forget they are provisional, that their task is to reflect on what God has done rather than providing the system within which God is to function. But theology is such an interesting realm of discourse, its issues so vital for the full and free life, its subject matter of such ultimate importance, that the pulpit can find it as seductive as it finds it intimidating. The preacher will, therefore, want to deal with the question of theology's relationship to preaching.

There are basically two ways in which one may reflect on this question: one is expressed in the phrase "theology and preaching" and the other in the phrase "theology of preaching." This latter phrase will be the subject of the next chapter. Major attention will be given to a theology of preaching because effective preaching sustained over a long period of time must have some sense of its own nature, its own significance, its own role in the redeeming and caring work of God in the world. What is preaching and what is its place in the larger purposes of God? These are theological questions which must be addressed by the one who preaches. The pulpit cannot survive on custom alone, however rich and sacred, or on personal preference: "I like to preach." A theology of preaching sustains and nourishes the pulpit with a constancy that survives the ebb and flow of the feelings of the one standing in it as well as the smiles and frowns of those who sit before it.

Therefore, for the remainder of this discussion of the theological context for preaching, we will attend to the former phrase, "theology and preaching." The relation of theology and preaching may be summarized in three statements. First, theology and preaching exist in a relationship of mutuality. On the one hand, theology is a careful reflection upon the preaching of the church. Theology provides the tools, the methods, and the categories by which the church can remain self-critical, listen to its own voice, and assess what is heard.

48

Only in this way can health be maintained; otherwise, the pulpit can yield to public pressures, follow false messiahs, be hushed in a fearful silence, or strut and preen itself in the warm sun of general approval. The light of Scripture, the life and mission of Jesus Christ, the preaching of the apostles, and the faith of the church through the ages—these are the resources for theology's reflection upon the faithfulness of the pulpit. Because preaching has a performative dimension and therefore must occupy itself with skills, it needs theology to keep front and center a concern for the truth by which both preacher and listener are to live. On the other hand, preaching fulfills theology, giving it a reason for being. Theology comes to fruition in the church's proclamation to itself and to the world. Without that purpose, theology's careful attention to the message would be pointless and sterile, and most likely would cease.

The second statement about the relation of theology to preaching can be expressed as a matter of size: theology prompts preaching to treat subjects of importance and avoid trivia. How easily sermons seem to err, not on the issue of truth but on the question as to whether what is said really matters. When preparing sermons, if preachers would write "So what?" at the top of the page, many little promotional talks or clever word games on "Salt Shakers and Light Bulbs" would quietly slip off the desk and hide in the wastebasket. Theology urges upon the pulpit a much larger agenda: creation, evil, grace, covenant, forgiveness, judgment, suffering, care of the earth and all God's creatures, justice, love, and the reconciliation of the world to God. It is not out of order for theology to ask of preaching, What ultimate vision is held before us? Are there words, deeds, and relationships by which we can move toward that vision? How does God look upon us in our stumbling and failure to embrace that vision? It is almost impossible for a sermon on a matter of major importance to the listeners to be totally uninteresting and without impact. But small topics are like pennies; even when polished to a high gloss, they are still pennies.

The third and final statement about theology and preaching has to do with language. Theology deals in concepts in working out its formulations while preaching uses more concrete and graphic vocabulary, words that evoke and create images, terms that stir the senses. Preachers, however, can become irresponsible in the use of words, captivated by the novel, the interesting, and the surprising, indulgent in language that tantalizes and titillates but carries no freight. Temptations in this direction are especially strong for those who discover in themselves that facility sometimes called "having a way with words." This is not said in order to bless poor and awkward speech. On the contrary, ability to use the language is a capacity much to be desired, but we need to alert ourselves that it is at the point of capacity, not incapacity, that temptations to pride and indulgence are strongest. Theology stands by to ask if the language of the sermon could be recast into a concept or concepts, not because concepts are more appropriate for the pulpit, but because, when framed as theological concepts, the words of our sermons prove their sound substance and good intent.

Preaching takes place in a theological context, but is itself also a theological act. But what does it mean to say that preaching is a theological act? To answer that requires a consideration other than the relation of theology and preaching; it requires a theology of preaching. To that matter we now turn.

three

A Theology of Preaching

Having a theology of preaching has been urged upon the reader. It is important that this not be understood as urging that one preach theology. Preaching theology could be offering in sermon form small pieces of the stuff of belief, with or without the authorization of biblical texts. Whatever merit there may be in such an exercise, it is not a theology of preaching because it leaves unexamined and unclear what one is doing when one preaches and in what way preaching relates to revelation. To assume that the sheer weight of the authority of the sacred texts, the faithful commitment of a regular audience, and the inspiration of a worship setting will sustain the pulpit without the preacher's own wrestling with the question of what it is we are doing is serious error. The emptiness at the center of such a ministry will have its hollow echo in the soul of the one who preaches, and that echo will not pass the ear of the church unnoticed. To do that wrestling until one walks away with the blessing of sufficient clarity to give reason and impetus to one's preaching ministry is what is being urged.

In the consideration before us in this chapter, preaching is understood as making present and appropriate to the hearers the revelation of God. Here revelation is used not in the sense of content, although content is certainly there, but in the sense of mode. If preaching is in any way a continuation into the present of God's revelation, then what we are doing and how we are doing it should be harmonious with our understanding of the mode of revelation. At the risk of sounding presumptuous, it can be said that we are learning our method of communicating from God. In other words, from the transaction we call revelation we understand and implement the transaction we call preaching. That is, the way of God's Word in the world is the way of the sermon in the world. The discussion which follows proceeds from that understanding and, therefore, in attempts to characterize that, revelation and preaching will be interwoven. To facilitate our thinking, the discussion will be framed on three phrases: proceeding from silence, heard in a whisper, shouted from the housetop.

Proceeding from Silence

How one understands a word as an event in the world of sound depends to a great extent upon whether that word is experienced against a backdrop of silence or in a room of many words. We have all experienced sound that breaks the silence: a ticking clock in a sickroom; a single cowbell at dusk; taps above a flag-draped casket; "hello" on a park bench; a whippoorwill outside a camper's tent; a baby's cry at three in the morning. When the house is shut down for the night except for the small light in the hall, when teeth are brushed, pajamas are on, and bedcovers have enfolded the child, then and only then comes the story. Much that we remember has been preserved as much in silence as in sound. " 'Twas the night before Christmas, when all through the house,/Not a creature was stirring"; "Once upon a midnight dreary, while I pondered weak and weary"; "Silent night, holy night, all is calm."

In fact, some of the persons who have most influenced us carried in them a silence that was the context for their words and actions. Theirs was not the silence of someone trying to be mysterious, but a silence that was a quality of character, part of the definition of who they were. It was as if they were aware that human life is from silence to silence, and that it was not necessary to fill every minute between with words, perhaps thereby to postpone silence. Rather, such persons carried silence comfortably, and when they spoke, their words were clear and distinct, having brought their own context rather than depending upon the one provided by circumstance.

Let us pause here to remind ourselves that silence is not to be praised as an unambiguous good. In fact, there are silences that are negative and sometimes painful: the silences of fear, of cowardice, of apathy, of guilt, of loneliness, of death. Nor can genuine silence be manufactured. Anyone who has said, "Sh-h-h," in a library knows how noisy are our attempts to create silence. Of course, we make our efforts with dramatic pauses in sermons, organ music to quiet chattering worshipers, and a call for a moment of silence to remember the deceased gladiators before the game begins. But a break in the noise is not the silence which we are considering.

The silence being affirmed here is a primal reality. We all speak freely and favorably of the Word of God, but we have also experienced, even if we do not speak of it, the silence of God. The silence of God is not solely a reference to our not hearing an answer to prayer or not receiving a word in response to an anguished, "Why?" God's silence is integral to God's revelation. God does not talk all the time.

Ancient Jewish and Christian writers commented with respect and awe on silence as a primal reality. Rabbis, commenting on Genesis 1:3, "And God said," asked and answered the question, What was there before God spoke? God's silence. Likewise, silence surrounded the coming of the Word or Wisdom into the world, according to a text which inspired "It Came upon a Midnight Clear": "For while gentle silence enveloped all things,/and night in its swift course was now half gone,/thy all-powerful word leaped from heaven, from the royal throne,/into the midst of the land" (Wisd. of Sol. 18:14-15). And in the end, the world will revert again to silence. "And it shall be after these years that my Son the Messiah shall die, and all in whom there is human breath. Then shall the world be turned into the primeval silence seven days, as at the first beginnings" (Apoc. Ezra 7:29-31). "Now when the Lamb broke the seventh seal, there was silence in heaven for what seemed half an hour" (Rev. 8:1 NEB).

But few Christian writers have reflected on silence as a fundamental reality quite as beautifully and as profoundly as Ignatius of Antioch. He wrote of the three mysteries of the faith: Mary's virginity, the birth of Jesus, and the cross as having been "wrought in the silence of God" (*Eph.* 19:2). Or again, "there is one God who manifested himself through Jesus Christ his Son, who is his word proceeding from silence" (*Magn.* 8:2). The two qualities, silence and the word, are expressed in the life of the church in the person of the bishop. Because the bishop is of God, says Ignatius, the bishop sometimes speaks and sometimes is silent. Both are authoritative (*Eph.* 6:1).

The Word proceeding out of silence—what an appropriate description, not only of Jesus Christ but also of preaching! The silence as well as the word of the bishop carrying authority—what an appropriate description not only of a bishop but also of a preacher! God breaking the silence with the Word—what an appropriate description not only of revelation but a sermon, a word tossed against the clear glass of silence behind which people sit waiting and asking, "Is there any word from the Lord?" The very characterization of preaching as breaking the silence should give to the one who so understands it a fresh respect for words. The words seeking employment in a sermon would then be screened carefully. Nouns which refused to stand straight and march out rather than slump off to the corner of the mouth could not be used. And so with verbs which stood around like adjectives instead of getting on with the business of the sentence. And the one whose sermon proceeds out of silence will know what to do with a sentence, whether it be short and nervous and anxious to stand, speak and sit down, or long and lingering, thinking and exploring as it meanders. Nor will there be any problem with accent, stress, and underscoring. Excessive volume, exaggerated gestures, and unnecessary accumulations of more words are the frantic devices of those whose words proceed not from silence but from noise, words thrown into rooms of words.

A preacher cannot decide some Sunday morning to be equally at home in silence as in breaking the silence. This is the case whether one had once been convinced that the call to preach was a call to speak at every hint of an opportunity, or had simply yielded to the pressure of every church gathering: "Oh, I see Reverend Brown has come in; I'm sure everyone would like to hear a few words from our pastor." Some, of course, are uncomfortable with silence and see no authority in it whatsoever. This is not a view peculiar to the ministry; all of us are in part products of a culture that has gone public with everything and is very suspicious of silence. Perhaps the sermon fared better in those times when there was concerted effort to silence it than in a society in which everything is talked about incessantly by everybody.

But a preacher can recover and reclaim the silence that he or she carries within, and out of that silence, speak the Word. It demands the realization that a minister's life does not consist in the abundance of words spoken. But most of all it requires embracing both silence and revelation in one's understanding of God, and developing a mode of preaching which honors that understanding by being in harmony with it.

Heard in a Whisper

The silence surrounding God's activity and purposes has been broken, not by our noisy opinions but by God's revelation. Revelation is not simply about grace but is itself an act of grace. The fundamental human appetite—the Gospel of John calls it hunger and thirst—is to know God, for to know God is life eternal (John 17:3). "Show us the Father, and we shall be satisfied" (John 14:8) is not the request of Philip alone but of us all. And the request has not gone unanswered. "No one has ever seen God; the only Son, who is in the bosom of the Father, he has made him known" (John 1:18).

But God's self-disclosure has not been obvious to everyone. As far as we know, God has not dipped a finger in a cloud and written across the sky, "I love you." If God rolled a ball of thunder from east to west, booming unmistakably "I love you," then some of us missed it. How, then, has God broken the silence? Not with a shout, but in a whisper; that is to say, in ways not all have heard. That God is revealed in creation is a clear, if minor, theme in Scripture. Paul says so plainly: "Ever since the creation of the world his invisible nature, namely, his eternal power and deity, has been clearly perceived in the things that have been made" (Rom. 1:20). Luke says so poetically: "Yet he did not leave himself without witness, for he did good and gave you from heaven rains and fruitful seasons, satisfying your hearts with food and gladness" (Acts 14:17). And, of course, the psalmist sings it: "The heavens are telling the glory of God;/and the firmament proclaims his handiwork./Day to day pours forth speech, and night to night declares knowledge" (Ps. 19:1-2). And were creation all daffodils and dogwood, sunsets and sailboats, trout streams and timbered trails, shocks of grain standing guard over sleeping pumpkins, and snowflakes on freckled noses, then all would agree: only a fool says there is no God. However, creation includes drought, flood, tidal wave, earthquake, and tornado, not to mention mosquitoes and crippling germs. When the legal profession speaks of "an act of God" it is usually talking to a family who has lost everything. God is revealed in creation, yes; but not in unambiguous ways.

The Scriptures, we believe, record the revelation of God. "In many and various ways God spoke of old to our fathers by the prophets" (Heb. 1:1). We read the sermons of Isaiah, Jeremiah, and Amos, and all seems perfectly clear. Why did not all Israel listen and believe? Because we are reading the oracles of the prophets whom history proved to be true, while Israel listened to them along with scores of prophets who proved to be false, most of whose names have been forgotten. But at the time, with a prophet on every corner crying, "Lo, here," and, "Lo, there," who could discern the Word of God? Is God's Word one of prosperity or doom for Israel? Of Jerusalem or of the wilderness? The true Word was heard, to be sure, but it did not come over the only loudspeaker on the street. Some might protest and say that the truth was corroborated by miracles so that true and false could be distinguished. In some cases, yes, but in others there were either no miracles, only the word, or the miracles provided uncertain testimony. For some time, the wizards of Egypt matched Moses miracle for miracle. When Jesus was accused of exorcising demons by Beelzebul, he asked his critics, "By whom do your sons cast them out?" (Luke 11:19). In fact, Jesus said that some would on the day of judgment be rejected as evildoers even though they had prophesied, cast out demons, and worked miracles (Matt. 7:21-23). In other words, miracles do not guarantee that one is of God, and so they certainly do not change the whisper of revelation into a clear shout of certainty.

In Jesus, says the Fourth Evangelist, God is revealed (1:18). One might think at last the whispered and fragmentary sentences, the refracted images half-veiled, would give way to the clear and unmistakable word and vision of God. But the whisper continues, for somewhere on the spectrum between opaque and transparent, the revelation of God in Jesus occurs. To experience Jesus was to experience the revealing/concealing of God. Jesus was a Galilean, of Nazareth, from a carpenter's home, a friend of tax collectors and sinners, often in conflict with the leaders and institutions of his own faith community. He taught primarily in parables, a literary form by which meanings are not made explicit and listeners must invest a great deal in the attempt to understand. Many did not, including his immediate disciples. According to Mark, his disciples did not understand Jesus' ministry, especially when he began to speak of his death. At the end, one denied him, one betrayed him, and they all abandoned him and fled. Jesus was crucified as politically dangerous. A Roman soldier confessed him to be the Son of God, and women of Galilee attended to his corpse. On the third day, he was seen alive again by various followers. According to the Gospels and Paul (I Cor. 15:1-8), Jesus appeared to women and to men, singly and in groups, up to as many as five hundred. But among non-believers in and around Jerusalem there is no record of seeing the risen Christ. In fact, according to Acts, the apostles preached that Jesus' life was public record and his death was public record, but of his resurrection, *"we* are witnesses" (3:15; 5:32).

Certainly this brief sketch is enough to remind us that the voice of God in Jesus was not a shout, so overwhelmingly self-evident and persuasive that even the disinterested and casual passerby was crushed into faith by the weight of the evidence. God in Jesus was "veiled in flesh." According to Matthew, when Simon Peter confessed Jesus to be the Christ, the Son of God, Jesus said that Peter's conclusion was not arrived at by observation; "flesh and blood has not revealed this to you, but my Father who is in heaven" (16:17). Later Paul was to say that no one could confess Jesus as Lord except by the Holy Spirit (I Cor. 12:3). This is to say, faith was not the end result of tallying up the evidence. Many did and to this day continue to experience God in the words, deeds, and presence of Jesus, but they did not and do not because God coerced faith as the unavoidable conclusion due to divine displays. Whoever has looked upon the crucified Jesus and said, "Son of God," has believed not just because of but also in spite of. The believer has chosen, has taken a risk, has said yes in a world of nos. The believer has leaned forward, heard the whisper, and trusted it to be the voice of God.

There are those who hold that the Gospel of John has turned the whisper of Bethlehem into a shout in Jerusalem in that the "of God, from God, to God, with God, like God" quality of Jesus is raised from a minor to a major key, enlarged from lower case to capitals. Thus, it is said, the veil has been removed and the revelation of God has been made a public announcement. Such a conclusion is understandable, given the prologue declaring Jesus the incarnation of the eternal Word, given the titles applied to Jesus, given the seven signs Jesus performs, and given the words of Jesus in which he speaks of coming from God and going again to God. But it must be kept in mind that there is a difference between what the writer and reader believe and declare about Jesus and what the characters around Jesus saw and heard. As we shall discuss shortly, once faith hears and embraces the whisper, the assurance of that faith shouts what had been heard. However, those who had not, and have not, believed still must listen, discern, and decide amid the because ofs and in spite ofs. As the writer says to the reader, "*we* have beheld his glory" (1:14), but Jesus' contemporaries did not have the prologue to read before they heard or observed Jesus. We who believe have beheld his glory, but what our faith has made so clear to us is not so clear to others. We say he is from God, but some say from Nazareth; we say he performed a sign of the Messiah at Cana, the steward said it was the best wine of the feast; we say he referred to his body as the temple destroyed and raised, his critics said it took forty-six years to build the temple; we say Jesus provides new birth, Nicodemus said he was already an old man; we say Jesus is the water of life, the woman said the well is deep and Jesus has no bucket; we say Jesus was before Abraham, they said he was not yet fifty years old; we say Jesus died as the Lamb of God, they said it is expedient that one man should die for the people.

It is so extremely important in preaching that we not be impatient or critical or condescending toward characters in the Gospels who did not see and hear what we see and hear. The eyes and ears of faith are not the eyes and ears of everyone. Lest we deride others and flatter ourselves, we should remember that flesh and blood did not provide the revelation of God in Jesus. We are believers not because we are more discerning of the evidence, more intelligent in our assessment. Consider, for example, those believers who made up the churches of Paul. The message that they heard was Christ crucified delivered by a preacher who had adopted the cruciform life, "always carrying in the body the death of Jesus" (II Cor. 4:10), slandered as "the refuse of the world" (I Cor. 4:13). Hardly the message and hardly the credentials to persuade and enlist those who expect the life of God in the world to be differently arrayed. Paul knew that his preaching Christ as the wisdom and power of God was foolishness and weakness and an obstacle to many, but he refused to turn the whisper into a shout by clever speech or subsidizing the gospel with eye-catching wonders. He was content with the understanding that the things of the Spirit are a secret hidden from those who think only in terms of the standards of the world (I Cor. 1:18–2:13).

These comments about revelation being heard as a whisper are in harmony with the nature of faith. The confidence and certainty that believers possess did not precede faith as though it were the reason for believing, as though they had said, "When we are absolutely sure, we will believe." The blessing of confidence, and the freedom that accompanies it, is the fruit of, not the prerequisite of, faith. We could wish for more, of course, and probably have on occasion asked for signs. Gideon is not the only one who puts out the fleece. It takes courage to witness to answered prayer when even one's close friends have referred to the experience as coincidence or good luck. Why does God not answer prayers on wide screen and in technicolor and get us off the hook? And very few ministers can honestly say their call came in a voice loud enough for the whole family to hear.

The plain, though often painful, truth about a whisper is that not everyone hears it. According to the accounts in Acts of Paul's call to be an apostle to the Gentiles (chapters 9, 22, 26), his experience of the risen Christ occurred in the company of fellow travelers. They seem to have seen a light but not Jesus, heard a sound but discerned no message. Too bad; Paul could have used some witnesses when he argued that he was an apostle by reason of that experience. When God responded to Jesus' prayer in John 12:27-29, "the crowd standing by heard it and said that it had thundered." The reasons some hear and some do not are varied, profound, and in some ways mysterious beyond our charting. According to John 7:17, a major factor is in one's willingness to obey, as if to say, those who will not, cannot. In the description of God's Servant in Isaiah 50:4-6, preparation for speaking included sufferings, and among the sufferings was God's opening the ear. The implication is that it is easier, less disturbing, less painful not to hear. Hearing certainly involves character. Those who choose to be small, petty, mean, and self-centered seem unable to grasp the big words of the faith, to sing the songs of Zion, to catch the vision of a world at peace before God. In order to hear the whisper of revelation, one must still have the capacity, however abused since Eden, to recognize the voice.

What, it is time to ask, does this have to do with preaching? To that matter we now turn.

Shouted from the Housetop

To say that God's Word is heard in a whisper is not simply to borrow a conversation from art, which is characterized by the desire both to tell and to withhold its secret. Nor is it to suggest that revelation is of such a nature that its preachers introduce in their deliveries the tones of tentativeness and uncertainty. Quite the contrary, to hear in a whisper does not at all mean one is to preach in a whisper. The Word of God *at the ear* is a whisper; *at the mouth* it is a shout. To preach in a whisper is to be seduced by a deadly and heretical equation: all do not hear = all cannot hear = all are not supposed to hear. Such a line of thought turns the gospel into a secret, the church into the elite, and Jesus into a riddle rather than a parable. True, some of the seed sown by the sower will fall along the path, some among weeds, some among rocks, and some in good soil, but that fact does not justify holding tightly to the seed until one has located the good soil that will guarantee a full harvest. We were not ordained to exercise such careful selectivity.

This selectivity is precisely the error of the early movement we refer to as Gnosticism. Instead of locating the whisper at the ear of the hearer, Gnostics placed the whisper on the lips of the speaker. It was not the case that some simply did not hear the Word; they were not judged worthy to hear and, therefore, not permitted to do so. Instead of the Word creating its own audience, these "spiritual ones" took that responsibility upon themselves. One is tempted to digress for a moment to remark upon the difficulty the church has always had in allowing the Word to create its own listeners rather than deciding on its own who is to hear and who is not. The church described in Acts learned quite early that the Word, when left to find its own mark, generates a response of trust in Samaritans, Greeks, Ethiopians, and Romans as well as Jews, a jolting surprise to the church in Jerusalem. The realization that God is "rich toward all" forced the church into a high-level conference. But we must resist the temptation and proceed with our train of thought. The tradition of shifting the whisper from hearing to speaking is represented in the Gospel of Thomas, a collection of "secret sayings of Jesus," and the Gospel of Philip. For example, in Philip 2:58, the writer characterizes Jesus' teaching: "His word hid itself from everyone." In some Gnostic circles the holy kiss was a means of communicating the Word in the circle of insiders without running the risk of it falling upon the wrong ears, a risk obviously attendant upon speaking aloud.

It is the position of the theology of preaching being presented here that the New Testament, which carries the Word as both a whisper and a shout, is best interpreted if one understands God's Word as being heard as a whisper and spoken as a shout. That is, at the ear the word of faith we preach is a whisper, for revelation is not simplistic and obvious, but at the mouth it is a shout. By "shout," of course, no indication of style of delivery is intended, but rather that what we preach is a public proclamation.

"What you hear whispered, proclaim upon the housetops" (Matt. 10:27*b*). These words of Jesus occur in the collection of warnings, encouragements, and instructions that constitute Matthew's account of the charge to the Twelve before sending them out to cleanse, heal, and preach. The instruction in verses 26-27 is framed upon the pattern of the eschatological reversal; that is, at the end time, the present state of affairs in the world will be overturned and reversed. Not only will good triumph over evil but the hidden will be revealed and that which was heard in a whisper will be shouted. But in its present context, the disciples are not to wait for that eschatological reversal; they are to participate in it, making present the future. Hope, then, has become a charge: they are to proclaim from the housetops what was, with great difficulty, struggle, and risk, heard and received with faith. The inner dynamic of that instruction merits our attention.

Coming to faith, leaning forward into the Word to hear, to discern, and to commit oneself in spite of risks and conditions arguing against belief, sometimes even against the counsel of those who love us but who listen to other voices: this experience we have described on the analogy of hearing a whisper. Once faith is born, an appropriate analogy is that of shouting from the roof. It is a shout of recognition of the Good News of God's grace, of release from the turmoil of indecision, of coming upon new vistas of clarity and confidence after arduous wrestling with values and vocation.

In the sense just described, the shout seems spontaneous and as irrepressibly easy as, "Eureka!" This is only partially true, for the shout from the roof is more than an expression of personal feeling; it is the charge to preach. And preaching does not wait upon feeling. The task to which we have been called is more important than how we happen to feel about it on any given day. If the pleasure principle is permitted to replace the prophet's burden as the impetus to mount the rooftop, then many Sundays would find the herald of God still below and not quite up to it today. Many ministers, however, testify to their most effective preaching on days when lack of sleep, personal woes, pounding temples, scattered attention, and unrequited investment in the lives of the broken and strayed, have left them feeling washed up at the foot of the pulpit. Such is the power of God at work through servants who do not mince and tiptoe among the likes and dislikes of the ministry.

There are other difficulties as well which tend to muzzle the shout. It is not always easy to shout. All of us are aware there are some matters we never shout; we are careful to wait for the right time, place, atmosphere, and persons. Why? Because the subject matter is personal and very, very important. But in saying that the matter is personal and very, very important, has not one perfectly described a sermon? Wrap it in worship and place it in a sanctuary among the faithful; even so, a sermon that will also be heard by the casual, the stranger, the visiting sermon-taster, and the twice-a-year member who is expecting "another good talk" is for some of us difficult to deliver.

Other forces also are arrayed against the shout. For example, cowardice, just plain cowardice. Times come when it is not enough to hold the coats of the prophets and apostles for twenty minutes, cheering them on; their opponents have sons and daughters in every community. According to the morning paper, Herod is still alive and the innocents continue to be slaughtered. Most of us, however, do not refer to our reticence as cowardice, and maybe at times it is not. The fact is, on issues of vital importance a sermon can disturb, upset, even radically affect relationships and behavior. Who has appetite for that? When old Simeon took the infant Jesus in his arms, he said to Mary, "Behold, this child is set for the fall and rising of many in Israel" (Luke 2:34). The realization that Christ makes such a difference, that some fall as well as rise, can muffle the shout in the hope that no one heard it.

The message to be shouted is the one that has been heard in a whisper. This eliminates the noisy borrowings of what others have heard. Also disqualified is the mock enthusiasm designed to give the impression of passion but which only momentarily convinces, and not even momentarily diverts attention from the lack of substance. "What you have heard" excludes also those hastily prepared, diffuse attacks in anger against the front page of the newspaper. Railing against the world is neither judgment nor grace, and putting boots and helmet on one's voice does not make one a crusader.

Even so, we do shout from the housetops, we do make public proclamation of the gospel, and properly so. Again, a reminder: shout is not to be taken literally but as a symbol for the open and universally available quality of preaching. It may, in fact, be loud or soft and still qualify. A quiet voice through a cabin door, "President Lincoln says we're free," is no less a shout than seventy-six trombones down Main Street on the Fourth of July.

This image of preaching as shouting from the housetops is appropriate to the task in at least four respects. One, it properly registers the importance and urgency of the message we speak. Two, its public nature witnesses against narrow sectarian or exclusive forces that arise now and then in the church. The pulpit cannot heed any person or group that says, "Keep your voice down or other races, economic groups, publicans, and sinners will hear and may come running." The shout, in biblical language, is to the ends of the earth. Three, the shout symbolizes the intensity and the tenacity of the love that not only is the message but impels the message. This word of love and care for every person derives its intensity from the indebtedness of every preacher toward all who have a right to know. And four, preaching in the image of one shouting serves, and has served since the time of Jesus, as an alert to all forces of evil: there is another voice to be heard, another claim for human life; God has not abandoned the poor, the stranger, the lonely, the captive and the desperate, to be victimized by those who traffic in greed and power. Mark portrays Jesus as the strong Son of God entering Satan's house and plundering it, casting out all the demons that cripple, suppress, frighten, alienate, and kill. In reciting the stories of Jesus' activity, Mark often pictures Jesus shouting at the demons: "Shut up and come out!" And it is very important, even to those in every village and city who are not attending worship on a given Sunday, to know that in faithfulness and with regularity that witness is being made with courage and grace.

The preacher knows, however, that the public proclamation always carries a whisper in its bosom, for one never forgets how faith had its beginnings. After all, we are not barkers at a sideshow or peddlers of the gospel. Even in times of impatience and exasperation, the point is not to get something off the chest but into the heart. To preach, then, is to shout a whisper.

What does it mean to shout a whisper? It means to speak boldly and clearly, but to trust the Word as the sower trusts the seed to carry its own future in itself and to make its own way into the heart. It means to proclaim what we have heard, being true to the received tradition, but being careful to frame it in the context of the listeners. The preacher cannot *make* them hear it, but he or she can at least remove some obstacles to hearing. In other words, the listeners will not have to pretend they live in another time and place in order to believe and to be Christians. They will recognize not only Jerusalem and Damascus but also their own town and streets in the sermon. And life will be presented as realistically as the Bible presents it. Not even Easter is all cheers in the Scriptures; only a child's world is all light with no shadows. The Bread of Life is broken and offered, but the hearers must be allowed to chew for themselves.

And shouting a whisper certainly means respecting the listener's resistance to the message. The forms of this resistance are many, and familiar: irregularity in attendance, criticism of petty and peripheral matters, inattention, raising other questions, attempts at humor, and many others. One must not forget that there are two kinds of preaching difficult to hear: poor preaching and good preaching. Why should a listener not resist? If a person recognizes in the sermon issues of ultimate importance, if embracing the message will affect relationships, uses of one's influence and resources, and perspectives on ethical and moral questions, if believing means entering into covenant with God and the community of faith, then, of course, there is resistance. Does not the patient on the operating table have the right to ask, "Doctor, what will I look like after the surgery?" Petty sermons and promotional pieces arouse no resistance; a sense of insult, maybe, but no resistance. Understand, nothing is intended here to encourage those feverish and frustration-born attacks on one's parishioners in order to provoke counterattack, in order to feed the martyr complex or to confirm that one is a prophet. The subject here is nothing other than preaching the gospel.

The final word to be said in any presentation of a theology of preaching is an acknowledgment of its provisional nature. Such a recognition is by no means a retraction of anything said. It is rather a statement which both reserves a person's right and makes no claim upon God. The right reserved for oneself is to grow, to continue learning and maturing through study, preaching, pastoring, and living one's faith. That process will necessitate continual modification of one's theology of preaching. That no claim is made on God is simply the recognition that a theology of preaching is no more than an attempt to discern the way of God's Word in the world and to align one's mode and matter of preaching accordingly. The minister never says, "This is the way God will work through preaching," but rather he or she says, "This is the way I work because of my understanding of the way God works." But even then, surprises wait at every corner. The disciples who prepared supper for a stranger at Emmaus had no idea the occasion would become a sacrament. Paul wrote to his friends at Philippi with no idea that his note would become sacred Scripture for millions. The would-be disciple who volunteered to follow Jesus "whithersoever" surely did not know how many places in the world are named "Whithersoever."

PART II

*Preaching: Having Something
to Say*

four

The Life of Study

The time has come for us to talk about the minister's study life, but the time has not yet come for us to talk about study directed toward the preparation of a particular sermon. When the life of study is confined to "getting up sermons," very likely those sermons are undernourished. They are the sermons of a preacher with the mind of a consumer, not a producer, the mind that looks upon life in and out of books in terms of usefulness for next Sunday. The last day of such a ministry is as the first, having enjoyed no real lasting or cumulative value in terms of the minister's own growth of mind, understanding, or sympathy. Studying only for the next sermon is very much like clearing out of the wilderness a small garden patch, only to discover the next week that the wilderness has again taken over. If the gardener is bitter and resentful, feeling that the time spent was wasted, the feelings are understandable and the assessment almost correct. There is, however, another way of viewing the role of study in the life of a minister, a way which is both fruitful and satisfying.

The Importance of the Life of Study

The minister is expected to be adequate for many occasions, both in and out of the congregation, and often without much advance notice. Though by no means an expert on every subject, the minister will want to be sufficiently informed to be respected when standing to speak and likewise respected when seated and silent. In most communities, this respect is accorded the minister in advance, but it can be sustained only by disciplined endeavor.

It is public knowledge that ministers' studies (not offices) all have a common address: at the intersection of the normative tradition, which the minister is obligated to interpret; the congregation, which the minister is obligated to lead and nourish; and the world, which the minister is obligated to serve and return to the renewing grace of God. Whether situated over garages, in basements, off foyers, or behind furnaces, the address is the same. Other professionals in town have studies, but none at so busy an intersection; not a physician, not a lawyer. There are exceptional persons among them who long for it, who wish and plan for those get-away times to take up again an ethical or philosophical question which arose in law or med school and which refuses to go away. The question does not ordinarily bear directly upon a normal day's work and, therefore, its pursuit lies somewhere between a side interest and a nagging insistence.

With the minister, such is not the case. Time spent in study is never *getting away* from daily work but *getting into* daily work. The hours of study bear directly and immediately on who the minister is and the minister's influence by word and action. It is in the study that so much of the minister's formation of character and faith takes place. There are many terms to describe this activity. Study is an act of obedience: "You shall love the Lord your God with all your mind." It is a time of worship: "An hour at study," said the rabbis, "is in the sight of the Holy One, Blessed be He, as an hour of prayer." What minister has not experienced a desk becoming an altar? It is a time of pastoral work; the entire congregation will benefit from the fruit of this labor. Study will protect the parishioners from the excessive influence of the minister's own opinions, prejudices, and feelings. Study is getting a second and third opinion before diagnosis and treatment. No minister has to do the world's thinking over again, but every minister needs to spend time with the writings of those who have for a lifetime wrestled with matters of importance. Study gives distance on the minister's own life as well as the congregation's and there is health in that. Unrelieved intimacy smothers and distorts.

Finally, study is a homiletical act: the confidence born of study (not the pseudo-confidence of personality or bravado) releases the powers of communication. To know one's subject and to believe it is important is to be free, and it is freedom that permits all one's faculties to have their finest hour in the service of speaking and hearing. Gone is the tendency to mumble, to draw in the breath while preaching as if to prevent one's words from reaching ears that may be informed on one's text or topic. Gone is the fear that someone may want to converse further about the sermon and discover that you have said all that was known, and more, about the subject. Rather, the preacher now welcomes such a conversation, not only as an extension of the pulpit's ministry, but also as the opportunity to share in more detail the matters of concern which study unearthed but which lay outside the thematic and temporal limits of the sermon.

Hindrances to the Life of Study

One of the ironies in the history of the church is the fact that the person who is expected to speak every week on issues of ultimate importance—God's will and human freedom, evil and suffering, grace and judgment, peace and covenant—has been in many quarters begrudged the study time necessary to prepare. Not everywhere, of course, but in many parishes there is strong resistance to granting a pastor any study leave. "If the minister wants to go study somewhere, why not use a week of vacation time?" "What do you mean, study? I thought you had already graduated." It would be comforting if such comments were rare, and exaggerated, but the one room in the house of God which, judging by its size, furnishings, and location, is an afterthought, is not the parlor but the pastor's study.

Let us hasten to add, however, that the laity are not alone to be indicted. Our culture has not accorded teachers, students, and schools the respect granted them in other societies. One should remember also that churches are institutions, and institutions are generally suspicious of investigation and exploration, the heart and soul of study. There is a felt threat buried in there somewhere. But even so, a few churches provide the pastor space and time for study, but to no avail. Many ministers struggle here. Some, of course, love to study, perhaps even to the point of hiding among the books to the neglect of persons. Others, however, creep like snails to the study, force themselves in, sit down, line up sheets of paper, sharpen pencils, go for coffee, rearrange the papers, resharpen the pencils, hope the phone rings, cock the ear to hear the bleating of a stray lamb lost somewhere in a dark ravine, and sure enough—! There are a thousand voices, and reasonable ones, too, which argue that the shepherd's place is among the flock. No one can counter that. And, in addition, with the flock is where the satisfactions are, the clear reminders that one is a minister. But, not until a minister is persuaded that working in the study *is* being among the flock, and not until the flock accepts that fact, can a ministry, and especially a preaching ministry, attain full stature and be consistently effective.

Why is it that this dimension of ministry is so often neglected if not actually downgraded within the clergy? The reasons are obviously many and varied. Some ministers have had problems and probably will have them all their lives, with disciplined and sustained patterns of study. The reasons may be totally outside the factors of intelligence and ability, and may be due to early school traumas, being made to study as punishment, or the association of study with being graded or evaluated. Even the seminary experience, coming at a time after some maturity is reached and primary commitments are made, may represent the kinds of activity a minister may not wish to continue. Many complaints about the irrelevant and unreal character of seminary education are unjustified; after all, even professional education has to be more than the wholesale outfitting of future retailers if it is to qualify as education at all. But even so, some seminary programs are unnecessarily distant from the practice of ministry.

It is sometimes the case that the life of study is a casualty of an unsatisfactory transition from school to parish. If in seminary a person did not establish good study habits that were portable to future locations, but only met the faculty's requirements and deadlines, then graduation was the withdrawal of the scaffolding for study. However much one may have complained about school demands, the fact is, those demands gave a pattern and structure to life. Recent graduates confess to wasting time and struggling with

72

the question, How do I spend Tuesdays? Older pastors may counsel the young pastor not to worry; Tuesdays and every other day will be filled and overflowing soon enough. That is true, but it is poor advice because it misses the point. The aim is not to fill all one's days with busyness, but rather to have sufficient discipline with priorities firm enough that the minister can sort through the countless claims on the available hours. Of course pastors are called to serve the needs of people, but to have their schedule totally dependent on the schedule of others is to undercut their own effectiveness in that very endeavor. There is a difference between being a servant and being servile.

A major contribution of the academic life, which is sorely missed later, is the ability to select quality reading materials. One can usually trust that books read under supervision and assignment represent the best in the field. Given the vast number of volumes being printed on every subject, that is no small benefit, however burdensome it may seem at the time. Care in choosing books is essential, because it saves time and money and helps a person from being overwhelmed by the numbers available. Behold the pained faces peering over the attractive displays of compelling titles in the book room at a church conference or minister's institute. Old patterns of study, now faded from neglect or shredded by anxious efforts to do everything at once, survive only as the dull ache of guilt. Full of high resolve, the minister gives the bookseller half the grocery budget and walks away with a heavy bag but with the light heart of a sinner leaving a confessional. Chances are good that three of the purchases will simply repeat what the minister already knows, and two are duplicates of books already owned but long unnoticed on the shelf. A few suggestions offered below may give some help to those who recognize themselves in this description.

Let us look at study straight in the face and call it what it is. Study is work, often hard work, and just as often having no immediate fruit in terms of solution to a problem, counsel to a parishioner, or message for next Sunday. Motivation has to be nourished by deep springs because frequently it is not the case that what we *have* to do can be transformed into what we *want* to do. One is reminded of the method of some art teachers who have their students struggle to paint with the wrong hand in order to seduce the right hand into more creativity. The work is hard, and sometimes accompanied by pain and fear. The pain in study is usually vague and ill-defined, but at its root is the fact that all learning involves giving up something. To attain to one understanding involves giving up another, and the one given up might have been ours since childhood, or endorsed by family and friends, or taught to us by someone loved and respected. Is discarding an interpretation an act of ingratitude or disloyalty to a parent, a Sunday school teacher, a beloved pastor, a respected professor? Those who continually call for change, glibly and cynically as though it were a simple and painless switch of the dial, surely have forgotten, or have yet to experience their first radical readjustment.

Unlike the pain, the fear is clearly identifiable; it is the fear of discovering that which will cause the pain. One fears to plow through a new volume if there is the chance that a favorite landscape will be bulldozed in the process. One fears discovering a truth which will demand rethinking several views and changing the mind. One fears that knowledge will somehow negate the pleasures of naïveté. One fears there may be some truth to the popular notion that study banks the fires of enthusiasm replacing zeal with knowledge and converting the impassioned preacher into a pale lecturer.

The preacher who continues to be a student does so in spite of two cultural elements that are erosive of that effort. One is the myth of experience as the true and adequate teacher. Experience can be a teacher and provide a perspective not gained otherwise. For example, a soldier in the trenches of the Civil War came to understand war in ways unavailable to non-combatants. However, that experience was also limiting; so limiting, in fact, that the soldier could hardly interpret that war to the nation and to subsequent generations. That task calls for another perspective; that is, another experience. Getting distance from an event and reflecting on it is experience as surely as being plunged into its swirling currents. Study is not an alternative to experience but is itself a form of experience that grants understanding, even expertise, on a range of subjects. Were that not the case, communities would be made up of isolated individuals unable to communicate and unable to help one another. All ministry, and preaching in particular, is predicated on the truth that a young woman can understand and be helpful to an old man; an older man can speak with insight to a teenage girl. Experience is indeed a teacher, but only as a member of a larger faculty.

The second element in our culture which tends to discourage the life of study is the premium placed on the spontaneous, the intuitive, the undisciplined impulse, the immediate sensation. This is not the place to offer a critique of the widespread insistence that activities and relationships be prompted by pleasure, with the anticipation of further pleasure. "Obligation" remains in the vocabulary of those who know the profound satisfaction that follows tasks often begun with no appetite and much anxiety. Nor is this the place to lament the general preference for ecstasy rather than awe. Ecstasy is the self's experience of delight; awe is the experience of that which is greater than the self and before which the self recedes. The present point is simply that study and knowledge do not dull one's capacity for the immediate or render one less appreciative of a full engagement of life. Of course, there are always the bad models, the caricatures of the thinker, equipped with impressive quotations, overloaded with information, and off to nowhere brilliantly. But the fact remains, study to the point of understanding sharpens rather than dulls one's appetite for and capacity to engage life with all one's faculties. To verify this, a person has only to attend a concert and note the difference in the responses of those who know music and those who do not or attend a lecture and observe which listeners know the subject and which do not. Or, for that matter, simply take a walk through the woods with someone who knows the flora and fauna. Not only will it be obvious that knowledge increases the pleasure and the appreciation of the forest, but also knowledge graciously shared is infectious, stirring in all of us the desire to know.

Suggestions for a Life of Study

The following suggestions are not offered on the assumption that the reader does not already possess a way of going about the task of study, nor are they offered as improvements upon present habits. What is presupposed here is that it is healthy to have one's patterns of work raised to the level of conscious reflection in order to own them intentionally, modify them, or shift to new patterns altogether.

For purposes of clarity, these suggestions will be itemized, with a brief discussion accompanying each.

1. At the beginning of a ministry, small or large, student or resident, inform the congregation of one's study schedule and explain that time in study is time spent with the entire congregation and with the community. Though every church understands that a minister's schedule includes time for small groups and individuals, it may not have thought of study as benefiting all the people through preaching, teaching, and counseling. Until they are helped to think in such terms, many parishioners are left with the simple equation: more time in study equals less time in ministry. How ministers spend their time is something of a mystery to the laity and many are hesitant to probe or to question, but they harbor strong suspicions. The minister who does not take time to enable understanding should not complain when there is misunderstanding. It goes without saying that the minister will choose study hours during the day and week when the flow of congregational life is at its lowest and demands on the minister's time are least.

2. Be realistic in one's expectations of the life of study. There is hardly an area of thought or activity that does not bear directly or indirectly upon ministry, and books are flowing from the presses every day. Pastors, especially those in remote areas, can sit in their studies and become depressed by the thought that there are many great new ideas circulating out there, but in what books are they to be found? Rather than being frustrated and immobilized on the one hand, or attempting the impossible on the other, a minister can do quality reading within the limits of time and the requirements of one's position. Quality reading means locating and carefully engaging the few really significant books in a field. In theology, biblical studies, preaching, pastoral care, and other related areas, there are one or two landmark books, in response to which there will follow scores of books for the next twenty years. Thoroughly digesting one such book can be immensely more valuable than racing through two dozen spin-offs and hasty revisits to the thoughts of the central figure in the discipline. To aid in that selection, the opinions of respected peers and seminary professors can be solicited. In addition, subscribing to a journal that provides good book reviews will be invaluable. Though a minister need not feel

76

guilty for not having read every book mentioned by lay and clergy, he or she should know the circles of thought and conversation out of which those books come. To have read the major works, to have reflected upon their contents, and to have weighed them carefully in relation to one's own views and convictions, is to gain the ear and earn the respect of those to whom one offers oneself as a leader.

3. Establish and maintain a routine of time and place of study. When hearing such a suggestion, some ministers voice the objection that ministry means being available, which means frequent interruptions of scheduled activity. The point is well made, but the point is lost on those who have no schedule to be interrupted, just as it is on those who go about seeking, encouraging, and advertising for interruption to justify failure to attend to study and reflection. The busy person has no better friend than routine and habit. Just imagine all the time wasted by those who are forever looking for "a good place" to study or "a good time" to study. Equally prodigal with time are those who study a bit here and a bit there, a little now and a little then. Such persons seem always to be studying but, in fact, are poor stewards of their time. Except for those rare individuals who can sink into deep thought and concentration anywhere at anytime, studying requires a good deal of time getting into and out of the subject matter. In fact, getting started is the major hurdle. Once into the process, the worth of the material and the satisfaction in thought usually provide sustaining power.

The greatest aid in reducing the time involved in getting started and later in coming to closure is placing oneself in a certain room, at a certain desk, at a certain time each day. Once the routine is established, the body, the mind, and the emotions know what that time and that place mean. Sights and sounds that once distracted do so no more. Negative adaptation has done its work; nothing is seen or heard except the task at hand. Routine has simplified life, and the minutes or hours of such total engagement are amazingly fruitful. In fact, not infrequently someone will remark, "When in your busy schedule did you find time to prepare so well?"

A second benefit of a routine is the new level of pleasure gained without any real change in life-style. The formula is simple: study when studying and play when playing. All of us can recall from college days times when we did not enjoy studying for thinking of our need for recreation and did not enjoy a party or a game for thinking about our need to study. Hence both study and play were robbed, each by the other, of both pleasure and effectiveness. A good schedule removes the debilitating guilt and releases all one's powers to enter fully into each moment.

4. Develop the ability to use small units of time. The word "develop" is used here because effort and patience will be required. There was a time with many of us when an hour between classes or events was regarded as insufficient to make any effort to study. We told ourselves that real study required larger blocks of time. That was not entirely self-deception; some of the tasks of study do require extended periods for thought and reflection. However, study also involves a number of acts which are important but which can be accomplished rather quickly. Reading brief journal articles, checking biblical references, assembling resources, using diction-aries and lexicons, sequencing materials to be read, and many other tasks can be cared for when only minutes are available. In fact, journalistic reading that informs us about denominational and general religious events and trends can well be done along with the reading of the daily paper and news magazines and does not need to be taken to the study at all. Now and then an article will be worth "elevating" in that room.

5. Regularly read novels, short stories, and poetry. Because such reading is so rewarding and pleasure-filled, it can be regarded as recreation, but for reasons stated below, it is classified here as study. First, let us be clear that we are referring to good literature, not thrill stuff that depends on a murder and a rape on each page to sustain the reader's attention. By great literature is meant that which has stood the test of time and remains on the list of recommended reading in literature classes. Those who are lacking a good high school or college education in this area, or those who have moved into ministry from fields more technical or otherwise narrowly defined, would do well to secure a reading list from a college literature class. There is no need to be embarrassed about reading Hardy, Maugham, Milton, Flaubert, and Dickinson while in or even after seminary. However, to allow fear of embarrassment to prevent one's reading the classics would be tragic indeed.

Lest anyone misunderstand, there is nothing intended here which even remotely resembles the vulgar practice of combing through literature for illustrations. To read Flaubert for sermon illustrations would be prostitution. Of course, what one reads enters directly and indirectly into one's speaking, but the reading is not done with usefulness in mind. Reading good literature enlarges one's capacities as a creative human being and has a cumulative effect on one's vocabulary, use of the language, and powers of imagination. Not by conscious imitation but through the subtle influence of these great storytellers and poets, a preacher becomes more adept at arranging the materials of the sermon so that by restraint and thematic control, interest, clarity, and persuasiveness will be served.

The ideal would be to begin in seminary the habit of reading such literature along with one's assignments in history, theology, and biblical studies, and then to maintain the practice through one's ministry. The reasons are two: first, seminary professors and classroom experiences so heavily influence the student not only as a thinker but as a communicator. However, the classroom lecture, properly designed to carry a heavy freight of information, is no model for the sermon. Second, the texts that are required reading of the curriculum were written by persons who are experts in the subject matter, but only rarely are they masters in the use of the language. In short, they do not write well. This is not a criticism but a fact, a fact that should prompt the students serious about preaching to supplement their reading with the works of master communicators. Since the short story is a first cousin of the sermon, the homiletics student could, for example, relieve the professor of the contradiction of having to assign such reading by taking the initiative to read at least one per week.

A major obstacle for the student is the feeling of guilt: there sits Aquinas on the shelf and I am indulging in Steinbeck. This guilt often leads the student to weigh the story and the poem in the same scales used for everything else, Will this be covered in the exam? Do we have to write reports? Will we discuss these in class? Since the answer is no on all counts, the reading becomes casualty to the oldest fiction in both academy and parish: I do not have the time. A large block of time? Probably not, but this is reading that can be done in brief time periods. The person who has a comfortable chair in a quiet corner beside which is always a book with a marker and who reads twenty minutes after dinner or before retiring will read dozens of books each year. The person who waits for time to read will, at the end of the year, have good intentions and sad regrets about the first one. The practice is not study in the heavy-browed, note-taking sense, but if the person whose primary business is communicating spends time each day with someone who has proven skills at that very point, it qualifies.

6. Resist the urge to cease study once a sermon idea emerges. The temptation to do so is strong; after all, motivation toward the sermon for Sunday is a very real factor in study and with the birth of a central idea for that sermon, motivation for continued study may sag. And, of course, there is that nagging fear that further study may prove that the idea was more flash than light. It is disappointing to have Matthew or Paul give one a sermon and then in the next few verses take it away. That possibility is, however, the very reason for continuing with one's study past the moment of insight. Will the insight stand the test of context and theological consistency? The claims of truth and appropriateness must be allowed to chase away tempters who whisper, "The congregation will never know."

The suggestion that study not stop with the birth of a sermon idea does, however, raise the question of the effective timing of breaks from study. Some ministers feel that once interest in a text or subject is generated, it is best to ride that momentum until interest or energy is spent. Such a pattern has its good points. There is truth in the old adage, "The iron, once cooled, is hard to heat again." Though taking a break after interest has ebbed and one's efforts seem not to be productive makes the return to the desk uninviting and starting again difficult, much can be said for stopping when interest is still high and ideas are flowing, whether one is reading, writing, taking notes, or reflecting. Resuming one's studies is a pleasant prospect and the desk attractive. One does not, however, simply stop at a peak; too much can be lost in the interim. A few notes sketching what is being done and thought and felt will offer threads that can be picked up again to carry the work to fruition. But again we remind ourselves that our rhythms of work differ, and we must honor schedule, habit, energy level, and abilities peculiar to ourselves.

7. Locate and take advantage of library facilities available. These resources will vary from place to place, but one should not conclude

without investigation that the absence of a seminary library leaves one intellectually stranded. Many public and small college libraries hold pleasant surprises, and some, even at great distances, have by-mail lending services. In any case, expenditures for one's own library can be happily reduced.

8. Set up your own library to function efficiently. Some ministers' libraries were apparently arranged by decorators. Cluttered does not necessarily mean functional, but neither does placing blue dust jackets near the pale yellow draperies. In order to maximize usefulness, three simple suggestions seem appropriate. One, when new books arrive, leave them on the desk until read. Once on the shelves they can be forgotten, but on the desk they get in the way, staring back at the one who tries to push them aside. Besides, the minister does not know which books to shelve until he or she knows their contents. Two, share books with others. The right book for the right person can be an extension of one's ministry. Other ministers might be willing to exchange books on a regular basis. Some books properly should be given away, not because they are of no value but because one has outgrown them. For them to remain on one minister's shelves is poor stewardship when they could be used effectively by a younger minister who is at a different point in his or her life and career. And finally, arrange the books for ease of use. Some reference books are used every week, so they need to be located for ready access. It is not difficult to think that a certain book is not all that important if it is located across the room or on a shelf accessible only by straining on tiptoes while perched atop the back of a swivel chair. The law of inertia is very strong, especially when it protects us from bodily harm. Other books also should be placed according to regularity of use. Their very presence prompts the minister to consult them more often.

9. Take advantage of available workshops, institutes, and seminars. These events are usually publicized in the journals, and most seminaries publish well in advance information on continuing education activities. One should strike a healthy balance between those events that address one's weaknesses and those that address one's strengths. Attending to one's lacks is vital for growth in ministry, but also vital is being confirmed and encouraged in areas of one's highest proficiency. In the meantime, for gain and

satisfaction, ministers can form peer groups that meet on a continuing basis. Agendas for these groups vary from book reviews to texts for sermons to evaluating tapes of one another's sermons to current issues before the church. These groups, if small and congenial, can be very stimulating and supportive.

10. Preserve the fruits of one's study. Methods here vary all the way from drawers filled with newspaper and magazine clippings to folders filed by topics, such as prayer, divorce, suicide, and Good Friday. If one does keep folders of materials, keeping one for each of the books of the Bible can also be a way of preserving the notes of research. Whether filing by topic or text or both, the point is to save materials for future use and avoid wasting time in duplicated efforts. It is a waste of time and energy to study for a lesson or sermon, and once the message is prepared, save only the message. The work done on Ephesians, for example, in preparation for a sermon, if preserved, will save much time and increase confidence when next returning to that book for a presentation. After years in the ministry, the cumulative value of such a file will radically reduce preparation time as well as increase the quality of your work. These folders do not have to contain all the information gained from research; in many cases, an entry indicating where appropriate materials can be located will suffice.

Preserving the fruits of study involves different kinds of note-taking. There are research notes, notes containing one's thoughts in response to research, and notes that move the research and the reflection upon it closer to a sermon in preparation. However, there are notes to be taken on ideas that are spawned in the course of one's study which are quite unrelated to the immediate purpose and direction of that study. It is characteristic of stimulating resources to generate such thoughts and ideas, sometimes an explosion of them, which move in many directions. Although tempted to do so, one cannot pursue every thought triggered by a text or article or personal experience. Neither should one take the time to evaluate their merits. The wise course is to make a note on the idea and place it in a card file or folder designated for further consideration. If it is clear that the thought belongs with a sermon or an occasion already in prospect, then, of course, take time to place it with the notes already beginning to cluster at that point. (More will be said about sermon calendars later.)

Some of these notes will wilt in the light of careful scrutiny later, but no matter. The important thing now is to make the note full enough to revive later the thought that prompted it. Otherwise, the note is not only worthless; it haunts the edges of one's mind like an almost-heard conversation in the next room. For example, one may have a flood of ideas generated by Jonah's resentment of God's grace and generous love. The thoughts are pulsating and fresh but off to one side of one's present course. So a note is made. The card says, "Jonah at Nineveh." Months or years later, the note says too much and too little. It is good for nothing except to be cast out and trodden underfoot. Or, on a drive down a country lane, you are so alert to the sights and sounds of nature that a mockingbird in a tree becomes a magnet drawing together a rush of thoughts and feelings. On a scrap of paper the moment is captured: "Bird in tree." A year later, you may stare for hours at that piece of paper and feel no racing of the blood, no pounding of the heart. Of course, at the time there seemed no possibility of ever forgetting.

Within the minister's life of study there lies one pressingly regular assignment: the preparation of a sermon. We move now to give full attention to that assignment.

five

Interpretation: The Listeners

The principle of procedure fundamental to the task of sermon preparation is this: the process of arriving at something to say is to be distinguished from the process of determining how to say it. This statement should be printed in placard-size letters suitable for cutting out and fastening across the top of the minister's desk. The failure to observe the principle can be credited for many dull and unimaginative sermons, not to mention the boredom of ministers who approach the sermon as a chore. Such a preacher sits in the study like a child sitting at the window on Saturday when friends come over to play. "I can't; I have to get up a sermon."

Behold a seminarian sitting in the library with books open all around. The seminarian is "getting up a sermon." How is that possible? How can one work on a sermon, which is designing the communication, when the message has not yet been determined? How can one work at arriving at the message when attention is being given to framing a sermon out of that message, which as yet is undetermined? The two processes cannot be collapsed into one. It can be said, however, that there will be times during the process of arriving at the message when the form of the sermon will suggest itself. One can hope that the text being interpreted will provide the key to the movement of the sermon. After all, to impose upon a message a sermon form alien to the text that yielded the message could result in preaching what the text does not say and doing with the sermon what the text does not do. But what is being said here concerns procedure, the way one goes about the task, and what is being urged is that the minister not attempt two things at once. Otherwise, both suffer in quality and the minister suffers in frustration.

The reason this is so is clear upon reflection. The work of interpretation, which is the heart of arriving at a message, and the work of deciding on design and movement for framing that message into a sermon are two processes with their own integrity, their own purposes, their own skills, and their own climaxes. The task of interpretation has its own "eureka!" The message for Sunday is clear; what one will seek to achieve in the pulpit has moved out of the mass of notes and the pre-dawn gray of the mind into sunshine. It is time to stand for the "Doxology." And how will this be communicated? What movement of the sermon will provide the experience of this message for the hearers? That task still lies ahead, but when it is done, again there will be "eureka!" Unless the minister has two eurekas, it is not likely the listeners will have one.

To facilitate the separation of the two phases of sermon preparation and hence to preserve the benefits just described, it is wise to take a break after the first and engage in some activity totally different from study and reflection. Time with family or friends, physical activity, or some pastoral duty that is comfortable and not too demanding would provide a rewarding interlude. There is no reason to fear loss of motivation or momentum. A desk on which lies the message for Sunday is inviting. It is the desk containing blank tablets like empty eyes staring up at the minister that is ever the grim prospect he/she seeks continually to postpone.

One begins, then, with study in order to have something to say. And of what does this study consist? There are two focuses and the distance between them. One focus is upon the listeners, including their contexts: personal, domestic, social, political, economic. The other is upon the biblical text, including its contexts: historical, theological, and literary. The distance between these two focuses is very real, consisting of factors of time, space, language, world view, and immediate circumstances. Through the processes of interpretation, or hermeneutics, the distance can be negotiated with some degree of confidence. What the listeners hear the text say in a fresh, appropriate, and indigenous way to them: that is the message for the sermon.

We shall discuss these three elements as distinct and separate, knowing all the while that they are not distinct and separate. Keeping them apart is for purposes of clarity and sharpened attention and not out of some notion that the text's and congregation's intrusion upon each other would somehow erode honesty and objectivity in our study. In fact, "intrusion" is the wrong word. The listeners are the church, and as the church, they can claim the Bible as its book prior to and apart from our efforts to offer the texts in sermon. And the texts are Scripture, and as such can insist that the church hear their messages prior to and apart from our interpretive work. The horizons of the two worlds of text and congregation meet sometimes prior to and apart from our attempts to bridge the distance. This is not to void our methods of investigation or to minimize the importance of the results of such careful efforts. It is rather to recognize that in both the text and the congregation there are real issues of life and death and purpose which reach out to each other, resonating with each other, asking help of each other. And when the preacher studies both there is enough imagination and creativity, not to mention pastoral empathy, to render all claims of objectivity only partially true.

We begin the discussion with attention to the listeners. If one wishes to begin with the text, no objections come to mind. The two will meet on down the road anyway, with neither one claiming to have had a head start.

The Listeners as Audience

To think of the listeners as an audience is to regard them as an assembly of men, women, youth, and children who will hear the sermon. It is to think of them as strangers, as if an usher were to say to the minister, "The people have gathered and are waiting, and I have never seen any of them before today." For a minister to regard the listeners in this way requires a disciplined act of imagination; after all, these are parishioners whose names, faces, lives, relationships, addresses, problems, pleasures, and abilities are known. They have a relationship of need for the minister's sermons, and, admit it, the minister needs them. It was the anticipation of their presence on Sunday that gave impetus to the hours alone in the study. Just as there is a tradition among actors to say in the final rehearsal, "This play needs an audience," so the preacher could as well acknowledge that the sermon needs an audience. But in the theater those attending are strangers to one another as well as to the actors; it is not so in the church. What possible value could there be in imagining otherwise, in thinking of the listeners as an audience?

The value is this: to get enough distance to understand and accept the listeners in and of themselves, apart from their relationship to the minister. It is a common human trait, but one especially evident in ministers, to evaluate and to define persons in terms of their responses to us. In a church, certain members like the minister, others do not; some support the minister, others do not; some agree with the minister, others do not; some like the sermons, others do not. In the course of time, these factors tend to become very pronounced in the minister's estimation of the parishioners. When preparing a sermon, a preacher may predict who will and who will not like this one. The fact which tends to be forgotten in the process is that who and what these people are they brought with them, quite independent of their relationship with the minister or the minister's opinion of them. No one person's value is in any way dependent on another person's assessment. Ministers know that as well as or better than anyone, and yet these likes and dislikes and personal relationships do have influence upon preaching.

It is, therefore, important for the health of one's preaching to submit to the discipline of distancing every once in awhile, to remind oneself that those who are to hear this sermon are who they are and have their worth as well as their needs intrinsically, whatever may be their attitude toward or their relation to the minister. The discipline works something like this: sit down to prepare a sermon and say, "The audience for this sermon next Sunday will be men, women, young people, and children whom I do not know. Their lives and experiences are totally their own, unrelated to who I am and what I do." Having said that, take a sheet of paper and itemize what can be assumed about these listeners. The list is very important because it provides the portrait of the persons to be addressed in the sermon.

Does the list contain sufficient items for the sermon to have any appropriateness, to make any real contact at all?

However slowly this discipline may begin, eventually it will become obvious that the listeners are not really unknown. They are creatures of God, every one of them. In fact, they are the crowning achievement of God's creation, God's masterpieces. When God looked upon sky, sea, and hills, upon fish, flowers, and squirrels, upon terrapin, zebra, and goose, God said, "It is good." When God looked upon man and woman, God said, "This is like looking in the mirror; these are my own image." Some of the listeners do not know this about themselves and others have forgotten, but the preacher knows and it is evident in the sermon. In all the listeners the image of God has become marred, in some more than others, but even so, there remains the faint recollection of Eden. Therefore, when the preacher speaks of love and hate, of trust and suspicion, of evil and good, and of forgiveness and new beginnings, the listeners will recognize it, even if they have never before been in a church. The sermon will awaken undercurrents of fear and desire, hope and dread which belong to all human beings. Once awakened, they will be addressed firmly and graciously.

The preacher knows also that regardless of who these listeners are, they want to be taken seriously. This does not mean they won't tolerate any humor. They are, in fact, complimented by humor, but they have neither time nor temperament for silliness. This is true especially at the point of their weaknesses and sins. There is no insult more painful than having one's flaws and failures, constant sources of disappointment in oneself, taken lightly or dismissed as nothing in comparison to the grosser evils of the world. Or to have grace poured like syrup over one's life with no diagnosis, no recommendation of surgery, no regimen for recovery. However, the preacher knows that these listeners can quickly discern the difference between being taken seriously and being viewed negatively or judgmentally.

Even more understanding of this unknown audience begins to come into focus. They are all seeking a place to stand, a place that feels like home. Many of them have had the ground pulled from beneath them, not only by circumstances but by broken promises, dashed hopes, and misplaced trust. They are very sensitive to any efforts to deceive, manipulate, or take unfair advantage. However, their presence can be taken as their being open to the possibility that in this place, among these worshipers, and in the words of this preacher trust may begin again, and trust will provide a place to stand for viewing life and the world.

These listeners are ceasing to be strangers to the minister. Their expectations of a sermon are common to all who sit before a pulpit anywhere. They expect to hear the old but in a new way, not simply to make it interesting but to help them look upon old landscapes with a new eye. Words can be strung together into sentences and piled into paragraphs, words that are religious, biblical, and true, and yet do nothing. They do not raise a window, open a door, build a fire, or offer a chair. They are said, they collect below the pulpit, and are swept out on Monday morning. Not carelessly; the housekeeper moves the broom slowly among them to see if any are still alive. They are not; like Lazarus they have been dead four days, and this is only Monday. This means that on Sunday when they were spoken, they were already—Yes.

So what does this audience want, oratory? No; they want some insight. Perhaps looking at their lives, their marriages, their studies, their jobs, their world through the lens of Scripture and theology, a fresh perspective can be found. That perspective could be the redemptive alternative which all but the fatalistic and very cynical believe exists, if only someone would point them to it.

The preacher's portrait of the listeners is more than a generalized sketch; details are being filled in as the list, which the preacher has now entitled, "What I Know About Those I Do Not Know," continues to grow. Another item: because they are free human beings, the listeners want room to say no to the sermon but a genuine invitation to say yes. The sermon will not, therefore, paint them into a corner or strip them of every defense except anger. Neither will the preacher build into the sermon the listener's response, "Of course, everyone agrees," or, "I know you will not accept this, but." Rather the sermon will be of such nature and delivered in such fashion that the listeners know the preacher understands that yes and no must be real options if there is to be genuine response.

The list, however short or long, is not complete until it includes the listener's desire to be brought into the presence of God. It is expected of the sermon as well as of the entire worship service. After all, in the final analysis it is before God that all stand. The sermon, then, will contain as well as facilitate a sense of wonder and awe. It may not be a comfortable experience. Some may, in fact, say, "I have no right to be in this place," while others feel more at home in the sanctuary than anywhere else. But if the sermon has an altar in it, all can say, "This is none other than the house of God, this is the gate of heaven."

If these listeners can leave the service with no sense of having been put down; if their self-worth has been affirmed or restored; if God's love and grace are seen as available realities; if they are convinced that repentance and trust are acceptable to God; if there is more awareness of other persons and more hunger for covenanted life; then even strangers will likely say to the preacher, "You understand us quite well."

The Listeners as Congregation

We referred to the listeners as an audience in the attempt to understand them as strangers and hence as persons, no more, no less. In other words, as an *audience*, the listeners were seen as a guest preacher would see them. As a *congregation*, the listeners are known as a pastor knows them.

The pastor-preacher needs to keep in mind, however, that what has been said about the listeners as audience does not cease to be true or appropriate now that he/she is moving to more familiar ground. It is refreshing on occasion to look upon the familiar as strange. We do not replace but build upon what we understand to be true of all persons. To that understanding concrete details of experience, circumstance, and relationships, as well as names, faces, and addresses can be added. In addition to being persons, the listeners are individuals, family units, and social groups. Differences and distinctions are understood by the preacher and are factored into the sermons.

No congregation is homogeneous, not even the small rural one which consists basically of three "main families." This is true not simply in terms of age, education, income, and personal experiences, but also in basic postures toward the Christian faith espoused by the congregation as a whole. Some listeners have a totally uncritical stance toward all matters of Christian doctrine, including their view of Scripture. Sermons that raise any questions in these areas, whether they are the preacher's own or those voiced by scholars for centuries, will be surprising to these hearers. In fact, they do not want to hear them. Others in the congregation will be trying to arrive at a faith of their own, giving careful attention to what has been read and heard in church school and from the pulpit. These will want discerning sermons, and the less secure preachers may be a bit intimidated by the questions, the probing, the pressing for more. Such listeners are to be distinguished from those trying to shake themselves free of some old beliefs standing in the way of a new life-style. Still other parishioners do not take Christian beliefs and traditions seriously. They have not tried, or have given up trying, to see meaningful connections between the historic faith and the way life is in their world. Yet they are present on Sunday, and some with surprising regularity, for reasons that lie in the family, in society, in memory, or in sentiment. Needless to say, these listeners are a huge challenge because they, in fact, are not listening.

To refer to the listeners as congregation is to say a great deal about their relationship to one another and to the minister. That a very strong relationship exists at all between a minister and a congregation is in many ways remarkable and that it is sometimes sustained over a long period of time is near miraculous. After all, religion is for many people a very incendiary subject, making congregational quarrels some of the bitterest in our society. In addition, the minister has to relate to the parishioners in a variety of ways: standing beside them, out front leading them, pushing from behind them, squaring off over against them. But the relationship does exist, and one characteristic of its complex nature that directly and powerfully influences preaching is the knowledge of the listeners which the minister comes to have.

The understanding of one's hearers both as individuals and as social units enables the minister to preach with a power and effectiveness unavailable to the guest speaker, whatever may be the skills, credentials, and reputation of that speaker. Much hoopla to the contrary, the most effective preachers in this or any generation are pastors, whose names we may or may not ever know. This is not a comment on oratorical skills nor is it a broad benediction on every pulpit effort by pastors. It is rather a recognition of the central importance of knowing one's hearers, a fact which makes it possible for the sermon to have that irreplaceable source of power: appropriateness. Many otherwise good sermons make no contact because they are to the wrong people at the wrong time. All of us know there is nothing so insulting or offensive as comments or behavior inappropriate to the occasion, the time, or the group present. On the other hand, who among us has not been stirred or perhaps even changed by the right word at the right time? Parishioners will request copies of sermons, funeral meditations, or wedding ceremonies, not because these excelled in every way all other such offerings by the minister, but because for the occasion or for the persons present, "it was so fitting." However one may define Word of God, this expression must be included: "it is fitting." The old Anglo-Saxon word "meet," as in "meet and right so to do," captured the idea precisely: the Word meets the listener; contact is made.

It must be said, however, that the general familiarity that develops between a minister and a congregation cannot be assumed to be understanding. As we all know, familiarity can blind one and prevent genuine knowledge and understanding. A minister will never stay in a parish long enough to render unnecessary the asking of very elementary but vital questions in the process of sermon preparation.

Who will hear the sermon? No general answer is satisfactory; close your eyes and see the people in the pews. They can be seen clearly because they sit in the same places every week. Let the names of the listeners come to mind and be formed by the lips. After a few minutes of this exercise, say to yourself, "These are the persons to whom I will give this message." Simplistic and routine to the pastor in the same pulpit for years? Perhaps, but cease doing it and both pastor and parishioners will be the losers. Of course, it goes without saying that this question will be pursued with care when one is invited to preach to groups other than the Sunday congregation: college students, other ministers, friends and family of the deceased, civic leaders, a conference of young people.

When will this sermon be heard? This is not a trite and useless question. If it is at the regular service of worship, many things can be known immediately about who will be there with what expectations. When set in a familiar pattern a sermon can take advantage of the security and comfort of that pattern and yet at the same time must fracture that comfort in order to get a fresh hearing. If the sermon is at a sunrise service or at a regular but early worship service, then the question, When? introduces special factors of audience and context. Every minister knows that identical services at 9:00 A.M. and 11:00 A.M. are not at all identical. And if the sermon is to be delivered at night it will be spoken in a different atmosphere. All activities after dark are quite unlike daytime events. One's mind can focus on the differences by reflecting on experiences of day and night meals, day and night parties, day and night ball games, day and night concerts. Think about it; "after dark" says a great deal about leaving home and getting to the church, going from the parking lot to the building, coming into light and security from the dark outside, not to mention dress and physical weariness after a day of activity. Nicodemus came to Jesus "at night." Astute politicians make modifications in their speeches according to the time of meeting; breakfast speeches, afternoon rally speeches, and evening speeches vary quite noticeably. The preface to James Agee's *Let Us Now Praise Famous Men* (Houghton Mifflin, 1960) asks those who take up the book to read it aloud and at night. The instructions show a sensitivity about communicating which preachers sometimes overlook.

Where will this sermon be heard? If the first two questions have been taken seriously, then this one is already in mind. If its answer is the sanctuary, the fellowship hall, the chapel, a high school auditorium, a private dining room of a restaurant, or the civic auditorium, then that fact will register in the preparation and will reflect in the length, mood, weight, and especially the introduction of the sermon.

The point of this discussion is to aid the preacher who has all the advantages of knowing the listeners to be alert so he or she will not lose those advantages by allowing a vague familiarity to pass for clear and concrete understanding. The methods by which a minister comes to know the listeners are basically three.

1. *Formal.* A preacher does not move into a ministry and expect to be consistently effective in the pulpit when he or she knows the parishioners solely by a process of gradual absorption. Initiative and

intentionality are essential, if for no other reason than to break the stereotypes we bring with us. More than we realize, novels, movies, and television have shaped our images of rural Appalachians, New York apartment dwellers, Florida retirees, southern county politicians, Texas spenders, and the unusual ones in California. In addition to reviewing our seminary studies in rural or urban sociology, more reading needs to be done. Most public and high school libraries contain short histories of the region, sometimes of the county and city. Chambers of Commerce usually have much information of a statistical nature about the community. The local newspaper will be a mine of information about life and death and the rituals for both. For example, a death notice containing the sentence, "Although the deceased had lived here only twenty years, he had made a number of friends," says many things about the community. Of course, the history of the local church and the membership rolls will be studied with extreme care.

A few key interviews quite soon after one's arrival in the community can hasten the beginnings of pastoral as well as pulpit effectiveness. Those to be interviewed should include a funeral director, the chief of police, an officer of the Chamber of Commerce, the school superintendent, and a tenured pastor of another church. Clear images of local citizens, including one's parishioners will soon emerge: how they earn their income, how they spend their leisure, what their attitudes are about themselves and others, what they most cherish, what they most fear, where the power lies officially and where it lies actually are among the questions which will be answered. One will wait, of course, on further experience and observation to determine if early images are framed by fact or prejudice, or both.

2. *Informal.* Hardly a day passes that does not provide many and varied human contacts and occasions to observe the activities and interactions of those to whom and among whom one ministers. In some of these the minister is intentionally and heavily engaged, as in a wedding, a funeral, a hospital visit, or a counseling session. In others, participation is more casual, as in attendance at civic, social, and recreational events, but in all situations, the minister is a listening and observing participant. This is in no way to suggest that any minister is to sit at life's curb and be a spectator of the drama

passing by. Nor does it even hint that a preacher could profitably move about among the populace like a vacuum cleaner, picking up human interest tidbits and illustrative materials to enliven the Sunday fare. To be a minister in a community is to be a resident, a citizen, a responsible leader, and one who shares the blame and the credit for the quality of life in that place. One preaches *in* and *out of* as well as *to* that community. What is being said here, however, is that the minister, as much or more than anyone else, has the opportunity to understand the people. By reason of education, professional skills, interest in and love for people, and that special entry into heart, home, and society granted to clergy, a pastor's preaching should touch life at the level of its deepest needs and profound joys.

Having an understanding of the currents of a community's life, its ways of relating to itself and to the world, its values, and the images of its fears and hopes, enables the minister to interpret the listeners to themselves and hold their lives under the judgment and blessing of the gospel. It is at this level that sermons carry an authority which is real, and human life is affected in lasting ways. The preacher whose contacts in and out of the congregation yield only anecdotes, inside jokes, and examples for homiletical use is operating at another level. On that level exist all the temptations to use what one has learned, sometimes in confidence, to curry favor, to exercise power over, to blackmail, to intimidate, or to coerce, and all from the pulpit. Violations of the human spirit occur in this way often enough, with results tragic enough, to serve as warning impressive enough, that nothing more need be said. Of course, preaching involves the sharing of concrete and particular instances of the beautiful and the ugly, the true and the false, the good and the evil, but never as a breach of confidence, never as an embarrassment or a put down, never in any spirit other than pastoral, and always told as in the presence of Christ. Otherwise preaching degenerates into gossip.

3. *Empathetic imagination.* Empathetic imagination is the capacity to achieve a large measure of understanding of another person without having had that person's experiences. The extent to which one cannot understand due to lack of similar experience has its compensation in the fact of one's distance from that experience. Sometimes persons are so trapped within and consumed by what is

95

happening to them that a person standing outside the event, but empathetic nevertheless, can offer a helpful perspective. Those approaches to helpfulness that assemble persons who have undergone the same difficulties can only partially succeed because no two people really have the same experience. Two people with terminal cancer may be having very different experiences; two people who have lost their spouses to others are very likely having different experiences. Seeking the counsel of someone who has "been through it" may be helpful, but it also may provide an ounce of understanding and a gallon of bitterness.

Empathetic imagination is, then, a modification of the partial truth that only those who have been there can really understand. Anyone who has lost a child or had cancer or lived alone or been fired can understand at a level of genuine helpfulness. When someone says, "Pastor, you can't understand, this has never happened to you," that person may be pleading in frustration for more insight. However, that person may also be protecting the pain from anyone's understanding as a way of maintaining the illusion that only one person in all the history of the human race has ever suffered so, and I have been destined to be that person. That illusion is a source of some pleasure during a difficult time and should not be shattered without a plan for helping the person move back into reality.

Being a minister does not automatically mean he or she has empathetic imagination, nor is it supplied by a solid course in seminary. In fact, being a minister for many years does not in itself supply this quality. The areas of persons' experiences may also be the areas in which they have developed the most callouses. As with other qualities for ministry, pastors have to be intentional, working past their own defenses against being hurt by the hurt of others, past their own impatience and need to pass judgment, past their own agenda for success, which gets delayed by human misery. Until they have a clear focus on the relation between pausing to pick up strays and cripples and marching to Zion, no formula for maintaining empathetic imagination will really work.

It goes without saying that listening and observing are irreplaceable keys to understanding; so also is reading for the insights of those who have subjected human behavior to more consistent and sustained observation with tested instruments for analyzing and reporting results. However, there is a simple exercise that helps maintain sensitivity and keep alive and functioning a minister's empathetic understanding of those to whom he or she preaches. This exercise takes only a few minutes per week and can be done profitably by seminarians and seasoned ministers alike. It is an effort of the imagination to bring to a specific human condition all that a person has heard, seen, read, felt, and experienced about that condition. The procedure is this: take a blank sheet of paper and write at the top, "What's It Like to Be?" Beneath that heading write a phrase descriptive of one concrete facet of human experience. Examples might be: "facing surgery," "living alone," "suddenly wealthy," "rejected by a sorority," "arrested for burglary," "going into the military," "fired from one's position," "graduating," "getting one's own apartment," "unable to read," "extremely poor," "fourteen years old." For the next fifteen minutes scribble on the page every thought, recollection, feeling, experience, name, place, sound, smell, or taste that comes to mind. The first few times may be slow and awkward, but it will not be long until the page fills easily and quickly. In fact, you will be surprised how much the relaxed and free association will dredge up and cluster around a single instance of human experience.

From such an exercise three quite satisfying results may follow. First, ministers will likely be surprised to discover how much understanding of the human condition they already have but which has not been adequately reflected in either the words or music of their preaching. It is regrettable how much preaching, including that of learned and capable ministers, shows little evidence of the seasoning that is provided only by thought and reflection. Apparently the first thing to be sacrificed to an overload of duties and activities is time for thinking. As a result, we have more intelligent sermons than wise ones.

Second, from this exercise one will reap a harvest of ideas, anecdotes, and even areas for further treatment in preaching. Of course, scribblings from this sheet will have to meet all the criteria of appropriateness before admission into a sermon, but those items that do enter will be immensely more fitting and valuable than the usual borrowings offered as illustrations with the hackneyed and apologetic "The story is often told—" Yes, too often.

And finally, the cumulative effect of this exercise can be the noticeable reduction in the number of sermons that either make no contact with the listener or make contact in ways unintended and often counterproductive. Empathy and understanding do not make the preacher "soft on sin" or lead to the loss of a person's prophetic indignation. Rather, the understanding preacher has come to see who the real enemy is and where the real battle lines are to be drawn. The scalpel replaces the ax and surgery replaces bruising. The preacher who spends a little time with the exercise, "What's it like to be extremely poor?" will no longer draw all illustrative materials from conversations on planes to San Francisco and sunsets on Caribbean beaches. The preacher who responds to the question, "What's it like to be fourteen years old?" will not likely preach one of those "The Trouble with Young People Today" broadsides which have the net effect of emptying the sanctuary of its last few teenagers. The loss is too tragic to be redeemed by a compliment from the shrew who is pleased that someone finally put the young people in their place.

Giving disciplined time and attention to the interpretation of one's listeners is critical for preaching. It in no way diminishes the importance of careful exegesis of texts, but then neither does any amount of work in a text make a sermon apart from this understanding. No book of theology, even if it is addressed to the modern mind; no biblical commentary, even if it moves the text toward the pulpit; no volume of sermons, packaged and ready for delivery, has the Word winged for the hearts and minds of a particular group of listeners. Only the minister there can properly do that. Whatever may be provided a preacher by any and all resources, it is only when local soil has been added that the sermon will take root and grow. Such work is blessed by the Holy Spirit with the result that each one hears in his or her own language (Acts 2:6-8).

six

Interpretation: The Text

In our discussion we are not yet to the point of preparing a sermon. Rather we are in the process of having something to say. Once this process is completed, framing that message into a sermon is the next but distinctly separate task. The purpose of this chapter is to sketch a procedure for listening to a text, or stated more actively, for interpreting a text. The phrase "*a* procedure" is used deliberately because there is no one right way of interpreting texts. Certain steps are common to all thorough procedures, but in the final analysis, one has to arrive at a method that is not only appropriate to the material being explored but also congenial to one's own processes of understanding. It is vital that one's procedure lead smoothly into and through a text and that it be simple enough to be followed almost unconsciously. This is to say, one should come to a point of investigating a text without being aware of the process as so many steps to be taken. A method will be most fruitful when it has become a habit as comfortable as an old sweater. Habit, universally criticized, remains a great liberator of the talents and faculties of busy and creative people. It will be appropriate, now and then, to raise one's procedure to the conscious level in order to evaluate it in the light of new research and scholarship—but not too frequently.

The nature of the process by which one interprets a text will depend to a large extent on how one understands the relation of the text to the sermon. Some preachers who derive sermon content primarily from topics, issues, and occasions, probably will not give lengthy consideration to investigating the text. Though scripture texts are read in the worship service, they may complete their duty simply by contributing to the atmosphere of the occasion and providing continuity with tradition. The texts therefore serve much like background music or the national anthem at a public function. So long as the tune is played or hummed, that is enough; knowing the words and their historical context is hardly necessary. In the preaching of others, the biblical texts move a little closer to the sermon. In some cases the text yields the subject, in others the introduction to the sermon, or perhaps a governing image or basic vocabulary.

In the opinions of many of the constituency, several of these types would be regarded as biblical preaching, especially if the sermon is sprinkled with words and phrases from Scripture. Whatever may be the intention of the preacher, however, there is here the illusion rather than the reality of listening to the text. The issue is not one of quantity of Scripture verses; sermons that carry a heavy load of passages from Genesis to Revelation often are only the result of the preacher's being seduced by the concordance, a seduction then passed along to the listeners. An attentive hearer will easily sense, however, that not one of the passages cited was investigated in a serious effort to listen to it. We are here considering a fundamental theological question of authority. The preacher is obligated, regardless of the kinds of sermons the parishioners may like, to ask and respond to the questions, What authorizes my sermons? If the authorization is by the Scriptures, in what way? How do I prepare so as to enter the pulpit with some confidence that my understanding of biblical preaching has been implemented with honesty and integrity?

One person cannot respond to these questions for another; answers that are truly answers must come in the wrestling. However, it is not likely that any preacher will arrive at a satisfactory position that does not involve serious grappling with the text of Scripture. What is offered here is one such effort. The process which in application moves along smoothly will here be presented step-by-step with supporting comments and examples where appropriate.

1. Selection of the Text

Text selection ordinarily occurs in one of two ways: by the preacher or by following the lectionary. When the preacher makes the choice, one or more patterns emerge: random selection influenced week by week by factors personal and pastoral; choices dictated by occasion or issues; choices of texts that inform and support the program of the church; series of texts for messages on books of the Bible or major biblical themes. All of these methods with the exception of random selection provide for some degree of advance planning and scheduling of sermons. Those who attempt to defend random selection usually speak of the pastoral obligation to be relevant and to meet needs as they arise, needs that cannot be known in advance. The assumption is that a planned preaching program would not be able to address those needs, an assumption not supported by reason or experience. Some ministers who use this method confess to anxieties about what to preach many weeks when no clear need worthy of pulpit treatment arises. One could also find oneself wishing for a crisis at least by Thursday, and then treating issues too quickly before adequate preparation is made, taking into the pulpit matters better handled by conversation, being too influenced by personal and subjective factors, and gravitating to those favorite texts when Sunday gets unavoidably near. Pastoral concern for the balanced diet of the parishioners gets lost in the scramble for "something for Sunday." But even those trapped in this method know that the cook's appetite for squash does not justify serving it three times every day.

As we will observe in further detail when discussing the method of following the lectionary, planning one's preaching program weeks and months in advance has several distinct advantages in addition to reducing the minister's weekly anxiety about what to preach and the congregation's receiving a more balanced diet. Sermons that grow and mature over a period of time are usually superior homiletically, theologically, and biblically—as well as in ease and freedom of delivery—to those "gotten up" just days or even hours prior to presentation. In addition, those who work with the minister in planning the worship service are able to do just that, work with the minister, rather than having to wait for a phone call, hoping that the now revealed text and subject do not tear the worship service from top to bottom like the curtain of the temple.

A primary reason that sermons preached in a planned preaching program are consistently better in every way than those planted, watered, and harvested in less than a week lies in the gathering of material in preparation. Assume that a minister has on the desk a loose-leaf notebook in which are pages, each containing a date, a text or texts, and perhaps a general statement of subject. These cover the occasions for preaching for the next three, six, or twelve months. Of course, as time moves along the texts and subjects become more specific, but such refinements can wait. To these pages the minister adds the seasons (Advent, Easter, Pentecost), any other special feature of a given Sunday, any program emphases for particular Sundays (Week of Compassion, World Day of Prayer, World Communion), as well as any notes of a pastoral or theological nature. From time to time, these pages, or at least the next several upcoming, are reviewed. The biblical texts are read and immediate responses in terms of questions, ideas, feelings, and recollections are recorded. Nothing more, certainly not any heavy preparation yet. However, what one has done is to fix in mind a few texts and a few embryonic ideas. In the meantime, as one reads, watches television, works on other material, plays, converses, or is otherwise engaged, those texts and ideas function as magnets to which other related ideas and observations are drawn. These, too, are recorded on the appropriate pages. By the time a particular Sunday draws near, there awaits the preacher a page of scribblings, from many sources and somewhat loosely related, but germinal and suggestive. With such a beginning, the specific and heavier task of preparation is not only inviting but already underway.

Picture the preacher who has no such method. With Sunday approaching and the minister staring at the most uninspiring object in a preacher's world, a blank sheet of paper, the search is on. More than once a voice whispers, "How about that good sermon you heard last week at the seminar?" or, "There are some sermons up there in that collection on the fourth shelf; why not?" Whether or not the preacher succumbs and tries to walk away with the blessing without wrestling with the angel will depend on many factors. Those who know the price one gradually pays for shortcuts will dig deeper, stay up later, and resolve to break out of this syndrome into a more disciplined life.

Perhaps an objection has already come to a reader's mind: but what if an event of major importance occurs in the community, arresting the attention and touching the lives of many parishioners? Does one continue on the planned and scheduled path? Certainly not. A preaching program is a servant not a master. However, having a sermon already on the drawing board is helpful in such situations. Whenever a crisis or some event of significance occurs in the church or the community, one has a choice: to go with one's schedule or to interrupt it. The crisis is weighed over against a sermon well along in its development. If the crisis is weighty enough to push one's plans aside, then it most likely is deserving of treatment from the pulpit. That is a fairly reasonable canon by which to make such decisions. However, if a preacher has no plan, no sermon well on the way to maturity, then the slightest noise in the community will sound like a cannon in the homiletically empty ear and the slightest ripple in the congregation will register like an earthquake on that blank paper on the minister's desk. Into the vacuum of no advance planning, with nothing against which to measure the emergency's right to the pulpit, rushes the hasty topic and another journalistic sermon is soon to be preached. As for those who decide to set aside a schedule in order to address a sudden need—and they will occur as long as tornadoes strike, floods rise, buildings burn, and trains hit school buses—there awaits the pleasant discovery that years of disciplined planning and study pay off. A reservoir of study and thought, though never before drawn to this particular problem, is a resource available and appropriate. The apparently sudden sermon is not really sudden at all.

A rapidly increasing number of ministers are following a lectionary in their preaching ministries. For some this is an unwavering procedure, for others a procedure with variations and departures, and yet others look at the lections each week as an option. There are also quite a few ministers who traditionally and personally looked upon the lectionary with some suspicion but who are now finding the recently available and quite excellent brief commentaries on the lectionary texts very helpful for preaching on those texts according to a schedule of their own choosing.

For those not yet familiar with them, lectionaries consist of four lections or readings for each Sunday and special worship day (such as, Ash Wednesday, Christmas, Good Friday); an Old Testament reading, a psalm, a reading from an epistle, and one from a Gospel. The readings are arranged on a three-year cycle, with the intention to have read in the worship of the church over a three-year period the biblical texts affirming the central themes of the Christian faith. Ancient precedent lay in the Jewish synagogue, which divided the Hebrew Scriptures into readings to be completed in three years (in some synagogue traditions, one year). As might be expected, the Gospel readings are most influential in the choice of the other texts. During the period from Advent to Pentecost, most lectionaries attempt to offer readings for each service which have thematic unity, even though that unity is not always easy to ascertain. Following Pentecost until Advent, efforts at thematic unity are relaxed in favor of extended continuous readings over a number of Sundays, inviting sermons in series on larger bodies of materials, such as, I Samuel, Isaiah, or Mark. Most modern lectionaries are based upon ancient ones, and the new common lectionary has been formed with the desire to embrace the principal values of all the major ones in use.

The benefits of following the lectionary are those which were described above for a planned preaching program, plus others. The lectionary assures the congregation will hear, and in many cases read along with the worship leader, much of the Bible. It is an unusual contradiction that in many churches that claim to be Bible-centered, often using the word Bible in their names, the only Scripture reading in the assembly consists of that brief selection on which the preacher bases the sermon. Perhaps this is the time to pause and remind ourselves of the obvious: a congregation which moves to the use of the lectionary should join that move to a concerted effort to improve the quality of the public reading of Scripture. Otherwise, the increase of reading will compound what is already in many worship services a misdemeanor, if not a felony. In addition to the amount of Scripture, the lectionary assures a breadth for both public reading and preaching, probably far greater than would be scheduled by the choices of a single minister. The pulpit is thereby nudged into corners of the canon into which it might not otherwise go if personal preference prevailed.

Think for a moment of other benefits. The lectionary not only provides the basis for a worship service, including the sermon, which is a seamless robe, but it can also join home and church together in Christian worship and thought. The family that uses the lectionary for devotions and study is more prepared for and hence more participatory in congregational life. In fact, families whose members worship at different churches can often join afterward in conversation because the same lectionary was followed in worship and sermon in their separate congregations. Increasingly across the country, ministers in small peer groups are finding the lectionary a common ground for worship, Bible study, and fruitful discussions in the direction of sermons. And an unanticipated benefit for many preachers has been the realization that the lectionary has provided a solid and broad base both in Scripture and in the larger church of which the lectionary is a voice for dealing with critical and sometimes incendiary issues. While the minister is responsible for what is said in the pulpit, lectionary or not, it is still the case that large portions of Scripture and those not of the minister's arbitrary choice, confront the church with its own tradition and confession rather than the lone voice of the preacher. Such preaching is not only more in keeping with the prophetic tradition but more powerful in its effect, being less likely to have its birth, and often its death, in the private opinions of the minister.

2. First Reading of the Text

In the translation decided upon as the most reliable rendering of the Hebrew and Greek texts, the Scripture for the sermon is read, several times silently and at least once aloud. Of course, the original languages are to be used if one has the facility. However, this is not the time to become superconscientious and try to resurrect that which has been dead longer than Lazarus.

This first reading is a spontaneous, even naïve, engagement with the text. All faculties of mind and heart are open, with no concern for what one ought to think, much less what one will say later in the sermon. This is the time to listen, think, feel, imagine, and ask. All responses should be jotted down; do not trust the memory or take time to weigh the merits of your thought. This process is most enjoyable, but one should not be deceived by the pleasure: serious preparation has begun. And by all means, no other books or study aids are to be used at this point; they will have their chance later. Second only to the fault of not doing adequate study is that of introducing into one's preparation too soon the secondary resources. When used at the proper time they are indispensable, but if too early opened, they take over. They suppress and intimidate the preacher. After all, who is going to venture a thought or an interpretation when at the very same desk are six internationally known Bible scholars? They intrude themselves between the text and the preacher and begin explaining everything. Some preachers who spend much time in study have confessed to having preached texts which they had not even read in the process of preparation.

During this first reading several important things are occurring. With this open and honest engagement with the text begins the process of owning the message to be preached later. In addition, one is identifying with the listeners who will also come to the text unaided except for their own thoughts, feelings, and needs. The minister who reads the text does so inescapably as pastor and preacher, sitting more among the parishioners than among the scholars. Later he or she will be surrounded by commentaries and lexicons, sitting among the doctors asking and answering questions. Very likely, however, the questions to be pursued will be those raised by the text itself in this first reading. It is also likely that these early notes will provide more than half one's introductions to sermons. And why not? After all, this is the way the preacher began to get into the text; the congregation could happily begin the same way. That would be a marked improvement over introductions which ask the listeners to begin with the conclusion the preacher arrived at after hours of study and thought.

Again let it be stressed that this beginning with the text will be of immeasurable benefit later when the secondary resources are consulted. The text has raised the questions to be pursued in those books, and therefore those volumes are servants, not masters. Because the minister knows the text and has spent time with it, he or she is more confident in opening and using books which otherwise might seem to be in another world. Now the minister sits among them as among colleagues, and not beneath them looking up with no comment except, yes, ma'am, and, no, sir.

There is no better time than now to begin this exercise. If the reader has no other biblical texts in mind, then the following three brief passages are offered for reading and response. Admittedly, these were selected because they can generate a variety of responses immediately; at least they have in a number of preaching seminars. Some texts are not as lively and require more work to achieve interaction, but these need only to be read. No suggestions, guidelines, or prompting questions are in order; the reader is left alone with the texts (I Chron. 11:15-19; I Cor. 7:32-35; Luke 9:57-62).

3. Establishing the Text

Simply stated, establishing the text means checking for any variant or alternative words or phrases in the text. This does not refer to differences in translation; of course, those will occur often. Variant readings in a text have to do with disagreements among the manuscripts from which all our translations are derived. Footnotes in one's translation of the Old Testament may occasionally say, "Meaning of the Hebrew uncertain here," or, "Text obscure here," or may simply provide the Hebrew word translated in the text so that a reader who so desires can work at other ways to translate the word. However, considering alternative readings among manuscripts is primarily a New Testament matter since we possess over five thousand whole or fragmentary Greek manuscripts.

If there is a step in the process of preparing to preach or teach that is frequently omitted, this is it. For some it is simply a matter of not feeling qualified for this kind of investigation. For others, it is a matter of faith: "I don't question the Bible." Generally, ministers assume qualified scholars have worked on these texts for years and have presented to us the best possible readings, so who are we to try to do over again everyone's thinking? That is not an unhealthy position; after all, the synagogue and the church have always had circles of scholars whose service to the larger community of faith is to preserve and to pass along the tradition uncorrupted and unaltered. Why, then, should a preacher take time to establish the text?

The reasons are several. In the first place, this kind of attention to the text is not an act of suspicion or distrust, but a way of honoring the text. It is this important. Second, one who is preaching a given text wants to be sure that the text being preached is what the author wrote. Third, it is of primary importance to maintain in preaching as in all one's work the pattern of careful honesty. There is an insidious evil that haunts every minister's study, and its unceasing whisper is, "But the congregation doesn't know the difference." If the minister knows and God knows, that constitutes an overwhelming majority. Fourth, there are cases in which decisions about the text affect *what* one preaches. Suppose, for example, that the lectionary readings for a certain Sunday include John 7:53–8:11 and the preacher notices a footnote: "The most ancient authorities omit 7:53–8:11." Perhaps one's prior study of the Fourth Gospel had led to the conclusion that this was a misplaced or even spurious passage. Now what? The same situation could arise with the troublesome Mark 16:9-20. Study involves not only reading and thinking; it also involves making decisions. In the fifth place, more and more worshipers follow the Scripture readings in pew Bibles. There are no more secrets. Now and then a family may pass back and forth a Bible, noting something unusual, or gather three or four copies to see if the same phenomenon is in all of them. Afterward at the door, the unofficial voice of the congregation, a skeptical and sometimes irreverent eleven-year-old, says, "Pastor, our Bibles are different from yours. Ours didn't have a verse four in the fifth chapter of John. It just skips from verse three to verse five." Somewhere in that event is a pastoral, teaching opportunity. And finally, as though it were not clear already, this attention to the text and the decisions made concerning it, contribute to that level of confidence that welcomes rather than dreads subsequent questions and comments from listeners. It is this same confidence that sets free the full powers of the preacher's faculties both in preparation and in delivery. Uncertainties and anxieties born of aborted preparation peek through the preacher's words, voice, face, and gestures, and when efforts to hide them are increased, they stick their heads out and make faces at the congregation.

How, then, does one establish the texts without making such an investigation a second career? Those who work regularly with the Greek text will not only have attention called to the variants, but they will also have before them the apparatus for making assessments of those variants. The footnotes in a good study Bible will introduce the major alternative readings to those using English exclusively. At this point a decision can be made as to the significance of the differences. On matters of importance the better commentaries will get into a discussion that will help in making a decision. Often, however, these weightier commentaries assume the reader already knows what the issues are and engage in the discussion as with a faculty colleague. When feeling left on the outside of such conversations, or wanting to avoid it in advance, the minister could well purchase and keep near at hand Bruce Metzger's *A Textual Commentary on the Greek New Testament.* (United Bible Societies, 1978). This small book lists and briefly presents the evidence for every significant text variant in the New Testament, and all are arranged by book, chapter, and verse. Greek words are used, but if the non-reader of Greek studies the introduction carefully, he or she will find help and will over a period of time learn a great deal of the Greek text.

One question regarding establishing the text remains, Should one include in the sermon any of this investigation and its results? The minister has to answer this anew in each situation, but it is not usually a problem for the one who has done the work and come to clarity about it. For these preachers it is a pastoral as well as a homiletical question. If the issue is important for the sermon or if the variants are evident to those who read the Bible with care, then the minister should prepare appropriate remarks. Some prefer to comment on text variations when they do not seem to be of much importance, thereby having a teachable moment when no one has to shed blood. This is not a bad practice. Not only do parishioners come to understand more about how the Bible came to be and lose some apprehensions about shadowy scholars somewhere tinkering with Holy Scripture, but they are also better prepared for the few occasions when text variants are of greater significance. If it is decided that comments do need to be made from the pulpit, then they should come quite early to clear the path for the sermon. The remarks need to be well-prepared, clear, brief, positive, and honest. There is no congregation so distant from biblical scholarship that it does not welcome information graciously when shared by one whom they trust. The minister can begin, "Perhaps you noticed in today's reading that Mark 9 does not have verses 44 and 46," and within sixty seconds be pastor and teacher as well as preacher. On the other hand, there is no congregation so learned and sophisticated that it appreciates condescending comments by a minister whose insensitivity to fragile faith is revealed in remarks, such as, "It's only a guess whether any of our Bible contains what the authors actually wrote." Such behavior is not a case of being honest and letting the chips fall where they may; it is irresponsible and destructive.

4. Determining the Parameters of the Text

To ask how much Scripture can properly be dealt with in one sermon is to raise the wrong question. Rather, one should ask if the text selected is a unit having its own integrity, and therefore providing focus and restraint for the sermon. Fuzziness at the edges of one's biblical text prophesies fuzziness at the edges of one's sermon. The text will, of course, be studied in its literary context but, even so, the chances of violating that context as well as the unit itself are greatly lessened if one's text has a beginning and an ending, and is not ripped out with broken sentences and dangling thoughts hanging loose on every side. It must be said also that one cannot assume that the lectionary readings have always been chosen with a concern for clear and defensible parameters. Other considerations figured in those decisions; therefore, the minister must give attention to the determination of the borders of one's text, even when respecting and following the lectionary. For example, on a given Sunday, some lectionaries offer Luke 4:16-21 as the Gospel for the day. That verse 16 is a distinct beginning is obvious, but is verse 21 an ending? Is verse 30 really the close of the narrative begun at verse 16?

The example above makes it clear that determination of parameters is substantive, not cosmetic. Consider two examples. Luke 10:25-37 is a clear unit, as is 10:38-42. Each contains a strong and certain message. But suppose one's text is Luke 10:25-42. Now one has a larger narrative in which two smaller units are set, the one urging initiative and action, the other insisting that there are times when being still and listening is "the good portion." The two together constitute a message different from that conveyed by either part or by the sum of the parts. Or again, parables offer a good example of the importance of determining parameters. Matthew uses the "first last, last first" saying as both the introduction and conclusion of the parable of laborers in the vineyard (19:30–20:16), a fact which underscores one line within the parable (verse 8). If one's sermon text is Matthew 19:30–20:16, then one will preach on Matthew's interpretation of the parable. However, if one's text is the parable itself, 20:1-15, then another message may announce itself, such as the problem of presenting God's generosity to others. Or again, how one understands the parable of the dishonest steward will depend to a large degree on the point at which one's text ends. Read the story beginning at Luke 16:1 and ending at verse 8*a*, then again at 8*b*, and at verse 9, at verse 12, and at verse 13. Where does the parable end and Luke's commentary begin? It makes a difference in what you say in the sermon.

Observing the parameters of a text often allows the preacher to isolate and treat smaller units of material without fear of violating the meaning of the text. Not only do the wisdom books of the Old Testament contain small units such as proverbs which are extractable and portable, having their meanings independent of context, such materials exist also in the New Testament. The Epistle of James is a piece of Christian wisdom, seldom sustaining an argument but being filled with proverb-like advice. In the Gospels there are units of sayings which may have been clustered around a common word or phrase (Mark 9:42-50) or under a particular topic, such as prayer (Luke 11:1-13). There is no violation if one chooses to treat one of these sayings, which once circulated separately but which now is lodged in a collection.

Ordinarily it is not difficult to locate the beginning and ending of a text. The preacher will want to do this work by direct engagement with the text, checking commentaries later for confirmation or correction. One thereby becomes even more at home in the text. The clues for beginnings and endings are usually of two kinds: thematic and literary. A single theme makes I Samuel 16:14-23 a unit, as is also the case with Matthew 6:25-33 and II Corinthians 9:1-15. Literary clues provided by the writers may be brief introductions to the material (Jer. 11:1), or notations as to time (Mark 1:32), place (Matt. 8:28), or occasion (John 5:1). It is also common for units to be rounded off with summary statements (Acts 16:5) or with a comment on the response to the preceding event (Mark 1:28). In the Gospels and in some narrative portions of the Old Testament, stories will show evidence of having been "talked smooth" during the period of oral circulation. Likewise, liturgical pieces can be rather easily identified (Deut. 26:6-10; Luke 1:68-79; Phil. 2:6-11).

The preacher is now ready to enter into fruitful conversation with the writers of commentaries. The preacher will also have arrived at a point of expecting from the commentaries something substantive and grounded in the text. There will be a new impatience with those thin discussions in books which once looked like the answer to a Saturday night prayer. But all is not lost; some of them go quickly in garage sales.

5. Setting the Text in Its Several Contexts

Through direct study of the text and in consultation with dictionaries, concordances, atlases, introductions, and commentaries, the preacher now places in context the passage that had so recently been isolated. The contexts which bear directly upon the meaning of a text are three:

(a) Historical. As far as is possible, the sermon's text is set within the time, place, and circumstance of its origin. For some biblical documents, such reconstructions are more easily done than for others. It is easier to recover Paul's relation to the church at Corinth, for instance, than to identify and situate the writer and the readers of the Gospel of Matthew. Even so, the effort must be made; honesty and respect for the texts demand it, not to mention the need to know what it is that Jeremiah or Mark or Paul is saying.

Many preachers confess to finding this task discouraging and distasteful, and they prefer to get on with the sermon. The reasons are primarily two. In the first place, there is felt, if not clearly defined, no little discomfort due to the dissonance between historical research and study leading to a sermon. In biblical studies, the historical disciplines have looked upon the text as the *result* of certain events and interactions, while the preacher looks upon the text as the *cause,* the generator, of events and interactions. It is no easy task to move from one to the other, much less to see the fruitfulness of the one for the other. Second, historical study makes one more keenly aware of the distance between the text and the present, giving one the distinct impression of moving away from rather than toward the pulpit. That distance is a fact, not an illusion. One might, therefore, in a sincere defense of the pulpit, argue by analogy that there is a great deal of meaning in "The Star-Spangled Banner" without any knowledge of the War of 1812, the British bombardment of Baltimore, and Francis Scott Key's night watch and morning watch from aboard a British ship in the harbor. The argument is, of course, partially valid; after all, it is characteristic of great music, poetry, and literature that they have a kind of life of their own and are not totally dependent upon historical context. However, who could deny that knowledge of the circumstances of the writing of the national anthem would not only thwart misapplication of its lines but also enrich them, giving meaning beyond sentiment to expressions such as "gave proof through the night" and "on that shore dimly seen"? In fact, it might be the case that a lack of historical reference contributes to the average American's inability to remember the words of the anthem.

It needs to be understood that historical recovery is in no way intended as an effort to find a firm footing in facts in order to preach with certainty rather than looking to faith's witness expressed in the text itself. On the contrary, it is faith's witness that one seeks to hear and to speak, but faith witnesses to specific persons, in specific places, under specific conditions. The gospel encounters culture, sometimes rejecting that culture's values and forms, sometimes embracing them, sometimes modifying them. To recover that meeting, to hear the interchanges, to know what issues are at stake: this is the understanding the preacher seeks. And much of it comes to the one who is not intimidated by the distance, who is not impatient to get quick relevance, but who takes time to sit nearby and overhear Israel's king and Israel's prophet in a fierce exchange, or Paul and the church at Corinth discuss what constitutes Christian worship. Before long one moves in closer and distances begin to collapse as ancient issues of life and death, faith and morals, sin and forgiveness, family and society begin to sound remarkably current.

(b) Literary. Some passages are tied inextricably to their contexts while others are more loosely joined. A sermon text from Acts will likely be set within a longer narrative; a text from the Epistle to the Hebrews will be a portion of a lengthy and well-designed oration or sermon, while Pauline texts are usually ingredient to a theological debate or to practical problem-solving. In all these cases, it is quite evident that one's sermon text is so integrally related to the context that its interpretation apart from that context is unthinkable. However, such seems not always to be the case in the Gospels. Some stories and sayings are joined with minimal editorial cement and, therefore, apparently may be lifted from their literary settings without fear of violating meaning. Both Old and New Testaments contain materials that enjoyed oral circulation prior to and apart from their present lodgings, their orality and easy portability making them especially attractive to preachers.

However, the quality described above may be more apparent than real. While an episode in one of the Gospels may seem hardly related at all to what precedes or follows, the very location of that episode may have been an interpretive act on the part of the writer. All of us know that an incident related in the introduction of a sermon can, though told in exactly the same words, have a far different meaning as a conclusion to that sermon. Arrangement of materials, whether in our sermons or in the Gospels, is an act of interpretation to which listeners and readers need to be alert. Consider several examples. Readers of Luke have long been intrigued and a bit puzzled by the fact that Luke places his account of John's imprisonment prior to his account of Jesus being baptized (3:18-22). Why does the writer remove John the Baptist from the scene before Jesus' baptism? In the arrangement, without comment, is a message. Jesus' rejection in his home synagogue at Nazareth appears rather late in the narratives of Mark and Matthew, but Luke places it at the beginning of Jesus' ministry (4:16-30). The story in Luke is a programmatic introduction to the whole of Jesus' mission. Mark locates the request of James and John for the chief seats in the kingdom immediately after Jesus' most detailed prediction of his approaching humiliation, suffering, and death (10:32-45). To treat the James and John episode apart from the dark contrast of that prediction would be to rob the text of much of its power. One final example: Jesus' lament, "O Jerusalem, Jerusalem . . .," occurs in Matthew at the close of the controversies with Jerusalem authorities just prior to Jesus' arrest (23:37-39). That lament ends with the words, "For I tell you, you will not see me again, until you say, 'Blessed is he who comes in the name of the Lord.' " To what does that last line refer? Luke, however, locates the lament on Jesus' journey to Jerusalem (13:34-35). Here the concluding words are, "And I tell you, you will not see me until you say, 'Blessed is he who comes in the name of the Lord!' " How does the different location affect the interpretation of that last line?

We are speaking of the importance of literary context for interpreting a text. The preacher may wish to pause here to make a note which may be useful later in the task of sermon construction. The note might remind the preacher to learn from the Gospel writers about arranging one's materials. Both interpretation and communicative impact are involved in decisions about the design of the sermon.

(c) Theological. One cannot arrive with any confidence at an interpretation of a text until that interpretation has been illuminated by the theology of the writer from whom the text was taken. Johannine texts are to be preached in a way consistent with the Johannine perspective, Pauline texts consistent with Paul's theology, and likewise with all others. This is not said out of some preference for the diversity of the Bible over its unity, but rather out of the conviction that one should be sensitive to and fair with a writer's intention. Intention is not always easy to ascertain, and even when it can be discovered, intention is not the sole canon by which to interpret a text. Some regard the search for intention unnecessary and its role in interpretation fallacious. And, indeed, it must be said that a mark of classic literature, the Bible included, is its surplus of meaning; that is, no single interpretation, even that which was intended by the author, exhausts all the meaning of a text. However, to disregard a writer's intention and to treat a text as totally autonomous, is to open the door to privatism and subjectivism, to which religion has a history of falling victim.

The need to stress interpreting texts in their appropriate theological contexts arises primarily out of the nature of the Bible itself. The Bible is, in a sense, an anthology and, therefore, is subject to the abuses peculiar to that kind of book. While anthologies of poetry or short stories are convenient and make easily accessible the works of many masters, the distinct and unique gifts, styles, and thoughts of each writer tend to get blurred and lost in the flipping of the pages. In an anthology, the turn of one page can mean a change, not only of writers, but of continents, centuries, and languages. The same is true of the Bible, and, therefore, one turns pages very thoughtfully. And one no more entertains the question, What does the Bible say? any more than one would ask, "What does the anthology say?" While a general unity does characterize the whole canon, the tallying of Scripture references in support of a point hardly qualifies as biblical preaching, nor does it honor the integrity of each writer and the ways in which the community of faith has argued with itself over matters of crucial importance.

Immediately there comes to mind the question as to the bearing of these remarks on lectionary preaching. It does not seem practical, perhaps not possible, to investigate each of the lections each week with the depth and care suggested above. For one text, yes; for four, hardly. Several remarks may be appropriate. First, to some extent the procedure suggested above must be followed in order to discern what is not at first usually apparent: a thematic unity at a deeper level. A cheap purchase of a superficial unity in pursuit of a sudden sermon destroys rather than fulfills the purpose of lectionary preaching. Second, it is not necessary to give equal time to all the texts. One text can play the central role while the others support, or question, or applaud, or stand aside, as their contents may warrant. Homogenizing the texts may serve the preacher for one year, but what happens when these texts return again and again and again? Observing and preserving the integrity of each separate text enables one to return to them again and again to hear a fresh and appropriate word. And finally, if the preacher preserves in some orderly fashion the fruit of research on these texts, the availability of quickly recovered thoughts and lines of investigation will, in the course of the years, not only remove the intimidation of three or four texts per week, but greatly enrich one's preaching.

The minister will want to be especially attentive to theological context when treating subjects that several biblical writers address. One thinks, for example, of the many perspectives reflected in Scriptures on such complex matters as suffering, poverty, eternal life, obedience to civil government, prayer, miracles, or the meaning of Jesus' death. Unless the preacher gets tangled up in the concordance, the different witnesses will be heard at different times in such ways as will quicken and enrich faith rather than confuse and checkmate at every point.

In concrete terms, then, the preacher will respect and seek to share with understanding the fact that Ruth and Ezra-Nehemiah look differently upon foreigners; that the chronicler and the author of Samuel and Kings have their own assessments of David; that Paul's call to faith and James' exhortation to works are not addressed to each other or to the same congregation, but to persons needing different corrections to their life-styles. The preacher will permit John to display the many signs Jesus performed as revelations of God without pressing Mark to change his mind about the demand for signs as the quest of an evil and non-trusting generation. The preacher will listen to both Mark and John tell their stories of Jesus healing the blind without getting into the pulpit the next Sunday and telling them as one story. The preacher will celebrate all the visions and miracles with which Luke fills his two volumes, and yet appreciate Paul's caution about the whole business, and his inability even to speak of his one ecstatic experience of the third heaven. Nor will the preacher who respects the theological integrity of each writer overstaff the Christmas sermon with all of Luke's poor shepherds plus Matthew's rich Wise Men from the East. After all, there will be another Sunday and another sermon.

6. *Being Aware of One's Point of Contact with the Text*

By the time one has reached this stage in the process, distances have collapsed and one is heavily engaged if not engrossed in the text. If this is indeed the case, then the process of withdrawing from the text and recovering one's distance from it should begin. No encounter with the text is healthy if either the text or the interpreter loses identity as a center of meaning, decision, and action.

117

This withdrawal can begin by becoming self-conscious about one's relation to the text. It is important to be very intentional about this because it bears directly not only upon the interpretation of the text but also upon the sermon soon to be designed. Awareness of one's relation to the text can be achieved by asking two questions:

1. At what level did I engage the text? "Level" used here does not refer to deep or shallow, nor is any value judgment implied. Rather, the term refers to the fact that many passages of Scripture contain materials that existed prior to their present use. In other words, if the biblical documents are thought of as preaching, then this preaching was often based on texts that both writer and readers considered authoritative for the community. For the New Testament the primary source for texts was the Old Testament, used both directly, as is best illustrated in Matthew, and allusively, as best illustrated in Luke. Sometimes a New Testament writer will not interpret an Old Testament text but will interpret an interpretation of the text, as Paul does in I Corinthians 10:1-5. That passage in First Corinthians, therefore, has three levels: Exodus 13, a later Jewish interpretation of Exodus 13, and Paul's use of it. In the preacher's investigation of this text, all this will be discovered. What is now being said is that the preacher needs to be quite aware of these levels and decide at which level the text will be preached. If, for instance, the decision is to remain at the level of Paul's message, then the two earlier levels can be used to illumine Paul's thought, but always in a subordinate way. An exegetical decision has to be made not only for the sake of the sermon's content but also in the service of clear communication. The listeners will be confused if not deceived if they are led up and down through three levels, or if the preacher authorizes a message derived from one level by comments made at another.

By the time the New Testament was written, however, the Christian communities had, in addition to the Old Testament, their own traditions to be interpreted. As early as Paul, creeds, hymns, and liturgical formulas were in use, and Paul quotes and interprets some of these in his letters. Among these are Romans 1:3-4; I Corinthians 8:6; II Corinthians 8:9; and Philippians 2:6-11. Suppose one were preaching on Philippians 2:5-11, which lectionaries use as the epistle reading every Passion/Palm Sunday.

At one level is the christological hymn Paul quotes; at another is Paul's use of the hymn in his instruction to the church. One cannot sustain two sermons at one time; one level must serve the other, and the preacher must decide to preach Christology or preach Christian attitude and conduct based upon that Christology.

The reader's mind has probably rushed ahead to the very clear examples of levels in a text provided by the Gospels. The Evangelists preserved and interpreted sayings and events from the ministry of Jesus. In addition, it is generally, though not unanimously, agreed that Matthew and Luke used Mark's narrative as a basic source for their own. One's investigation of a text in Matthew, therefore, may reveal that Matthew is interpreting for his church a passage from Mark which is a record of a saying of Jesus. The preacher may choose to recover the saying of Jesus as the message of the sermon. However, it may be decided that the appropriate word for the parishioners is the tradition Matthew received about the saying, or perhaps Matthew's interpretation of the tradition. A decision must be made; otherwise, one may be giving the hearers the impression that Matthew's interpretation is the exact wording from Jesus.

Again, let the preacher be clear about what is being said: nothing here refers to levels of profundity or levels of authority. It is rather to say that preaching which is biblical recognizes the Bible for what it is: the faith community's preservation, interpretation, and continued interpetation of its own life and tradition. The tradition and its interpretation for believers generation after generation was heard as Word of God. Biblical preaching does not confuse or deceive the congregation about that, nor does it remove itself from the continuity of that process of preserving and interpreting. In other words, biblical preaching is listening for and speaking the Word of God.

2. At what point did I identify within the text? This is the second of the two questions by which the preacher can become aware of the relation to the text which has developed in the process of the exegetical work. A major purpose of making oneself aware of that relationship is to begin to distance oneself from the text and to begin thinking of oneself as the person who will share with the church what the text says.

Usually in the course of intense engagement with a text the

interpreter, quite unconsciously, identifies with or is against particular persons or actions in the text. Become conscious now of that point of identification, or if identification is too strong a word to express the relation to the text, become conscious of the place where you stood in the text as the interpretation was developing. Paul is discussing with the Corinthian church the role of women in the worship assembly. Where do I now realize I have been standing during the study of the text? Beside Paul? Among the women? Near the rear of the room wondering what is going on? Jesus is responding to critics of his practice of eating with sinners. Have I identified with those critics and have heard all too clearly his indictment, or am I one of the sinners awed, thrilled, but feeling awkward at the table with Jesus? Perhaps I have, without realizing it, assumed the place of Jesus with everyone else being among either the sinners or the critics. Or suppose the text being interpreted is the parable of the prodigal son. There are three characters in the story. In working with the text, where am I? Am I the father who loves his sons, both of whom need forgiveness; or the younger son, standing awkwardly at the punch bowl, the guest of honor at a forgiveness party; or the older brother, still out back unable to see the fairness in parties for prodigals? It could be that I assumed I was Jesus telling the story, or a Pharisee listening to it, or a neighbor who has just been invited to a strange party and who is wondering if it is proper to go.

It is not the intent of these remarks to advise as to where the preacher *should* stand in any given text. Rather it is the invitation to become aware and intentional as one moves gradually away from the text and turns toward the sermon. If this step is not taken deliberately, it is very likely that the sermons will be prepared and delivered from the choice places in the texts. The congregation will hear loud and clear what is not stated but implied: today our preacher is Jesus and we are the Pharisees; today our preacher is Paul and we are the Corinthians; today our preacher is the loving father and we are the older son pouting on the back porch. Once one realizes this tendency of preachers to gravitate to the best seats in the text, a wholesome and, congregationally speaking, welcome shift might be made. The preacher may return to the text and *listen* to Paul or Jesus rather than repeat their lines. It will make a world of difference in the sermon.

7. Putting the Text in One's Own Words

This final step in the process completes the withdrawal from the text and compels the preacher to assume full responsibility for what has been heard in the text and, therefore, what will be carried forward to the sermon. In other words, one is at this point fully aware of the burden of being an interpreter-preacher, one who cannot avoid that responsibility either by remaining in the text, repeating Bible words and phrases, or by remaining with the listeners, repeating their opinions about the Bible but never seriously investigating the text. Those who remain outside the text through the "study" of it will not, of course, need this final step. However, those who are intensely involved in the first six steps will.

We often talk of how important it is to get into the text but not often about a responsible and intentional exit. The exit is vital not simply in order to return to the contemporary scene so that the sermon will be relevant and appropriate to one's hearers; of course, that is to be done. However, the interpreter's getting distance from the text is essential—let it be said again—to owning the sermon which will follow one's interpretive work. Otherwise, you have preachers entering the pulpit on someone else's ticket, and all the while seeming very humble because the sermon is offered as really what Amos, Elijah, John, Paul, or Jesus "is saying to us today." The following are examples of opening remarks by preachers who hid in the text and refused to come out and accept responsibility for either the interpretation of the text or the sermon based on it:

"Friends, I am not going to preach today. I can see that some of you are pleased. Our guest preacher today is the prophet Samuel, so I am going to keep myself out of it and just let Samuel say what he wants you to hear."

"Some of you may get upset today, but don't get upset with me. The word today is not from me but from Jesus."

"You have heard me many times give you my views and understandings on many issues and some of you have disagreed with me. But today there is no place for disagreement because this sermon is pure Scripture, straight from Paul himself."

These comments may strike the reader as caricatured, but they represent a pulpit transaction not at all uncommon. In whatever words it may be expressed, the illusion being entertained here is very real: it is the illusion of innocence and non-responsibility for one's sermons. Some listeners may buy and welcome such "pure and untouched" preaching; others may reject it as a case of using a pulpit mask in order to borrow authority; still others will feel uncomfortable but not know why. But the preacher, unless already a victim of much self-deception about what it means to accept the call to ministry, knows what is being attempted and sooner or later must face up to it.

There is nothing complex or unusual about this final step; it is simply stating what one heard and experienced in the text. This can be facilitated by asking and answering two questions.

1. What is the text saying? In one sentence, and as simply as possible, state the message of the text. This should be in one's own words, and as an affirmation. By making the sentence an affirmation one is more likely to capture the Good News than if stated in the hortatory terms that too often characterize entire sermons: we must, we ought, we should, let us, let us not. Exhortations are appropriate to preaching, of course; there is an imperative in the gospel. However, exhortations follow the message as an "and therefore" and are not themselves the message.

At the bottom of a page on which one has scribbled notes from research and reflection, the preacher will write a sentence such as: "Every Christian is a charismatic," or, "Acting like a Christian may lead to becoming one," or, "Hope can survive on almost nothing," or "Prayer is a learned experience," or, "The resurrection of Jesus is God's vindication of self-giving love," or "God's grace seems unfair because it is impartial." Writing that sentence marks a genuine achievement, rewarded not only by a sense of satisfaction but by a new appetite for the next task: the sermon itself.

2. What is the text doing? Because a text is a communication from one person to another or to others, the text is doing as well as saying. A mother talking to a child is not just saying; she is doing, as is a physician at a bedside, a comedian before an audience, a politician before a crowd, friends over dinner, and a preacher in the pulpit. As things are being said, persons are informing, correcting, encouraging, confessing, celebrating, covenanting, punishing, confirming, debating, or persuading. Here, then, one is simply asking what the

text is doing. This question is not only identifying the nature and function of the text but is also providing an early guideline for the sermon to come. After all, the preacher will want to be clear not only about what is being said in the sermon but also about what is being done in the sermon. And just as one's message is informed by what the text is saying, the sermon's function is informed by what the text is doing. If, for example, one were to state as what the text is saying, "Every Christian is a charismatic," and as what the text is doing, "Encouraging those believers who felt second-class," then content and tone and purpose of the sermon have come into focus.

What a text is doing is usually derived from the historical and literary contexts or from the form of the text. In most cases, knowledge of contexts yields knowledge of function, but uncertainty about the one means uncertainty about the other. For example, in Matthew 10:34-36 Jesus speaks of bringing a sword, not peace, of dividing family members, and creating foes within one's household. If the context for those statements is apathy and compromise, then what is the text doing? It is calling the reader to primary loyalty and unwavering commitment regardless of the cost even within the family. However, if the context for those words is a church already paying a heavy social and domestic price for its discipleship, what is the text doing? The text is encouraging, saying Jesus told us these conditions would arise. We should not feel that we are being punished for something, but feel ourselves in the company of the crucified Christ himself. In other words, it is one thing for a text to scare; it is another to speak to those already scared.

Whether a text is correcting, instructing, celebrating, or probing will often be revealed by its form; that is, whether it is a doxology, a creed, a confession, a proverb, a parable, a debate, or a beatitude. If the minister wants the sermon to do what the text does, then he or she will want to hold on to the form, since form captures and conveys function, not only during the interpretation of the text but during the designing of the sermon as well. While the sermon form may not be the same as the text; that is, a sermon on a psalm may not itself be a psalm, still one does not want to move too far from the form of the text. Much preaching that aims at propositions and themes and outlines does just that: the minister boils off all the water and then preaches the stain in the bottom of the cup. Until recent times, this was a common violation of parables, much in the manner of a father who replaces the children's bedtime story with, "The gist of what I want to say to you tonight is this." Perhaps it is enough at this point to alert ourselves in advance about the seriousness of altering form, which may alter function, which may alter content. If "blessed are the poor in spirit" is allowed to become "we ought to be poor in spirit"; if the drama of Jesus and the blind man in John 9 is reshaped into "there is a lot of blindness in the world; the world cannot heal its own blindness; but Jesus opens the eyes of the blind," then many true and Christian things can be said in the sermon, but the preacher may be taken to court for violating a text.

We have now come to what was earlier called an "eureka" point. The preacher now has something to say and something to do. Unless totally driven and unable to stop work at this point, he or she should take a break. The body, mind, and spirit would welcome some relaxing and refreshing activity. There is no reason to be anxious about the sermon; after all, the preacher now has something to say.

seven

Interpretation: Between Text and Listener

We have considered the twin tasks of interpreting the listeners and interpreting the text, and in the process have become very aware of the distance between. The negotiation of that distance is central to the preaching and teaching ministry of the church. Interpretation—or more commonly in the academy, hermeneutics—is the process of ascertaining for a reader or readers the meaning of a document written to another reader or readers. When applied to the Bible, and especially to certain portions of the Bible, that distance of time, space, language, historical circumstances, and world view seems to be "a great gulf fixed." However, we have already seen a narrowing of the gulf in the very process of investigating the listeners and the text. The listeners and the text do not suddenly at some point along the way look across the chasm and dimly see each other; they are aware of each other from the outset. To pretend or to wish otherwise out of devotion to pure objectivity would be neither desirable nor fruitful.

As a matter of fact, moving back and forth between the text and the listeners is not in all ways a conscious act. One might even argue that the process is healthiest when it is not conscious of itself. Empathy, intuition, and imagination move in and out of the most disciplined and calculated procedures of interpretation. This is not to say that one's methods in this and in other acts of ministry should not be brought to the level of awareness and placed under careful scrutiny. The question is simply one of timing, When do learning and improving occur? Of the three moments of an activity— rehearsal, the activity proper, and reflection—the moment of the activity least commends itself. To sit on one's own shoulder doing an analysis while preaching, teaching, counseling, or studying hardly qualifies as either analysis or ministry. It is one purpose of rehearsals, and this includes homiletics classes, to set one free for undivided engagement in the events for which preparations are being made. But there is a quality of non-seriousness, of not being the real thing, in rehearsals, and this includes homiletics classes, which limits the learning and invites postponement of the thoroughness appropriate to ministry. This leads us to post-activity reflection as the time for learning by critical examination of one's methods with a view to necessary modification.

So much of a pejorative nature has been said and written about reflection as hindsight or understanding which comes too late that it is difficult for many to appreciate it as a learning posture. But the fact is, the Bible is a product of reflection. Its portraits of Jesus are offered after a time of remembering and experiencing what was *really* going on. The disciples did not understand at the time, say the Evangelists, but after the resurrection they remembered. The eucharist is interpreted, not for those who have never been to the table, but for those who have. Baptism is beautifully presented to those who have already been baptized and who need to appropriate anew their own experience. Even the Bible's visions of the future are reworked memories. So the reflective posture is no less vital and no less fruitful for learning and improving in the task before us now: interpretation for preaching.

Therefore, this chapter is not being offered to the reader as a *step*, a stage in the movement toward the sermon. This is to say, one should not expect to find here a sketch of what to do between the processes suggested in the previous chapter and those in the next. The nature of the interpretive task as the negotiation of the distance between past and present will be discussed, to be sure, and a number of methods for going about that task will be presented. Therefore, the reader who is in rehearsal for the pulpit, the one for whom preaching is still a future prospect, is certainly in mind in the discussion, and this chapter can appropriately be read at this point in the process of sermon preparation. But more importantly for such a reader and for those already engaged in a preaching ministry, greater benefit might be derived from returning to this and to similar discussions elsewhere following the preparation of a sermon. As one of the disciplines of a preaching ministry, one should sit down with a sermon recently preached and ask, How did the listeners and the text engage each other in this sermon? Was the text interpreted with these parishioners in mind? Were the hearers led into and out of the text and returned to their own addresses? What principles and methods of interpretation were employed, and am I satisfied that they are honest, valid, and appropriate to the text which the sermon was designed to continue as a living and present voice? In addition to its value in its present location in the interpretive process, this chapter is offered in the service of such a discipline of critical appraisal and continuing growth as a preacher.

The Task of the Preacher as Interpreter of Scripture

We will consider the preacher's task as interpreter of Scripture in terms of the necessity, the difficulty, and the possibility of interpreting biblical texts.

1. *The Necessity of Interpretation.* In the job description of the minister as preacher, teacher, and leader of a community of believers, interpreting Scripture is integral, not optional. Five facts descriptive of the nature and function of that community make this conclusion persuasively clear.

First, the church spends a considerable portion of its time in assembly and in small groups pondering and discussing written documents; that is, texts. The moment any communication is written down, it is separated from its writer, its intended readers, and its original context. In other words, a text of any kind, whether religious or not, whether significant or not, has an identity and life of its own, no longer moored but passing through many hands, before many eyes, under many circumstances. Removed from the persons and conditions of its origin, a text almost automatically prompts questions. What does this mean? Who wrote this? For whom is the message intended? These questions would arise in response to a letter found along the path that no longer carried the identities of writer or receiver. It is no different with biblical documents; no different, that is, except in the seriousness and intensity with which those questions are pursued. The leader of the community is expected to be able and willing to lead also in this endeavor.

Second, the task of interpretation is made necessary by the fact that these texts to which the church gives careful and continuing attention constitute the community's canon of Scripture. Of the many documents produced by and circulating within Jewish and Christian circles, these alone came to be received as the Word of God, to be read and heard as the work of the Holy Spirit and normative for faith and life. To say these texts are canon is to say they are the authoritative rule by which to measure belief and conduct; to say they are Scripture is to say they are living documents, addressing believers in every age and place with a word that is fresh and appropriate as well as authoritative. However, general agreement with this affirmation does not automatically yield a concrete and practical word in each situation upon which the whole church agrees. Discerning the norm that is truly the norm and hearing the message that is truly God's Word for a particular time and place never has, nor does it now come, without diligence in probing, asking, praying, and listening. In other words, the Word comes through interpreting the Word.

The third fact making interpretation essential has been implied in the comments above but needs to be stated clearly: the church has a closed canon but serves a living and leading God. Voices calling for an open canon with new documents being added as witnesses to God's continuing revelation have been heard theoretically but never heeded. For reasons historical, practical, and theological the canon is closed and will not be opened. However, as long as interpretation continues, the canon remains theologically open because new hearings of the Word are possible. A closed canon does not mean a silent God if interpretation of Scripture remains a vital enterprise of the church.

The fourth fact about the Christian community which not only permits but necessitates interpretation of biblical texts lies in the relationship between the church and the Scriptures, a relationship which is by no means simple. While the church exists under the authority of Scripture that informs, corrects, confirms, encourages, and judges, it is also the case that the Bible is the church's book in that its documents were, apart from the Old Testament, written by and for the church. In addition, it was the church, led by the Holy Spirit, which made the informal and formal decisions involved in the selection and collection of the contents of the canon. The church makes no claim of being superior to or above the authority of Scripture, but historically and theologically the community and the book belong together in a relationship of reciprocity. This means the church does not sit passively before the Scriptures but rigorously and honestly engages its texts with the best available methods of interpretation, not to dilute or deflect its message but to hear and obey. As pastor, teacher, and preacher, the minister can neither avoid the role of interpreter nor leave it to "the experts." As the interpreter of Scripture for a particular group of parishioners, the minister *is* the expert.

The fifth and final fact placing the interpretation of biblical texts inescapably within the minister's job description is the nature of the texts themselves. The Scriptures are the products of the community's interpretation and reinterpretation of its own traditions and experiences of God. Deuteronomy is a new interpretation of the law of Moses for Israel in the time of King Josiah. Second Isaiah interprets the Exodus for Israel in exile, and Mark reinterprets the Exodus for his readers (1:1-8), as does Paul for the church at Corinth (I Cor. 10). The Chronicles reinterpret the role of David in Israelite history, and Luke reinterprets that role in the light of his faith in Jesus as Messiah of the line of David. Paul interprets the traditions about Abraham and Moses in discussing law and grace. Matthew and Luke not only interpret Jesus' words and deeds but they interpret Mark's presentation of those words and deeds. The Pastorals interpret Paul, Second Peter reinterprets the tradition about an imminent Parousia, and on it goes. Psalm 110 alone receives more than thirty-five interpretations by New Testament writers. All of this is to say that the Scriptures are located within a process of interpretation and hence, by their very nature, invite the continuation of that process. The biblical texts themselves offer ample testimony that no single interpretation exhausts the meaning of a passage.

2. *The Difficulty of Interpretation.* The difficulty inherent in the task of interpretation lies in part in the text and in part in the

interpreter. As for the text, its quality of historical particularity seems to withhold it from availability or relevance for later readers. Most, though not all biblical texts (Proverbs, for example) are fixed in time, place, and circumstance and, therefore, seem to possess a uniqueness, a quality of "once but never again." Such events, relationships, or words apparently hold little if any hermeneutical potential. After all, what meaning is there for believers in Toledo or Singapore in Ruth's accompanying Naomi on her return to Bethlehem? Or when will circumstances be such as to warrant telling about Abraham raising his knife to offer Isaac, his young and only son to God? Or to what condition in the church would a preacher appropriately offer Jesus' encounter with a demoniac haunting the cemeteries of Gerasa and chilling the citizens with hideous howlings? If the preacher operates on the principle of analogy, applying texts to events and conditions of demonstrable similarity, would not many of the biblical records have to remain under glass, visited and viewed, but untouched?

Very likely the minds of many readers have raced ahead of these remarks to object: historical particularity only *seems* to mean uniqueness with no transfer value for persons outside that particularity. The truth of the matter lies rather in a statement to the contrary: it is in the particularity of a text that its universality lies. Because the listeners live in concrete circumstances, they find analogies and points of identification in the specifics of recorded events and relationships. An eighty-year-old woman will find more meaning in a specific incident in the life of a twelve-year-old Galilean boy than in facile attempts to be timeless and universal by speaking in general to everyone about everything. After all, once names, dates, and places have been changed, love is love, hate is hate, grief is grief, fear is fear, joy is joy, and forgiveness is forgiveness.

Even so, Old Testament texts may present special problems for the preacher. The reason will lie partially, but only partially, in the greater distance in time between these texts and the preacher. After all, when the chasm is two thousand years at its narrowest, what is another century or two? The reason will also lie partially, but only partially, in the fact that Old Testament texts generally possess greater historical concreteness than do New Testament texts. In fact, the preacher may be attracted to the particularity, the vividness, even the earthiness of many Old Testament stories, especially if one is inclined to be more playful here than in the New. Some preachers enjoy a theologically dubious freedom when interpreting the Old Testament, a freedom born of an unspoken but very evident attitude which says to the congregation, "After all, it's only the Old Testament; we are not in the sanctuary of the gospel."

This cavalier attitude, this acting as though it does not matter about the flowers since we are playing on someone else's lawn, points up the reason Old Testament texts may present special problems for the preacher: a theological issue is at stake. How is the Old Testament to be treated in the Christian pulpit? Each preacher has to think through the question and arrive at a view congenial with the church's position on the Old Testament and one's own theology. Historically, the church rejected as heresy Marcion's effort to exclude the Hebrew Scriptures from the Christian canon, but it did so fully aware that a complex of interpretive issues would be the legacy of every generation of believers. At the heart of that complex is the question, Must one preach Christ even when using a text from the Old Testament? In other words, is the pulpit value of such texts to be found only in their direct or indirect witness to Christ, in the absence of which they would have to be corrected or supplemented by passages from the New Testament? Or, could one properly and adequately permit Old Testament texts to remain in their own historical and literary contexts, drawing from them such instruction and inspiration as analogies between Israel and the church would justify?

It is of some help and no small comfort to realize that New Testament writers experienced the same struggle over the continuity and discontinuity between Old and New, between synagogue and church. The documents reflect not only varying degrees of tension between the Jewish and Christian communities, but also thoughtful efforts to affirm, behind and beneath those tensions, faith in the one God from whom, through whom, and to whom are all things. Matthew's Christ came to fulfill the law and the prophets, and upon the authority of the Law of Moses erected the Sermon on the Mount with its call for a righteousness surpassing that produced by the Law. The writer of the Epistle to the Hebrews developed his argument *a fortiori*, from the lesser to the greater. In times past God was revealed in different manners and degrees, but in these last days he is revealed in a Son. If, therefore, the former word was sure in its reward and punishment, how much more so is the word delivered through the divine Son. Paul placed himself and the Christian community in direct continuity with Abraham and Sarah, of whom all who believe are children, but Paul was in sharp discontinuity with those who placed Moses and the Law at the center of Judaism. Luke, on the other hand, set Christ and the church within the story begun with Adam, continued through Israel, and proclaimed finally by the apostles and Christian evangelists. The Acts of the Apostles is the story of Israel properly understood, being opposed by Israel which had misinterpreted its mission and its Scriptures. Luke, then, finds it most appropriate to locate Jesus and the apostles in the synagogue and in the temple, obedient to the regulations of God's Law. Somewhere among these and other positions not here described the preacher will stand to read and to preach from Old Testament texts. For further pursuit of the issues involved and for suggestions toward resolution, the bibliography provided at the conclusion of this volume may prove helpful.

As was stated above, the difficulty in interpreting may lie in the interpreter as well as in the text. For preachers there is, of course, the vocational hazard of going to the text not to listen but to get a sermon, or perhaps even to go in search of a text to authorize a sermon already in mind. Such utilitarianism is the enemy of interpretation, and, as a result, of preaching itself. Some interpreters are inhibited by their profound respect for the sacred text and, therefore, are hesitant to engage the Scriptures vigorously with all faculties at work. Perhaps what is really at work here is not a concern for the fragility of the text but for the fragility of one's faith, a fear that investigation may turn over a stone and make a discovery that will unseat a favorite notion. Some sensitive pastors are cautious before the text because they know how easy it is to manipulate parishioners made vulnerable by their strong predisposition to believe what is said from the pulpit, especially when the message is laced with Scripture. This is a proper caution but unhealthy if it immobilizes.

Perhaps a word needs to be said about an obstacle to sound

biblical interpretation erected as a result of an unhappy, disenchanting, and even destructive encounter with the critical methods of biblical study. Some never make peace with the term "biblical criticism," even though the writer or instructor may have explained that criticism is used not in the sense of a negative value judgment but in the scientific sense of careful and methodical investigation. The classroom is not in and of itself the enemy of the pulpit, but the net result of critical biblical study upon preaching depends on how one is introduced to such study and whether there is instructional help in the methods by which one moves from exegesis to sermon. Such a move requires thought and work, and the frightened and the lazy find it easier to forget instruction in exegesis and return after seminary to a pre-seminary naïveté. It must be acknowledged that not all failures of seminary education are the fault of the student. Some of us who teach lack instruction in good teaching methods and, therefore, bring graduate school notes into the seminary classroom. And cases of professors passing on to the students their own anger and unresolved battles with critical scholarship are not completely unheard of. It should be repeated, however, that some recent trends in biblical studies have been more friendly to the pulpit in that they have not approached the text on the principle of suspicion but on the principle of assent, and even of anticipation; that is, with the expectation that the text will yield an important word to the interpreter.

In the meantime, however, a popular reaction against critical study of the Bible has been the uncritical embrace of intuition and feeling as the key that unlocks the text. This approach has been supported in some quarters by the notion that intuition and feeling provide immediate access to meaning—access which is pure, unpolluted, and uncensored by education, culture, and society. This view implies that meaning apprehended by exercises in thought is not immediate but mediated through channels censored and corrupted by academy and culture. The fiction at work here is the assumption that we have faculties for laying hold of truth and meaning which are untouched and uninfluenced by other factors. As important as intuition and feeling are in discerning and seizing the true and real, they can be as tyrannical and as biased as the processes of intellectual pursuit. The fact is, understanding is best

133

served if all our faculties engage not only the text but each other on the way to the pulpit.

3. *The Possibility of Interpretation.* Having said that negotiating the distance between the ancient text and the present listeners is a task necessary but fraught with difficulties, we need now to assure ourselves that interpretation is possible, not grudgingly, but with promise of clarity and confidence. This possibility rests upon five favorable factors. First, the distance between ourselves and the original readers of the text is in a measure bridged by our common humanity. Understanding Paul or one of the Gospels does not so much require that we think like first-century persons as it requires simply that we think. Probing through and beneath the trappings peculiar to an incident or saying reveals the human situation being addressed. When that is done, present listeners recognize the truth of the text, themselves, and their situation. Once the moment of recognition occurs, listeners need little further help in the way of explanations, urgings, applications, and exhortations.

Consider an example. On Sunday afternoon a young minister was conducting services on the ambulatory floor of a nursing care facility. For the message to the two dozen elderly worshipers, the minister read Mark 10:13-16, Jesus receiving and blessing the children. The text about little children seemed as distant from that congregation as any that could have been selected. The minister focused attention on the disciples' efforts to prevent the children being brought to Jesus. Why hinder their coming? Several possible reasons were briefly entertained: the children were in the way; they required special attention; they could offer no help for the program of Jesus; they had no money to contribute; in fact, some who could contribute had their time and money diverted to the care of the children. As this exploration continued, those wheelchair listeners recognized themselves and their situation in the description of the children. Therefore, when the preacher concluded with the gracious word of Jesus correcting the disciples, embracing and blessing the children, smiles, nods, and soft "amens" signaled the joy and peace which filled the room. How unnecessary; in fact, how painfully out of place would have been efforts to "apply" the text: "How like those children are many of us here today." Without the factor of recognition of our common lot, the preacher cannot build enough bridges between text and listener; with the factor of recognition, those structures are unnecessary.

The second favorable factor is the continuity of the church and its tradition of interpreting the texts. In other words, the interpreter is not staring at the text across twenty centuries of silence, but is receiving the text from a church that brings generations of efforts at understanding the Scripture. These predecessors are friends and associates in the task. The image of one person sitting alone with the Bible is both unreal and undesirable.

The third favorable factor making interpretation of ancient texts possible is the existence within the church of the community of scholars whose service to the church is to preserve the text as it has been received and to aid the church in understanding the text. It is important to remember that the church was born in the synagogue, a "house of instruction," and everywhere the church has gone it has formed an academy, a critical community in the service of the faith. This fact of the church's life is sometimes forgotten because of the tension that usually exists between the church at worship and prayer and the church at study. That these scholars of the church do not always agree with one another is not a flaw in the fabric of the faith, but rather it invigorates, teasing the whole church into active thought, preventing the oppression of a single perspective, and avoiding the deadening effect of premature finality. The preacher-interpreter should welcome these colleagues and hear them before drawing conclusions about the meaning of a text.

The fourth factor enabling interpretation is the presence of the Holy Spirit in the church. According to the Fourth Gospel, the continuity of the word of Christ in the church is assured not only through the apostles but through the other Counselor, the Spirit of truth, which God sends to abide forever with the church (14:16-17). Among the ministries of the Spirit is that of revealer and interpreter. "I have yet many things to say to you, but you cannot bear them now. When the Spirit of truth comes, he will guide you into all truth; for he will not speak on his own authority, but whatever he hears he will speak, and he will declare to you the things that are to come" (16:12-13). It was Paul's conviction that the Spirit of God enabled the believer to recognize and understand the things of God (I Cor. 2:10-13). Through the centuries the church has variously

135

understood the revealing and interpreting work of the Spirit. In fact, the belief in the Spirit as continuing revealer has often been problematic, opening the door for the admission of all manner of conduct and thought in the name of the Spirit. Such difficulties notwithstanding, it is unreasonable to believe that the Spirit was active in the writing and preserving of the canon and then abandoned the church that had to interpret these texts as a living voice to guide believers.

The fifth and final factor contributing to interpretation as a vital and fruitful endeavor is the text itself. The biblical texts not only have survived all our grappling efforts to understand them, but they continue to provoke, confirm, and reject our efforts. In ways uncharted and uncalculated, the text challenges and modifies our views, not only of the text itself but also of ourselves and our world. In the final analysis, it is the text's claim on the interpreter that keeps it alive in our knowing and unknowing hands.

Methods Available to the Preacher as Interpreter

We are here discussing interpretation as the process of negotiating the distance, or more precisely the various kinds of distance, between the text and the listeners to the sermon. Assumed in this discussion is that both the text in its contexts and the listeners in theirs have been given a close reading and have been carefully investigated. It is important not to think of interpretation as solely the exploration into what the ancient writer said to the intended readers. It is equally important not to think of interpretation as solely the modernizing or updating of that message. The problem is not one of time alone. Putting a statement into the currently popular idiom and tagging it with this morning's date and time does not fulfill the task of interpretation. Reading or hearing a sermon someone preached this very day does not necessarily mean it was addressed to *me*. The question is, Did it *fit?* Was it appropriate? Interpretation is truly interpretation when it is for particular persons in a particular situation. In other words, we do not interpret Scripture; we interpret Scripture *for someone somewhere*. For this reason published sermons have limited value. They have value for students who can examine how someone else did it. They have value for historians and sociologists who use such documents to profile an era. And they have some value for any reader on the ground that our common humanity gives a message intended for one person a degree of appropriateness to another. But as sermons, as interpretations of Scripture for particular listeners, their broader value waits upon yet new interpretations of those sermons. Interpretations and sermons therefrom have names and addresses on them and are not sent out to "Resident" or "Boxholder" or "To Whom It May Concern." This means that no instructor and no book can carry to its completion the work of interpreting texts. Only the one who delivers the message, the one who knows the names and addresses, in other words, only the preacher is in a position to do that. Discussions of methods are therefore theoretical and penultimate, awaiting final adjustment and use.

Even so, as was stated earlier in this chapter, there is real benefit to the preacher in surveying and assessing methods available to and employed by others. This benefit is not inconsiderable if one selects one of the methods and applies it in charting the course of a sermon in preparation. However, the value is greater if one lays alongside a list of interpretive methods a sermon already prepared and preached and asks the question, How did I get from Hebron to Biloxi? From Antioch to Munich? From Galatia to Jamaica? The pedagogical assumption here is that while the preacher, like the artist or the actor, needs instruction in fundamental methods, there is further need to assimilate these methods in ways congenial to one's own gifts and talents. When one reaches the point of not being conscious of which method is being used, then learning and growth come by critical reflection, evaluation, and modification.

What follows, therefore, is a kind of checklist of widely used methods of getting from text to listener. With each method will be a brief description, an example for clarification, and at times a value judgment. The reader will observe that some of the methods are similar, that variations and combinations are possible, and that others may be added to the list. These, however, with whatever modifications they may have undergone, represent the principal methods followed in classroom and pulpit.

1. *The direct and uncritical transfer of the text to the listener.* This method consists simply of reading a passage of Scripture and then

137

treating it in the sermon as though it had been written with this audience in mind. On the face of it, such application of Scripture seems to carry the direct authority of the Bible and the authenticity of "telling it like it is." It is a method easy and uncomplicated for the preacher and welcomed by parishioners who are weary of being led through philosophical and theological twilight zones. Such listeners often encourage this use of Scripture to the preacher by commenting, "You preached the Bible today." There is no question but that this method can be not only refreshing and forceful in its directness, but also congenial to the very nature of some texts. For example, Matthew 5:44 seems to call for such treatment: "Love your enemies and pray for those who persecute you." But shall the preacher do the same with I Timothy 2:11: "Let a woman learn in silence with all submissiveness," or Mark 10:21: "Go, sell what you have, and give to the poor"? These texts seem to address the listener as directly as Matthew 5:44. Or, why not a sermon on qualifications for ministry from Leviticus 21:17: "None of your descendants throughout their generations who has a blemish may approach to offer the bread of his God"?

It is obvious from these examples that this method can be appropriate, but it also may be pernicious and destructive. How, then, is one to know whether or not to transfer directly to the listeners the statement of the text? The minister cannot know unless he or she has first applied to the text the procedures of careful exegesis of a text. Under such investigation some texts will stand firm and speak to the present listener as it did to the original, while others will prove to have been relativized by the peculiar circumstances of time, place, and the audience addressed. In other words, this method is no shortcut, no way to bypass the work of interpreting text and listener. When used without such work, the preacher and the congregation are prey to their own preferences in choosing texts. One can imagine a chaotic church which chooses to have the Bible tell the women to be silent and submissive but never chooses to have the Bible demand that disciples sell everything and give to the poor.

2. *Allegorical interpretation of the text.* An allegory is a literary form by which one says something other than what one seems to be saying. To allegorize is to find a message behind the generally

138

understood meaning of the words and phrases. By this means a text is cut loose from its moorings of time, place, and historical circumstance and given a timeless, spiritual meaning. Allegorically, "and Abram went out from Ur of the Chaldees" could be interpreted, "and the soul left the confines of the body" or, "You shall not eat birds of prey" could become "You shall not prey upon your neighbors." Jesus' parable of the woman seeking the lost coin (Luke 15:8-10) has been preached allegorically so that her lighting a lamp becomes a reference to the true doctrine of the church. The lamp is the church, the wick is the Scripture, the oil is prayer, and the flame is the Holy Spirit of truth.

Historically, the allegorical method has enjoyed the prestige of rabbinic and early Christian use and was widely popular for sixteen centuries. Perhaps the clearest New Testament example is Paul's use of the Sarah and Hagar story to argue his point about slavery and freedom (Gal. 4:22-31). Paul, in fact, calls the story an allegory (verse 24). In the Gospels, parables and miracle stories attracted allegorical treatments quite early. In the case of the parable of the sower (Mark 4:3-9), an allegorical interpretation follows the parable (verses 14-20), whereas with others, the parables themselves show evidence of allegorical expansion as a way of interpreting the parables for new historical circumstances. For example, look at Matthew's parable of the banquet (22:2-14) in contrast to Luke's briefer and simpler story (14:16-24). Likewise, the parable of the vineyard (Mark 12:1-11) bears the marks of allegorical expansion by a church interpreting the story in the light of Jesus' rejection and death. The parable was made into an allegory in which the various elements of the story represent identifiable persons and events outside the story. As for a miracle story turned allegory, it is difficult not to believe that Matthew was *really* talking of the church facing the world in fear and in faith in his account of Jesus coming to his disciples in the storm and of Peter's effort to go to Jesus (14:22-33).

One can see immediately the delights and advantages this method offers the preacher. The wings of allegory have easily transported texts to different situations with immediate and clear application to the new audience. All historical particularities fall away when the preacher is able to state what a text is *really* saying: "The temple in Jerusalem is really a human life. The Holy of Holies is the spirit, the

Holy Place is the soul, the courtyard is the mind, and the outside area is the body." By such a move the whole of Israel's history, life, and worship is left behind; the time is now; the place is here. Allegory finds no text too obscure, too cruel, too culturally bound, too unsavory to yield a clear and certain word to the believers. A preacher could luxuriate in the belief that every sentence, every phrase, every word, every syllable in the Bible, properly understood, carries the gospel in its bosom. And parishioners have no reason to worry if the sermon text concerns the dimensions of the tabernacle, a list of David's officers, a genealogy, or the distance from Jerusalem to Emmaus: the word of God will leap from such texts as readily as from the cross and empty tomb. In fact, allegorical interpretation gives to the pulpit a kind of mystique and to the preacher the prestige and authority befitting one able to discern the mysteries of difficult texts.

But the problems inherent in this method are apparent. The erosion of the fundamental tenet of biblical revelation—that God acts and speaks through concrete events, historical persons, and human relationships—is totally unacceptable, and the extent to which allegorizing does just that renders it an unacceptable interpretive method. This is especially so when allegorical flights into the blue skies of "higher" or "more spiritual" meanings threatens the central affirmation of the incarnation and its implications for the Christian life as life in the world. And where are the restraints upon such a method that could conceivably prove anything and preach anything as the *real* sense of a text? The relatively meager amount of allegorizing in the Bible justifies the conclusion that both synagogue and church applied restraints, perhaps both theological and practical. After the closing of the canon, the development of creedal formulas and of ecclesiastical structures for providing acceptable readings of Scripture functioned to prevent excesses. That other and no less dangerous excesses in interpretation were thereby introduced does not deny the need for theological guidelines for the community's interpretation of its own sacred texts. In those quarters of Protestantism in which private interpretation apart from the historical community is not only permitted but celebrated, allegorizing continues as a means of authorizing pulpit opinions and exhorting the believers in certain matters of life-style.

3. *Typological interpretation of the text.* Typology is a way of addressing present listeners with an ancient text by discerning in that text events or conditions having clear correspondence to those of the listeners. In other words, something occurs or is experienced in the history of Israel or of the early church which is a type of the present community's experience, and therefore, present listeners can properly be instructed, encouraged, or warned by that past occurrence or experience. The foundation upon which typological interpretation is structured is analogy. Unlike allegory, however, typology does not discard concrete history in the pursuit of hidden, timeless, spiritual truths for the listeners. On the contrary, history is taken seriously and remains history throughout the interpretive process. This is the key. The particular historical circumstances of the people of God *was* real and *is* real, and therefore, can yield fruitful analogies.

Perhaps two examples from the New Testament will suffice for purposes of clarity. One is provided by John 3:14-15: "And as Moses lifted up the serpent in the wilderness, so must the Son of man be lifted up, that whoever believes in him may have eternal life." The writer has seen in Moses' elevation of a bronze serpent on a pole set up in the camp of an unbelieving and complaining Israel (Num. 21:4-9) a type of the central redeeming act of God in the elevation of Jesus upon the cross. Elements in the one case are typical and therefore instructive for the other. A more extensive use of typology is in I Corinthians 10:1-13 in which Paul exhorts the Corinthian Christians on the ground that the wilderness experience of Israel was typical. Israel had been baptized at the Red Sea and had subsequently partaken of the God-given meal, but baptism and eucharist were not guarantees that the Promised Land would automatically be theirs. Between the Red Sea and the Jordan lay the wilderness, teeming with struggles and temptations. In these ancient circumstances Paul saw the condition of the church at Corinth, and so, by typological interpretation, used the past to speak clearly to the present.

Even in these brief comments, the strengths of this method are evident. The interpreter does not read past or around or beneath or above the text, but the biblical record and its relation to the history of a people are permitted to speak again to a new generation of believers. This method also assumes what is widely recognized to be true, that there is a commonality in human experience, and therefore it is not unnatural, it is not a homiletical gimmick, to see in one time and place an event or experience that is typical. As a typical experience, it has hermeneutical potential for persons at other times and places. In addition, this approach to the text affirms the continuity of the believing community and the wisdom of listening to and interpreting ever anew its own life and faith.

One would do well, however, to be alert to flaws and weaknesses in typological interpretation. A principal difficulty arises when one presses a text for types of experience that are not really typical. When the experience or event in the biblical record is not really analogous to the life and circumstance of present listeners, then the congregation is misread so that the text will fit. Or conversely, a text may be misread in the effort to make what it describes analogous to the condition of the congregation. When types are not types, diagnoses are false and therapy is not therapeutic. Or, it may be that a text yields a type of experience which can fruitfully address the present audience, but the interpreter continues to forage in the text for more details to extend the analogy beyond reason or sound exegesis. Exegetically, the text loses its edge and its witness is muffled by the multiplication of subpoints. Homiletically, the sermon surfeits from the effort to say more than can be said, and hence its wealth becomes its poverty. The careful investigation of both text and listener as sketched in earlier chapters will protect against such degeneration of an otherwise helpful and valid method of moving between past and present. The preacher often needs to be warned, however, that typology lives next door to allegory. The pressure to legitimate a sermon with a Scripture text can be rather intense, and preachers otherwise sober and thoughtful have been known to wander off beyond the restraints of their usual paths of interpretation.

4. *Interpretation of the intent of a text.* Although it is not true in all cases, there are texts that make their intentions accessible to the interpreter. The intent may be made available through the context, as in the case of Romans 13:1-7. Paul's application of the principle

of justification by faith begins at 12:1 and covers a range of practical and concrete instructions for the Christian community. Among these is the matter of the believer's relationship to secular authorities. It is clear that the intent of 13:1-7 is to delineate the nature of responsible Christian conduct toward governmental power. The intent of a text may also be stated directly to the reader, as in Luke 18:9-14. "He also told this parable to some who trusted in themselves that they were righteous and despised others" (verse 9) is Luke's introduction and statement of the intent of the parable of the Pharisee and the tax collector.

For purposes of preaching, this interpretive method seeks to authorize the sermon not by the content of a text but by its intent. In the case of Romans 13:1-7, for example, the sermon would be compelled by the text's intent to address the matter of responsible Christian behavior toward governmental authority. There would not be an attempt, however, to transfer to present listeners what Paul told the Roman Christians to do. This method insists that radically altered circumstances regarding church and state call for new understandings of what constitutes responsible Christian conduct. In other words, the concern and intent of the text governs preaching but not the conclusions reached by Paul in his effort to implement that concern. Or, in the case of the parable of the Pharisee and the tax collector, Luke says the intent of the story was to address the problem of exalting self while putting others down. Those who hold that *intent* and not *content* is the normative element in Scripture are guided by the intent of this text to address not only cases of self-righteous piety which despises sinners, but also other and quite different examples of such an attitude. For instance, it is not uncommon in our culture to hear and read of a kind of reverse self-righteousness of sinners who boast of honesty and frankness while despising upright and churchgoing citizens. Movies, novels, and even some sermons make heroes and heroines of the affable thief, the sympathetic prostitute, and the generous embezzler who are viewed as social victims of the real villains who work hard, pay their debts, keep commitments, and worship God. How, then, shall the preacher address the "tax collectors" who thank God they are not as the "Pharisees"? Not with the content of the parable but with its intent.

There is much to be said for this method of bringing the ancient text into the present. It has the courage to recognize that simply reciting texts is neither biblical nor responsible. A change of audience is a vital hermeneutical fact, and therefore, a message said to one group, when repeated verbatim to another, is entirely different. Every parent knows this. Words to an older daughter do not carry the same message when repeated to a younger son. And all of us know by experience that we can misquote by changing listeners as certainly as by changing the words. Therefore, in order to say the same thing, a person may have to say something different. Such realities in communicating make the focus upon intent very important as the preserver of integrity and continuity.

However, the preacher-interpreter needs to proceed with caution. In some cases, the intent of the writer is simply not recoverable except in a broad and general sense, and in such cases the generality may be, in careless hands, an endorsement for whatever needs to be said. In all cases the minister will have to be very discerning in reading both the text and the present condition to see to what extent there is a real common concern beneath the cultural and social differences. If the preaching on a text continues its intent, the design and movement of the sermon should be such as to enable the listeners to follow clearly the hermeneutical process. This is to say, the hearers should not be led to think that the *content* of the sermon is an expression of the *content* of the text, but rather that text and sermon have a common intent but address it differently. The preacher must be prepared to respond to some criticism of the adequacy of this interpretive method.

As a final suggestion, let the preacher study further to determine if this text is really the one most properly to be treated in this fashion in this sermon. Other texts may provide not only intent but also content for the message. For example, Jesus called many to full commitment as disciples but he did not say the same thing to all. In some he met enthusiasm which lacked thought and planning, while in others he met thought and planning but also hesitation. Both situations have to do with discipleship; the question is, Which is more appropriate for one's listeners? The intent of many texts is to present the claim of discipleship, but with care and study the preacher will probably discover the passages that will meet in both intent and content the condition of the listeners. While both may not be thought necessary for valid preaching, double authorization by the text will hardly weaken the message.

5. *Thematic interpretation of the text.* By thematic interpretation is meant the interpretation of individual texts in the light of the major themes of the Bible. This is to say, the whole interprets the parts, the entire canon being the theological context for each passage. In a sense, the whole of Scripture is distilled into the great and essential affirmations of the faith: God is one; God creates, sustains, judges, and redeems creation; God loves all persons but at the same time calls for ethical earnestness and responsible relationships among us; creation, history, and prophets reveal God, but in Jesus of Nazareth, crucified, risen, and glorified, God is known supremely; God's Spirit dwells with the faithful community to comfort, guide, correct, and purify; God is not only the source but the end and meaning of all life which is purposefully moving toward God's good and final purpose. Of course, these statements are made for purposes of clarification and may say more or less than any one interpreter may deem central to biblical faith. The point is, each particular text is interpreted as a concrete expression of one or more of these major themes, expressions that may be framed as praise, as doubt, as struggle, as affirmation, or as some other real encounter with and response to the God who both confirms and confronts us.

Thematically interpreted, Psalm 23 praises the providence of God; Isaiah 40 declares that God restores and renews the faithful; Jeremiah 31 promises that God continually enters into covenants with those who trust; Jonah reaffirms that God's love and forgiveness knows no limits; Matthew 5–7 asserts God's righteousness and calls for behavior appropriate to those who trust such a God; Mark 15 describes suffering and death as revelations of God's way in the world, in Christ, and among Christ's people; Luke 15 tells again the story of God's seeking love; Acts 2 celebrates God's gifts of repentance, forgiveness, and the Spirit; I Corinthians 12 details the plenteous gifts with which God equips and enables the church; Galatians 3 assures that trust in a gracious God genuinely liberates; Revelation 21 lifts the promise of God's renewing love above the finally subdued forces of evil, and on and on the themes unfold.

One can hardly imagine a more beautiful or more satisfying method for dealing with texts! Here there is no bogging down in the irrelevant details of ancient history and the thought world of rather primitive peoples. Here is no confusing mixtures of messages that so emphasize the diversity in the Bible that laypeople are afraid to open it anymore. This method celebrates the unity of the Bible and impresses upon the listeners that God is the subject of every single text. By thematic interpretation, every text, and every sermon derived from the text, is presented with a theological adequacy and carries in it the fullness of the Word. Unlike some preaching on single texts, which barely qualifies as Christian in scope and perspective, preaching that is informed by this method has size; it is never small and narrowly focused. Thematic interpretation attends to matters vital to and embraced by all believers, and offers no occasions for splintering and dividing God's people in quarrels over non-essential and peripheral topics.

And finally, in its favor is the fact that the Bible itself frequently backs off from the particular topic under consideration, reminds itself of the grand themes, and resumes the discussion within the context of that theological affirmation. Into the story of Jonah the prophet himself inserts the ancient creed with which he had struggled in anger: "For I knew that thou art a gracious God and merciful, slow to anger, and abounding in steadfast love, and repentest of evil" (4:2). Paul responded to a church quarreling over its menu by setting the matter in a larger context: "Yet for us there is one God, the Father, from whom are all things and for whom we exist, and one Lord, Jesus Christ, through whom are all things and through whom we exist" (I Cor. 8:6). Rather than enter into the world of those Philippians who thought too much and too often of self, Paul sang for them a hymn they knew but did not know, and he sang all stanzas (2:6-11). The Christ hymn is of such size and scope as to silence in embarrassment all petty disputes. Lifting up the great and central themes of Scripture is an act of primary pastoral and homiletical importance.

However, problems inherent in the approach must be honestly faced. The Bible is not, in fact, a compend of sweeping theological affirmations and to transform it into such would be a kind of reductionism. Some texts and even some entire books sit uneasily side by side, testifying to the continuing struggles of faith to apprehend and to embody the will of God. To obscure that fact would be to put a false face on faith's history and nature and to give a biblical blessing to unreality and artificiality in the church. When Tatian prepared his *Diatessaron,* a harmonious weaving of the four Gospels into one, the church rejected it, just as it must continue to reject attempts to flatten out the richly diverse contours of Scripture into a simplistic formula, "The Bible says." The historical particularities ingredient to the Bible provide the concrete variables, making possible resonance and identification by many different readers in an endless continuum of new and fresh appropriations of the texts. When the Scriptures are converted too smoothly into themes, this experience is denied listeners to sermons which, by this process, all tend to become very much the same. In addition, thematic interpretation fails to respect and preserve the literary forms of texts. Making a paraphrase of the Song of Deborah or Psalm 139 or the parable of wise and foolish maidens is not simply a literary fallacy; it is to rob such passages of their power to generate new meaning by means of their form. And finally, this method could encourage laziness among preacher-interpreters. The translation of a thorny text into a broad theme about God's love or a call to hopefulness could be taken as a shortcut to the sermon, bypassing the troublesome details of dietary regulations, birth narratives, exorcisms, and apocalyptic visions. The real tragedy in such shortened exercises would not lie so much in the lamentable study habits of the minister as in the impoverished diet of those parishioners denied the rich fare almost every text offers, but only with persistent effort.

6. *Interpretation by translation of the text.* Every interpretation is a translation, but this method seeks to interpret by freeing the text to speak to the reader or listener by removing the barriers that are due to difficulties with language. The conviction underlying this approach is that the text is like a seed because it carries in its own bosom the capacity to generate life. The images, stories, songs, sayings, and historical recitations of the text are able to create in the listeners experiences not unlike those that are recorded in the Scriptures. That is, revelation spawns revelation. The task of the interpreter is not to transform, explain, apply, or otherwise build

bridges from the text to the listeners. Rather, the task is to release the text upon the listener's ear by translating it into the language of the listener. One's hearers will need help with furlong, first-century agriculture, sheep gate, a three-level universe, demons, bloodletting, Midianites, veiled women, and the denarius. After all, the offense of the gospel should not be located at cultural, geographical, and linguistic barriers, but where it belongs: God's addressing us in judgment and grace in Jesus Christ. The interpreter, therefore, seeks to remove with minimal loss of meaning the false barriers and then to let the text do what it will. For those preacher-interpreters who are able to do so, this will involve some original translating from Hebrew and Greek. For others, translation and clarification will come from research in dictionaries, commentaries, and atlases. The Anchor Bible, as originally conceived, was to be an interpretation by translation. It was not to be a commentary upon the text but a fresh translation with as few notes as clarity and honesty demanded. This intention was partially implemented in some volumes, such as the one on the Gospel of Matthew.

Who could say nay to such a method, to the fresh and trusting act of introducing the text and the listener to each other and walking away? There is no room here for imperialistic moves on the part of the interpreter; only a clearing of the way for the moment of recognition to occur. Here there is no forced steerage of text and listener in each other's direction with instructions on who says what to whom. The text that has a surplus of meaning, as the history of interpretation and preaching amply testifies, is permitted to be multivalent, to address the different listeners in their own different needs and circumstances. After all, is not the real event in preaching the creation of new meaning at the point of intersection between text and listener rather than in the carting of information from one to the other? Every preacher knows from experience what literary critics tell us, that a text has a life of its own, transcending our explanations, resisting our paraphrases, and breaking through the corrals of our thorough outlines. Then why not allow our procedures to give full rein to the text; after all, the parishioners have been asking all along for more Bible in our sermons. There seems to be no interpretive method more congenial to the belief that the Word can and will create its own audience if its primary language is not replaced by our secondary and tertiary discussions, explanations, and applications.

Even so, the question persists, Is this enough? Of course, powerful transactions and transformations occur without a sermon at all, triggered by the clear and unadorned reading of Scripture. Who has not on occasion, following the reading of the biblical texts in worship, whispered inaudibly, "Please, Preacher, don't confuse it"? Still it must be asked, Is this enough? After granting the text's own engagement of the listener at varying levels of emotion, memory, sentiment, and thought, distances between past and present remain, and without further interpretation, one can hardly argue that speaking and hearing the Word have been maximal. Communication is always difficult, and the office of preaching demands more responsible involvement in the process than just letting happen whatever will happen.

Consider three examples from the New Testament. According to Luke 4:16-30, Jesus read Isaiah 61:1-2 in the Sabbath service of his home synagogue and made a single statement in closing. His gracious words were complimented by those in attendance. Why did he not leave it at that? The text and the listeners had met. Apparently, Jesus concluded that they had not *heard* the text, and so he interpreted it. Their responses to his sermon demonstrated they had not heard, and they did not want to hear. A good, clear reading of the Bible they enjoyed, but its meaning they found disturbing. As a second example, look at I Corinthians 7:10-16. To the church members who were married, Paul recited his text from the Jesus tradition: stay married, do not divorce (verses 10-11). But Paul did not just quote the Bible and leave it with them. Some members had spouses who were pagans. Their question was, Are Christians to continue to live in marriage union with unbelieving mates? Paul's response is an interpretation of his text (the word from Jesus) in light of his listeners' situation. They needed help to negotiate the distance. And finally, recall the discussion of the Lord's Supper in I Corinthians 11:17-34. Paul addresses the problem of a confused and chaotic eucharistic meal by first quoting his text, which was the words of institution given by "the Lord Jesus on the night when he was betrayed" (verses 23-25). Paul is sensitive, however, to the distance between the upper room with Jesus and the noisy assembly in Corinth. He therefore interprets the text (the eucharistic tradition) and applies it to the Corinthian situation. Christian leadership sometimes demands more than introducing the text and the listeners to each other; sometimes one has to get a conversation started. Interpretation seeks to do just that.

That the process of interpreting, whether by the methods sketched here or by others, calls for a kind of audacity, that interpreting is an act of courage, is evident to all. In cautious respect for the text, yes; in paralyzing fear of the text, no. After all, the Scripture will remain after our efforts to interpret it have long ceased.

We have now discussed interpreting the listeners, interpreting the text, and negotiating the distance between. It remains now for us to turn to the sermon itself.

PART III

Preaching: Shaping the Message into a Sermon

eight

Qualities to Be Sought in the Sermon

At the risk of banalizing our discussion by excessive repetition, let it be said once more that we have not as yet been working on a sermon as such. Arriving at something to say and crafting that message into a sermon are two separate processes with quite different demands and dynamics. Our efforts thus far have been in pursuit of the message itself. Before us now is the task of shaping and designing that message in order that it may be heard and appropriated. Here all the person's art and skill as a communicator join his or her care and understanding as a minister in the creation of the sermon. That the preacher has a message does not mean that the listeners will get the message.

The readers of this book do not need to be persuaded that communicating is difficult, even under the best of circumstances. In conversations within a family or among close friends, it is not uncommon to hear such phrases as, "If I hear you correctly," or, "Perhaps I misunderstood you, but. . . ." Enlarge that circle, include strangers, widen the age range, diversify the capacities, interests, values, and motives of the group, insert variables beyond control or even prediction, and then you begin to sense the nature of the challenge of communicating through preaching. However, there may be someone reading this book who is persuaded that sermon crafting is a concession to human sin in that the preacher is trying to lure and tease the listeners' resistant ears, and therefore is an exercise in unbelief in that the preacher is not trusting the power of

God. The twin convictions that a message of burning significance will, without art or skill, cut its own path to the hearer's heart, and that the Holy Spirit, without human contrivance, opens the listener's ear, are widely and firmly embraced. And not without reason. There is enough truth in both of them to give pause and correction to any who become enamored with their own artistry. However, there is enough deception in both of them to alert any preacher to the danger of allowing healthy convictions to replace healthy work habits. Those who pray as though all depends upon God still bear the burden of working as though all depends upon themselves.

To insist that studying to have a message and framing that message into a sermon are separate tasks is an invitation to discipline and a promise of realistic returns at the close of each process. It is not, however, to be blind to the fact that occasionally flashes of insight, moments of inspiration, sudden perceptions into the nature of things will send the mind leaping over walls, breaking down distinctions between what to say and how to say it. When with the message comes also a clear design for the sermon itself, welcome the moment and be grateful. Arriving at a message and discovering it is already a sermon, born full grown, is a gift refreshing and rare, but not a reason to abandon the disciplines that put us week by week into the pulpit without apology. If one permits an impatience to have a sermon to bleed back into the prior process of studying for a message, then most likely the thoroughness of that study will be aborted, and the degree of objectivity appropriate to such discourse seriously subverted.

Before moving to the process of shaping the sermon, it will be helpful to remind ourselves of the qualities we seek in the sermon. How is a message congenial to the gospel, to the listeners, to the context, and to sound principles of communication, to be characterized? Of course, there are always plenty of old adjectives unemployed, sitting around waiting to be used in a description of a good sermon, adjectives such as lively, interesting, biblical, personal, brief, enthusiastic, relevant. Our purposes are better served, however, if we back off from those too available words and locate more comprehensive terms, few in number but specific enough both to release and to govern our creativity. In the list offered below it is already assumed that in terms of content the sermon is faithful in its witness and is of a piece with the entire service of worship in the proclamation of the gospel.

1. Unity

We have already concluded that, for purposes of preaching, the fruit of interpretation (of text, of listeners, and negotiating the distances between) is the statement of the message in a simple, affirmative sentence. That one is able to do this is the clearest evidence of the adequacy of that study which, in turn, gives permission to proceed to attending to the sermon itself. That sentence is the theme, the statement, the governing idea of the sermon. It is probably wise not to refer to it as the "proposition" since that term is drawn from the realm of debate and argumentation and, therefore, might prejudice the form and nature of the sermon in that direction. Some sermons may focus on a proposition, if indeed argument toward persuasion is the purpose, but certainly not all sermons have that intent, and therefore, need no statement of a proposition.

It has already been said that the message is best stated in the affirmative rather than the imperative lest the sermon be too hortatory and scolding, and in the positive rather than the negative lest the sermon be too much an indictment without the announcement of good news. What now needs to be emphasized is that the message statement be a simple rather than a compound or complex sentence in order to maintain unity and singularity of direction. Permit a few conjunctions into that sentence, a semicolon or two, perhaps an et cetera, and what happens? Fuzziness replaces focus and through the cracks between the poorly joined and disparate units of that overextended statement will creep every cause crying out for a little pulpit publicity and every announcement with its hand in the air insisting on a few lines in the sermon. We have all heard such sermons: they touch upon many topics, make some good comments, promote God and all worthy causes, intend for everyone the benefits of heaven, honor the Scriptures, and revere the saints, but they have an uncertain Alpha and no Omega at all.

Most preachers confess to having difficulty stating the message in

155

one simple sentence. For some the difficulty lies in the fact that the discipline here involves decision, not only about what will be said but also about what will not be said. To say one thing is to decide not to say something else. It is to accept the conclusion that on a given Sunday, many wonderful Christian things will not be said. Perhaps the pain involved is similar to that of walking into a disaster area and realizing that turning toward one person in helpfulness is turning one's back to another. Others complain that the Scripture text is too multifaceted, too filled with messages to be reduced to one message. That many texts hold a surplus of meaning is true, but not everything can be said at once. There will be occasions to return to these passages again and again. Yet other preachers point to the many needs represented in the congregation as an argument against the single focus. Such pastoral concern cannot be faulted, but as an argument for unfocused preaching, it lacks the support of both reason and experience. To aim at nothing is to miss everything, but to be specific and clear in one's presentation is to make direct contact with many whose ages, circumstances, and apparent needs are widely divergent. Listeners to sharply focused sermons have an amazing capacity to perceive that the sermon was prepared with them specifically in mind.

Why is it that the unity provided by this theme statement is so vital to preaching? The reasons are many. Among them are these: having in mind a clear message gives confidence to the preacher through the preparation and the delivery of the sermon; sensing that the preacher is well prepared sets the hearers free to listen more attentively; being specific in one's focus releases the imagination of the preacher for creating and for gathering enriching materials; having a single theme provides the assurance of where one is going in the message, which is the key to movement; the restraint of one idea adds to listener interest because energies are not dissipated on side trips to nowhere; a single governing theme enables the preacher to hold the message in mind more easily and therefore to be less dependent on a manuscript or notes; and the one central idea provides a natural control over which materials are admissible into the sermon and which are not, the theme serving as a magnet to attract only the appropriate.

At several points in the process of shaping the sermon the

preacher has opportunity to reassess and even to sharpen the unity of the sermon. For example, putting the theme into an even briefer form as a sermon subject is an excellent exercise in checking for extraneous or excessive content. A sermon subject is a brief—two to five words usually—phrasing of what the sermon is about, and should be a distillation of the theme sentence. The subject may serve as the title of the sermon, but quite often the subject is stated only for the one preaching and not for the public. For this reason, titles are subjects which are rephrased in order to attract attention and stimulate interest. As a final check of the unity and integrity of one's sermon, the following simple procedure may prove helpful: as the text yields the theme, so the theme yields the subject, and the subject yields the title. When arranged in this fashion, the unity of the sermon can be displayed before the preacher's eyes as a guard against meandering or including in the sermon that good story which does not quite fit. Two examples will suffice to make the procedure clearer.

(a) *Text:* Matthew 5:21-27
   Theme: In the church, relationships take precedence over ritual.
   Subject: Reconciliation as Priority
   Title: Leaving Before the Benediction

(b) *Text:* Romans 13:11-14
   Theme: Acting like a Christian is one path to becoming a Christian.
   Subject: Doing and Being
   Title: A Good Word for Hypocrisy

Such information, written on a card or sheet of paper and placed in the center of one's desk, will immediately take charge of the most disorderly scattering of notes and bring order out of chaos.

2. Memory

To urge that a sermon have a memory is to say that it should be set within the tradition of the believing community. A message that is thus contexted is prepared and delivered in a cloud of witnesses, and in its subject matter, struggles, affirmations, and recitals of faith and praise, intentionally makes contact with that tradition. By tradition is meant not only that portion which is normative, the Scriptures, but

157

also the continuing life of the people of God. No Christian community, regardless of its claim, is shaped solely by the Bible; it is also shaped by the endless line of those who sought to understand and to live the faith that they had received as a heritage. Preaching that has a memory does not forget Goshen, Jerusalem, Nazareth and Antioch, but neither does it forget Chalcedon, Wittenberg, London, and Plymouth; it does not forget Abraham, Sarah, Mary, and Simon, but neither does it forget Aquinas, Luther, Wesley, and Theresa. To use the imagery of Paul, such preaching grafts the listeners into the olive tree, the roots of which are Abraham, Isaac, and Jacob. To be a Christian is to be enrolled in a story that gives to each person and to the community a sense of identity and purpose which transcends the remembered experiences of those who worship at any given time and place. Faith that can only witness to events within the parentheses of one's own birth and death is undernourished and poorly resourced.

The quality in preaching that we are here considering does not call for a sentimental or uncritical embrace of tradition. Certainly not. Memory listens, reflects, sifts, and learns; otherwise we deny the present, cut off the future, and halt the growth toward maturity which should characterize the people of God. But preaching that has a memory is not guilty of that monumental conceit which reads the Bible as though it had never been read before, and enters the pulpit as though none had ever stood in that place. Neither does preaching that has a memory mean filling our sermons with stories from the old days and forcing the congregation to carry the bones of Joseph every step of the way to the Promised Land. There are many ways by which the listeners can be made aware of and put in touch with its tradition.

Consider, for example, the methods by which biblical texts are ingredient to sermons and therefore become a part of the congregation's thinking, feeling, deciding and doing. The most intensive and extensive use of a text is its *exposition* in the sermon. By this means the words, phrases, thoughts, and images of the Scripture are so integrally woven into the message that the listeners are hearing and thinking and experiencing the text. A less intensive use of Scripture in a sermon is the *quotation* without comment. Quoting Scripture passages is on the decline in many pulpits.

Perhaps the demise of memorizing in public pedagogy has been a contributing factor, as is the reaction of many to the thoughtless, concordance preaching of those whose sermons are little more than accumulations of unrelated verses. Such a reaction is understandable but hardly justifies denying one's parishioners the experience of hearing appropriately selected and arranged quotations of Scripture. Granted, such texts may be recalled by few and their functions in the sermon by even fewer, but quotations contribute to the texture of the listener's world and to the memory that nourishes life at a level deeper than anyone's capacity to recall. A third means of putting listeners in contact with Scripture is the *allusion*. By alluding to persons, stories, events, or even lines from the Bible, the preacher assumes a knowledge on the part of the hearers, a knowledge upon which the full value of the allusion depends. Allusions are not lost on those who are unfamiliar with the Scripture because the allusion usually carries its own meaning. For example, one does not have to know Daniel 5 to understand a preacher who says, "He saw 'the handwriting on the wall' and resigned from the company." However, for those who do, the allusion is not only richer in meaning, but they enjoy the compliment paid them by the preachers' assumption that they knew. A final method of nourishing a congregation on its tradition is the *echo* of Scripture. The echo is a mild form of allusion in which the preacher does not assume or depend on the listener's knowledge of what is being echoed. Ministers who have spent years with the Scriptures often season their sermons, almost unconsciously, with words, phrases, names, and fragments of ideas from biblical texts. These are echoes, and though faint and fragmentary, they add to the mood and tone of the occasion and to one's experience of the message.

These four modes of using Scripture illustrate how a preacher, without monotony or trivializing repetition, can draw upon the church's memory to enrich the church's memory and to nourish its faith.

3. Recognition

Since preaching is *for* the church as well as *to* the church, since the gospel is *from* the community of faith as well as *to* it, the parishioners must recognize in the sermon their own confession of sin and repentance, their own affirmation of faith, their own vision and hope, their own burst of praise. Unless there is an "amen" built into the message, how can the people ever say "amen?" Of course, this sounds like a formula for boredom ("Here we go again"), but not necessarily. The power and effectiveness in all public speaking, including preaching, lies in the mixture of the familiar and the new. Some of the new is in informational content, but ordinarily that should never exceed 10 percent of the message. Oral presentations should not carry to the ear more freight than that lest the overload overwhelm and the ear be closed in self-defense. Most of the new, however, consists of a different perspective upon the familiar. A rearrangement of the familiar can make it as interesting as the new yet as satisfying as the old.

Another way of expressing this characteristic of good preaching is to say that the *nod* of recognition precedes the *shock* of recognition. In fact, without the nod, that is, the sense of already knowing and agreeing, the shock of recognition, that is, the sudden realization that I am the one called, the one addressed, the one guilty, the one responsible, the one commissioned, is not even possible. The new alone can inform and may even interest a listener, but it cannot convict a listener. The Bible brims with examples of this very dynamic of nod and shock. It was because David so totally agreed that a rich man's slaughter of a poor man's lamb was an act of pitiless injustice that Nathan was able so effectively to say, "You are the man" (II Sam. 12:1-15). The religious reforms of King Josiah were prompted by and based upon the recovery of the book of the law, the reclaiming of tradition (II Kings 22–23). The familiar, the law and covenant at Sinai, is stated anew (Deuteronomy) with the power to change a nation. When listeners to Jesus said, "Did not our hearts burn within us while he talked to us on the road?" they were not referring to entirely new subjects on the lips of Jesus but to the fact that "he opened to us the scriptures" (Luke 24:32). Biblical writers do not regard rehearsals of the familiar as hollow and dull. Luke wrote: "That you may know the truth concerning the things *of which you have been informed*" (Luke 1:4, italics added). Paul wrote: "Now *I would remind you*, brethren, in what terms I preached to you the gospel, *which you received*" (I Cor. 15:1, italics added). John wrote:

"I write to you, not because you do not know the truth, but *because you know it*" (I John 2:21, italics added).

We are here thinking of the quality of recognition in practical terms, as that which can be implemented in the designing of the sermon. Were we to pursue the matter theologically, we would, no doubt, be led into discussions of human nature and the capacity of listeners to the gospel to recognize it even if they have never heard it before. Apparently the gospel speaks to that faint recollection of Eden in all of us and to that remembrance, sin distorted to be sure, of who we really are. However, on the level of plain speaking about shaping sermons, no view of human nature can negate the fact that the parishioners have banked experiences which, though unavailable to recall, can be evoked by preaching. Consistently good preaching trusts that this is so and, therefore, writes checks, so to speak, on those deposits of experience and knowledge. The preacher does not name the dynamic at work or call attention to it in the process of the sermon; the preacher simply does it. After all, some truths and values survive only if they are assumed. When focused upon and analyzed, they die, not from falsity but from attention.

Some preachers will perhaps object, saying the quality of recognition is valueless in their situations because most of their parishioners do not know the Bible or the tradition and, therefore, can recognize nothing. The church's biblical illiteracy is everywhere lamented and surely with justification. But here we are thinking recognition, not recall. Without question, some persons who passed with honors a curriculum in Bible three years ago would be embarrassed by their scores on a test of recall today. But that fact is unrelated to the point here. What is being urged is a way of preaching that assumes the listeners' recognition of much of the material. And how does that assumption function in designing the sermon? First, it means that the preacher will share, not omit, details. For example, it is a common fault of ministers to allow the listeners' familiarity with a passage to eliminate details, perhaps out of fear of boredom. The principle of recognition says no to such a practice. If treating the story of Jesus raising Lazarus, for instance, covering the details of the narrative to activate recognition produces the nod necessary for the shock of its impact. If some present do not know the narrative at all, then they have learned, and that is no small benefit.

Second, assuming listener recognition means presenting the familiar with interest and enthusiasm. Again, some ministers are full of excitement when covering daily news and telling stories, but drag through the biblical expositions in chorelike fashion. Why? One reason is the assumption that parishioners have heard it before and therefore are uninterested. To assume lack of interest can produce delivery with lack of interest which, like any self-fulfilling prophecy, creates lack of interest, making the preacher accessory to the condition being lamented. The renewal of biblical preaching waits not only on more and better exegesis, but on abandoning the pulpit attitude that comes across to the listener as, "If you will be patient and sit through the biblical stuff, I promise to tell you very soon now the interesting story about Uncle Clyde surviving a plane crash." The principle of recognition liberates the preacher to move through familiar territory with more, not less, conviction and enthusiasm.

4. Identification

Those who write plays and movie scripts know that the key to holding interest and making an impact upon an audience lies in the identification of the audience with characters and critical events portrayed. They also know that persons are drawn into, not instructed or exhorted into, identification. Therefore, they do not write instructions into the script for a director or producer to come on stage to interrupt the play now and then in order to address the audience: "Aren't many of us like Mary here, early victims of domestic strife?" "How many of us have experienced the same frustrated ambition that Harry is suffering?" "Who among us has not known Edith's longing to confess everything and start life anew?" "If we were honest, wouldn't we all have to acknowledge we are no less pretentious and hypocritical than Edward in our play tonight?"

Enough of this. Those among us who are not thinking of plays and playwrights but of sermons and preachers plead guilty, knowing that were our small endeavors set in that arena, we would very soon empty the theater. Having confessed to futile and perhaps even offensive attempts at effecting identification, our question is, How do we draw and hold the listeners in the bonds of identification so that the message may do its work on mind and heart? At least six qualities characterize preaching which is able to effect identification.

(*a*) The human condition is presented with genuine insight. Journalistic sermons that report on current events and place those events under the judgment and promise of the gospel have a certain appeal and value but listeners do not become interior to them or personally identify with them. Such appropriation of sermons occurs when human behavior or relationships are probed and revealed with such perception that hearers say, "Yes, that is really the way it is. I did not know anyone else really understood." Such preaching touches upon grief, joy, jealousy, fear, shame, anger, love, trust, betrayal, hope, and countless other contours of human experience and holds them up to the light of God's grace. Such messages are personally embraced and usually with life-changing results.

(*b*) Primary attention is given to the specific and particular rather than the general. When sermons are filled with expressions such as "modern society," "scientists today," "today's youth," "global conflict," "many marriages," "Europeans tell us," or "farm life in America," no pulse races, no nerves twitch, no parishioner leans forward in rapt attention. Life is not experienced or known in general. However, listeners are capable of generalizing appropriately once they have identified with specific persons involved in concrete events in certain places at certain times.

(*c*) Sermon materials are realistic rather than contrived for homiletical purposes. One does not have to be especially clever to discern homiletical distortions of descriptions, narrations, and characterizations in order to make life fit the point being made in a sermon. Materials thus bent out of shape telegraph ahead the illustrative or hortatory purposes to which they will be put and further convince some hearers that preachers live in a different world. With the people and furniture of that world none of them can identify. Sometimes zeal for applying an idea to everyone or trying too hard to achieve everyone's identification with an experience leads to a kind of artificiality in narration. For example, suppose a minister is wanting to describe the most enjoyable rest one can have. An analogy is drawn from an experience from student days. The student is sound asleep, the alarm having already been shut off. Suddenly the student sits upright, looks at the clock, it is five before eight and class begins at eight. Dashing madly to the bathroom, the student suddenly realizes it is Saturday, breathes a relaxing sigh, and sinks back into a bed still warm. Everyone can identify with that, but our nervous preacher wants to be sure. So the story is enlarged by having the late sleeper say, "Oh, my goodness, I'll be late for class, or work, or the doctor's appointment, or the bus, or whatever has to be done." What could have been a real account of a real experience is thus destroyed by the homiletical anxiety to do everyone's identifying.

There is probably no more common obstacle to listener identification than sermonic portraits of sin. For the sermon to be effective it is necessary that the hearers identify with, see themselves in, the persons, the attitudes, or the actions that are sinful. However, who will listen to a description of sin as foul, loathesome, scaly, serpentine, full of stench, and obvious from ten miles away, and then say, "Lord, is it I?" If the text is Jesus' word to Pharisees and in the sermon the Pharisees are caricatured, no one in the audience will say that the word of Jesus is to *me*. None of us identifies with the unreal, the exaggerated, the artificial.

(*d*) Narration and description are with emotional restraint and an economy of words. This counsel continues the caution about realism but needs to be underscored. Listeners tend to lean into narratives which have emotional force but which are presented with emotional restraint. If a speaker tries to milk all the emotion out of an event, emotion becomes emotionalism, and listeners sense the exploitation. They then recoil, at first instinctively, and then in embarrassment, disgust, and anger. The same is true with description. Too many adjectives in effect tell the listeners what to see and hear and how they are to respond to what is described. To be told in advance that a joke is absolutely hilarious is to put the audience on the defensive: "Let's just see if it is." The listeners do not see an overdescribed bluebird; they are handed one. They do not hear an overdescribed train whistle; it is shoved into the ear.

(*e*) Events are viewed from a single perspective unless the hearer is instructed otherwise. When treating an event or narrative, biblical or otherwise, it is best for the preacher to stand in one place throughout the message. If the truth is best served by moving to a second or a third position, then the audience needs to be led to the new angle of vision. Otherwise, confusion destroys identification and the hearers feel the disadvantage. For example, suppose one is dealing with the parable of the laborers in the vineyard (Matt. 20:1-15). The preacher may stand back from it and view all the characters, or the householder, or the early workers, or the late workers. The choice of perspective is determined by the desire to hear and receive the story, but once the choice is made, looking at the parable from other angles should be reserved for other sermons. No one can experience a concert from the wings, the balcony, the orchestra pit, and a front seat all at once. Neither can one experience a sermon and identify with anyone or anything if the perspective is altered frequently.

(*f*) As much as possible, the sermon material is reexperienced as it is related. In other words, the speaker functions from within the sermon, the result being that the hearer tends to do the same. Of course, some of the content is information and historical reporting, but even much of that can be presented with empathetic imagination. At times, experiencing the sermon as it is preached can be emotionally demanding and each preacher has to determine and respect emotional thresholds. However, the great advantage of this mode of moving through the material is that emotions are always congenial to the content; there are no manufactured feelings. To this genuineness, whether joy, anger, sorrow, disgust, or indignation, listeners naturally respond, and usually with some degree of identification.

5. Anticipation

Given the fact that listening to a sermon requires time and no small effort, and may even make demands on one's life and resources, how can a preacher expect anyone to give attention with sustained interest? To say that commitment and habit hold many listeners long past the merits of either content or delivery is only a partial answer, and not always true. Preachers do expect people to listen, and very likely the primary reason is the importance of the subject matter. But a second reason supports the expectation of many preachers: they have worked hard to shape sermons which create and sustain anticipation. To effect the quality of anticipation is a primary burden of movement in a sermon. It might even be said that an important subject notwithstanding, a sermon arranged in its parts so as to dull the edge of curiosity cannot hold the attention even of the committed parishioner.

It is difficult to overstate the vital role of anticipation in human life. Anticipation enables us to ride out the storm, endure periods of pain and privation, stick with distasteful and boring tasks, maintain sanity in chaos, and survive disappointments and delays in the pursuit of our goals. In addition, it is probably the human spirit's greatest source of pleasure, often exceeding that provided by the fulfillment of one's anticipation. The preacher understands the dynamic of anticipation, and therefore designs sermons which create expectation with their early promise, but which will delay the fulfillment of that promise until the listener is sufficiently engaged to own the message and take responsibility for what is heard. The preacher utilizes a climactic arrangement so as to arrest and hold the hearer's attention until the hearer is as involved in the message as is the speaker. All of this has one end in view: that the hearer be moved to respond with attitudinal or behavioral change.

One has only to read short stories to discern how materials can be arranged so as to create and sustain anticipation. In one a tension straining all nerves and threatening all relationships finally breaks in the joy of reconciliation. In another a gross injustice angers the reader who grows impatient for a fair resolution. In yet another some ambiguity clouds and haunts the action until the reader both demands and pleads for clarification. Perhaps an innocent person waits upon exoneration or a hapless victim will surely soon be pulled from beneath the wheel of misfortune. These examples are a bit dramatic, to be sure, but the principles by which writers capture and hold readers are available to the preacher. However, availability is one thing, employment is another. The difference often lies in the preacher's doubt about the advisability or admissibility of artistry and imaginative skill in preparing sermons. The old fiction that awkwardness, crudity, and tastelessness are more honest, prophetic, and Christian than skill, timing, and appropriateness is alive and well, and probably will remain so as long as laziness can disguise itself acceptably as religious conviction.

Actually we are not at all speaking of literary gloss and imaginative

166

embroidery. Building anticipation into one's preaching simply calls for one basic understanding of the task of the pulpit: the goal is not to get something said but to get something heard. One minister sits before the Sunday text: Adam and Eve being evicted from Eden, Joseph forgiving his brothers, David mourning the death of Solomon, Ruth's love for Naomi, Jesus sending demons into swine, Peter preaching for the first time to Gentiles, Paul saying farewell to the elders of Ephesus, John's vision of the new Jerusalem. The minister growls: "This again? How can I say it one more time?" Another minister sits before the same text and thinks: "How can I capture and hold their attention long enough for them to hear and experience this text?" For this second minister, achievement of the goal requires basically two factors: having a message—that is, knowing the end toward which the sermon will move—and exercising restraint in the journey to it.

Since we began this chapter assuming that study had yielded a message, let us dwell a moment on that second factor: restraint. If one's whole point has been stated in the introduction or fully made five minutes into the sermon, why should anyone continue to listen? Time drags the sermon like a dead body toward the noon hour, and restless children are assured it will soon be over. What is the problem? Is the sermon not true? Of course it is true. Is Scripture not being used? Of course there is plenty of Scripture. Is the preacher a pretender, a charlatan? Of course not; there has never been a hint of question about faith and character. What then? The presentation is completely without anticipation.

Near the end of his life, Carl Sandburg, historian, poet and entertainer, was asked by a reporter, "What in your opinion is the ugliest word in the English language?" Mr. Sandburg drew his brow thoughtfully over his face and repeated the phrase, "The ugliest word in the English language." The reporter and television audience waited. Mr. Sandburg gathered his face into a circle of concentration and said slowly, "The ugliest word?" Everyone waited. Mr. Sandburg looked away as if searching the room for a word written somewhere on a wall, pursed his lips and almost mumbled, "Ugliest? The ugliest word?" The reporter and millions continued to lean forward. The pause seemed long, but alive and promising. Mr. Sandburg turned back to the reporter. "The ugliest

167

word," he said, "the ugliest word is [pause] 'exclusive.' " Into a nest of anticipation, built entirely of restraint, he dropped the word, and years later, in the memory of many, it lies there yet, still vivid, fresh, and strong.

6. Intimacy

A group is never so large as to negate an audience's expectation that a sermon both assume and create a personal relationship between speaker and hearer. Were someone to inquire about the nature of that relationship, most likely he or she would hear among the responses a frequent recurrence of the words care, trust, and respect. The expectation is neither unreal nor out of order. The proverb makers remind us that part of the sound one hears in a seashell is created by the pulse and throb of the hand holding it. So one cannot totally separate what one hears in a sermon from the one who delivers it. This quality we refer to here as intimacy.

Genuine intimacy is not a planned creation of the preacher, as though at a certain point in preparation he could say, "Now I must add a touch of intimacy." This quality is enhanced but not created by eye contact. Eye contact has been much overrated. It must be congenial to content and happily married to the texture and mood of the sermon at every point. Otherwise, indiscriminate eye contact is nothing more than public staring. Neither is intimacy constructed of stories of self-disclosure. Most parishioners welcome some self-revelations by the preacher if the accounts are brief, not too frequent, and integrally related to the matter at hand. However, too many references to self, to spouse, or to children can be heard as an ego trip, a plea for approval, or as an apology; after all, see how human your minister is! Intimacy is not a quality put into a sermon but a quality out of which preaching is done. And it always has some distance in it. Speaker and listener are committed to each other but with enough detachment to be healthy and non-possessive. Emotion is ingredient to the relationship but never of such nature or degree that freedom is eroded, freedom for decisions, alternative views, and interpretive options.

A major contributor to intimacy is the fact that the sermon is an

168

oral presentation. To say a sermon is oral is not to say simply that it is spoken but that it is prepared with principles of orality closely observed. This is the case even if the minister preaches from a manuscript, even though it should be noted now that the manuscript is an obstacle to intimacy. Principles of orality and the matter of using notes or a manuscript will be considered in the next two chapters. Our present concern is with the psychodynamics of orality and its power to socialize and create intimacy. The human voice, released into a group of persons whose lives are interrelated in many ways, is an extraordinary force. Unlike readers of written words, listeners are drawn to participate in what a speaker says and even to imitate the act of speaking. Unconsciously intense listeners respond bodily with eye, facial, and lip movements which, even if barely visible, register the degree of involvement. When the preacher and the parishioners give themselves fully to the content and dynamics of the sermon, all are vulnerable, speaker and listener, to each other. Intimacy thrives in the climate of vulnerability. And this is in addition to the socializing and community-forming activities of congregational singing, prayer, and unison responses.

Also unlike textuality, orality generates intimacy, in that speaker and listener experience a sense of being on the "inside" of something very important. Visit any church on a given Sunday and observe the ways in which preacher and congregation engage, sometimes playfully, sometimes seriously, in inside jokes, inside problems, inside understandings, and even inside conspiracies against the evil forces outside. Such intimacy can, of course, be manufactured, exploited, and in gross contradiction of the universal, without distinction, love of God. Preachers must be on guard lest they operate in such an atmosphere to create dependent satellite relationships. Such corruptions notwithstanding, healthy intimacy is a quality vital to preaching, contributing as it does to the context of trust and care essential to effective speaking and to the hearing of the gospel.

As we enter into the sermon-designing process, we shall not, then, be thinking about "getting up a good sermon," but how to effect hearing and appropriating the message. Toward that end, the listeners will experience a sermon that will, to the extent we are able to provide them, possess these six qualities: unity, memory, recognition, identification, anticipation, and intimacy.

nine

The Formation of the Sermon

The Many Functions of Form

There is no form that can be identified as "sermon." To speak of a novel, short story, sonnet, limerick, poem, or parable is to draw upon a fairly common understanding of form, but to speak of a sermon it is not so. Of course, those persons who have listened to the same type of sermon for many years think they know what a sermon form is. They may even assume that seminaries uniformly instruct the students to shape their messages in that fashion; after all, a sermon is a sermon. However, there is no evidence that the Jewish or Christian communities created an oral form and called it a sermon. In preparing written materials, the church adopted with appropriate modifications available forms such as the epistle, the apocalypse, and perhaps even patterned the Gospel form after that of biographies of heroes. Likewise, Greek rhetoric was employed as a form for proclamation of the gospel. Even though that rhetoric dominated the field of homiletics for centuries, not even that pattern for oral presentations can justifiably be called *the* form of a sermon. It remains the case to this day that a sermon is defined more by content and purpose than by form.

This is certainly not said to advance an argument for formlessness. Whenever a single form has dominated preaching for a long time, a revolt by young preachers may seem to favor, or may in fact openly call for, abolition of form. In the late 1960s, until the late 1970s, it was not uncommon to hear sermons which consisted of gatherings of material that defied all canons of form and movement, seeming more akin to the collage or multimedia blitz, or perhaps to the stream of consciousness. This period of reaction and experimentation was not unusual; there is usually, between the razing of the old structure and the building of the new, a time for tents hastily erected on the vacant lot. Nor was the sermon the sole target for a revolution: music, art, architecture, even value structures were no less affected. Now that the dust has settled, many acknowledge that the old sermon forms were not all that inadequate, nor is there a single, agreed upon replacement. The primary abiding value of the transition period is the recognition, impressed anew upon preaching, that the search for form must continue as a search for designs which will not only be congenial to the gospel but also to the ways we order, understand, and appropriate reality.

The early church existed as an oral community prior to and parallel to its life as a writing and reading community, and the New Testament carries over into its texts the oral forms in which the faith was shared. In the Gospels, miracle stories, parables, proverbs, aphorisms, pronouncements, and resurrection stories bear the marks of oral circulation. But in the letters, too, one meets units of material drawn from the oral life of the community, such as hymns, creeds, baptismal formulas, prayers, and doxologies. In addition, because letters were read in the assemblies and therefore prepared for the ear rather than the eye, they employ literary forms designed to aid the listener's understanding and memory. Paul, for example, makes frequent use of the inclusion (units that close as they begin), the chiasm (inverted parallelism on the a b b a pattern), tables of household duties, antitheses, and other noticeable literary patterns. After all, in a culture primarily oral, the survival of its message depended very largely on form.

Consider, in addition to memory, some of the functions of the forms of early Christian traditions and stories. One form fairly common in both testaments is the farewell speech. Moses, Joshua, Paul, Stephen, and Jesus all give farewell addresses, and all have a common function: to join the tradition to the present life of the community, to have the past speak to the present. Jesus' farewell discourses (John 14–16), for example, tie the word of the historical Jesus to the word the living Christ continues to speak to the church.

Another form found often in the Fourth Gospel is the conversation: Jesus and Nicodemus, Jesus and the Samaritan woman, Jesus and Martha and Mary. In each case, what begins as a private conversation gradually enlarges to address the reader and all who will hear the witness of faith. Whatever may be the topic as the conversation begins, the ending is always a revelation of God giving life eternal to those who believe. In other words, the Johannine conversation is a proclamation form, a sermonic design. In the Pauline and post-Pauline letters, a familiar form for treating the apostle's own life could be called the "formerly but now" pattern. The radical contrast between Paul's former and present life had strong evangelistic appeal and, in time, came to be the most popular form of preaching for conversions. A favorite form in Luke is the journey, of Jesus in the Gospel and of Paul in Acts. The journey form not only functions to present the image of the pilgrim life, but serves also as a device for unifying separate and disparate units of tradition about Jesus and about Paul. The journey remains today a viable form for preaching. For a final example of form fitted to function, recall the courtroom scenes in Acts. There are many of them. What better form could make the case for Christianity as a legitimate religion than the one pronounced "not guilty" by Rome? With a little imagination, one can think of certain subject matter and certain circumstances today that might well justify sermons framed as addresses, as it were, to a jury, asking for judgment on the basis of the evidence.

These examples call attention not only to the variety of forms used in the early church (there are many more in the New Testament not mentioned here) but also to ways in which forms function. Form is not simply a rack, a hanger, a line over which to drape one's presentation, but the form itself is active, contributing to what the speaker wishes to say and do, sometimes no less persuasive than the content itself. With the growth of sophistication and complexity in the communication field, attention to the importance of form and to what form can accomplish remains a priority for anyone who wishes to be heard. As a frame does for a picture, the pattern for the sermon serves to arrest, accent, focus, and aid the listener's apprehension of the message. Let us, then, keep in mind that:

Form gains and holds interest. For example, observing the

principle of end stress withholds the point of primary interest until the end. Recall two examples. The parables of Luke 15 concern the lost and found. In the parable of the prodigal son, this central interest is accented by placing the words "lost and found" at the very end of the father's speech, even *after* the normally more serious words "dead and alive." "For this my son was dead, and is alive again; he was lost, and is found" (verse 24; also verse 32). In John 19, soldiers are ordered to break the legs of the three who were crucified. Jesus is in the middle, but in telling the story, the writer says they broke the legs of the first, then the third, and finally they came to Jesus. The reason lies, of course, in the desire to draw attention to Jesus. Who would be interested in hearing about the third person *after* the discussion of the treatment of Jesus? Dramatic stress overrules logical sequence.

Form shapes the listener's experience of the material. As one can walk into a room and anticipate by the arrangement of the furniture what experience lies ahead, so does the shape of a presentation affect the listener. In fact, one can sometimes hear the opening phrase, discern the form and settle down to the experience to follow. The following phrases clearly signal familiar experiences: "Once upon a time"; "There was a certain man"; "Dearly beloved, we are gathered here"; "There were these two Irishmen, Pat and Mike"; "I, being of sound mind, do hereby"; "Inasmuch as the party of the first part has testified." To confuse forms by trying, for example, to introduce historical facts with the words, "Once upon a time," would be to confuse the hearers and waste the information.

Form shapes the listener's faith. It is likely that few preachers are aware how influential sermon form is on the quality of the parishioners' faith. Ministers who, week after week, frame their sermons as arguments, syllogisms armed for debate, tend to give that form to the faith perspective of regular listeners. Being a Christian is proving you are right. Those who consistently use the "before/after" pattern impress upon hearers that conversion is the normative model for becoming a believer. Sermons which invariably place before the congregation the "either/or" format as the way to see the issues before them contribute to oversimplification, inflexibility, and the notion that faith is always an urgent decision. In contrast, "both/and" sermons tend to broaden horizons and sympathies but never confront the listener with a crisp decision. Form is so extremely important. Regardless of the subjects being treated, a preacher can thereby nourish rigidity or openness, legalism or graciousness, inclusiveness or exclusiveness, adversarial or conciliating mentality, willingness to discuss or demand immediate answers. Ministers who are called to pulpits long occupied by preachers whose sermons were framed on the same invariable pattern soon discover how poorly sermons with different forms are received. With most listeners, a change of form is equivalent to a change of content. "But it didn't seem like a sermon," they said of the new minister's message, which was no less biblical, no less relevant, no less theologically sound than those to which they were accustomed.

Form determines the degree of participation demanded of the hearers. Some forms make no demands of the listeners. The old pattern of stating the sermon in digest at the outset, developing the sermon, and then summarizing in conclusion is such a form. In contrast, the pattern, "Not this, nor this, nor this, but this" expects the hearers to remain thoughtfully engaged to the end. It is possible to frame the same message in several different forms, each making the listener do more or less work than the others. A riddle, for example, because it is so nearly opaque, places such a heavy burden on the hearer that it would only very rarely be congenial to preaching. A parable makes a lesser demand but yet enough that the listener is responsible for what is heard and for the values discerned and embraced. A proverb, being the distilled wisdom of common experience, is usually embraced without struggle, although some proverbs possess parable-like potential. "A lie will take you far but will not take you home" is a proverb, but almost parabolic in its triggering of the mind. A slogan lies completely opposite the riddle and asks nothing of the hearer but that it be repeated. Wisdom in discerning how much work one's parishioners must do during a sermon calls not only for homiletical skill but also for pastoral insight.

Having said all this to underscore the vital importance of form, we now owe it to ourselves to state a modifier: some forms are more or less classic and therefore are capable of performing many different functions and creating many different impacts. Consider the rich variety of uses to which one can put the familiar format, "the king and the peasant" (in the New Testament, "the master and the servant"). Upon this frame one can place messages of justice, injustice, humility and role reversal, grace, forgiveness, deception, and on and on. The same is true of "the employer who went on a journey of uncertain length" form so familiar in the New Testament. Into that mold many important messages can be poured, without violation.

One final example is the refrain, the recurring phrase or line more common to church music than to preaching, even though it holds real promise for sermons. The refrain can function as an amen, a word of confirmation or agreement, spoken by either preacher or congregation. It may also serve to unify a number of units of material which have a common theme. A clear example is Psalm 107:1-32, which begins with the refrain, then moves through four episodes, each of which concludes with the refrain. One sometimes hears a sermon which uses a key line from the text as a unifying refrain. The refrain may serve to build intensity of feeling in the listeners, either for or against an issue. Recall the speech of Mark Antony at Caesar's funeral in Shakespeare's *Julius Caesar:* the refrain "and Brutus is an honorable man" builds in the crowd a tide of hostility against Brutus. On the other hand, a refrain, because it is a repetition, can banalize and empty an occasion of meaning and feeling by a kind of reduction to the absurdly obvious. In an entirely different use, the refrain can create anticipation for action or insight yet to unfold. A secular example—if a saloon song be permitted here—occurs in the ballad "Frankie and Johnnie":

> Frankie, she was a good woman, and
> Johnnie, he was her man.
> Every silver dollar that Frankie made
> Went straight into Johnnie's hand.
> *Refrain:* He was her man, but he done her wrong.

Already in the opening stanza the refrain anticipates trouble, and by its repetition builds toward the crisis. Within the New Testament, Luke's recurring phrase, "And Mary pondered all these things in her heart," prepares the reader for profound, unusual, and painful events to come. One wonders why more sermons do not employ this very versatile form.

Having persuaded ourselves that there are forms aplenty with many functions, the question that presses itself now is this, How does one decide on a form for the sermon being prepared?

The Selection of a Form

It is the practice of some to choose from a stock of outlines a form for the sermon being prepared. This is to say that some preachers, when arriving at the point of asking, "How, then, shall I say this?" turn to a file of available forms and select one for that particular message. This procedure sounds rather arbitrary, to be sure, but there is nothing about it which rules out choosing forms that are both adequate and congenial to the message and the experience to be generated by the sermon. To speak of *adequacy* of form is to imply that some are not, which is true. For example, the question and answer form, especially the objective type often found in a classroom, is not adequate to carry major theological freight, much less to create the experience of that theology. To speak of *congeniality* of form is to imply that some are not, which also is true. A sermon with three points, for instance, would not be congenial to a message that intended to set the hearers before an "either/or" decision as in the "Choose this day whom you will serve" speech of Joshua (Josh. 24:14-15) or in the wide or narrow gates offered as alternatives in the Sermon on the Mount (Matt. 7:13-14). Such a message would be blurred and confused by anything other than a twofold structure.

The method of selecting a form from a supply readily available, while unattractive in its arbitrariness and measure of artificiality, should not be dismissed lightly or rejected in advance of thought. One could do worse. Consider two positive features.

First, the forms of which we speak are and have been for centuries the common store of writers and public speakers. In other words, these structures have demonstrated repeatedly that they can carry the burden of truth with clarity, thoroughness, and interest, and, therefore, have come to be regarded as standard. From such a supply of forms, many of us recognize and perhaps have used some of the following:

What is it? What is it worth? How does one get it?
Explore, explain, apply
The problem, the solution
What it is not, what it is
Either/or
Both/and
Promise, fulfillment
Ambiguity, clarity
Major premise, minor premise, conclusion
Not this, nor this, nor this, nor this, but this
The flashback (from present to past to present)
From the lesser, to the greater

No small amount of biblical, theological, and pastoral instruction, encouragement, and urging can be framed on these forms with a minimum of distortion, reduction, or dullness.

A second positive feature of this method is its guarantee of variety. No form is so good that it does not eventually become wearisome to both listener and speaker. There is in all communication that amount of repetition dictated by the need for clarity and the limits of common vocabulary. But even that repetition tends to erode its own purpose by dulling the ear and effecting the loss of vitality in once lively words and phrases. The preacher wishes, therefore, short of trading truth for novelty, to find and employ new forms for the familiar. It is only the person of rare gifts who can fit the message week after week on the same frame and not have the listeners assume "same old form" means "same old sermon." And even a preacher of such exceptional ability might improve with the kind of variety afforded by the possession and use of a dozen or so different sermon forms.

With a growing number of ministers, the selection of a design for a sermon sends them not to a storehouse of forms commonly held by preachers and other public speakers but to the Scriptures, and more particularly, to the biblical text from which the message is drawn. Attention to the form of a passage has long been regarded as essential to thorough exegesis. In addition, form in a biblical text has also provided historians with clues to the life and activity of both Israelite and early Christian communities to the extent that form reflects function; that is, materials were shaped for worship, debate, evangelization, initiation into the group, and instruction of new members, as well as for special occasions. However, until recently the identification by form and function of units such as proverbs, parables, diatribes, pronouncements, blessings, thanksgivings, farewells, and apostrophes had only minimally affected sermon design. This testifies to the extent to which Aristotelian logical discourse had become imbedded in homiletical tradition and instruction. Very few questioned the practice of placing the same outline on a biblical passage for preaching purposes, regardless of the form of that passage. With the increased dialogue between biblical and literary studies, however, preachers are paying more attention to how a text makes a point and creates a reader experience and, as a result, are often looking to the text for the how as well as the what of the sermon.

The values of permitting the biblical text to instruct the sermon on form as well as content are evident. All the benefits of variety in form as mentioned above are provided in this procedure as well. In addition, there is more assurance of integrity in the sermon if both design and substance come from the same source rather than having a message from one source and the form for its delivery from another. This is not to say that the shape of the sermon *must* come from the text: a text that is a prayer does not necessitate a sermon in prayer form, or a proverb in a proverb form, a pronouncement in pronouncement form, and so forth. Sometimes the shape of the text will carry over into the sermon quite well, as in the case of certain parables or the apostrophe in James 5:1-6. However, more important is attending to the form of the text to discern what it achieves—praise, correction, judgment, encouragement, defense, reconciliation, instruction—and then asking if the sermon is designed with that end in mind. If the preacher has some other purpose in view; that is, if a text originally framed as a judgment is now, due to altered circumstances, read and heard as a confirmation, then the preacher has made an interpretive and homiletical decision and bears the responsibility for it. Decision is a vast improvement over default, that is, paying no attention to what the text was seeking to do, and over deception, that is, giving the listeners the impression that the purpose of the text and the purpose of the sermon are one and the same. Such careful attention to form, both in the text and in the sermon, will usually raise the question which keeps sentinel watch over texts in the hands of preachers, Will a change of form from text to sermon alter the meaning of the text for the listeners? For example, a sermon on "blessed are the poor in spirit" (a blessing) which comes across as "we must be poor in spirit" (an exhortation) represents a shift not only in form but also in meaning. A sermon on a blessing should pronounce the blessing.

In order to confirm our understanding as to how a text might inform both the shape and substance of a sermon, let us look briefly at a few examples. The Gospel of John tells of an appearance of the arrested Jesus before the high priest Annas (18:12-27). However, the brief account is twice interrupted by turning the reader's attention to Simon Peter outside in the courtyard. The sequence is: Jesus is before Annas; Simon is with the servants and officers outside; Jesus testifies to the truth even though it brings punishment and death; Simon denied the truth to protect himself. By moving the camera back and forth from Jesus to Simon, the action of each is sharpened by the contrast. What preacher would abandon that form in favor of some other? A pattern common in Mark is the split story. One of several is found in 5:21-43. Between the two parts of the account of Jesus raising Jairus' daughter is inserted the healing of another "daughter" (verse 34). Each story aids in interpreting the other while the arrangement provides drama and suspense. Returning at the end to complete the event with which the writer began gives to the whole a satisfying symmetry and closure. In this format Mark proves to be a preacher worthy of emulation. Sometimes a writer will pack into a small space a number of different forms, indicating that units once existing separately in the church's preaching are now thematically collected. Consider, for example, Luke 16:10-13. Verses 10-12 are framed on the familiar and widely used format of arguing from the lesser to the greater (a favorite of the writer of Hebrews), but verse 13 shifts to the "either/or" form. The preacher would do well to preserve Luke's form in both subunits but would be ill-advised to try to fit all four verses on one frame in one sermon. Occasionally one encounters in a text a simple and straightforward but irreplaceably useful structure. Such is the case in I Corinthians 11:17-34. The Christians at Corinth wrote Paul about problems in their worship assembly, especially as it involved the Lord's Supper (problem), and Paul responded with clear reminders and directives (solution). The form of the passage remains today as helpful as its content. The preacher will want to be careful, however, to maintain a balance between the two parts; many of us seem more lively and articulate when presenting problems than when offering solutions. Other passages are more dramatically but no less adequately and usefully structured. John 9 is a case in point. The pattern to the story of the healing of a blind man is itself a theological statement. Notice: Jesus heals a man and then disappears from the scene. The man, able to see after a lifetime of blindness finds himself in an unsympathetic and hostile world. His neighbors are skeptical, his family is afraid, his religious leaders are trapped in the logic of their own theology and resort to ridicule and persecution. In the closing scene, Jesus returns and vindicates the man's faith. What an extraordinarily forceful way to address the church on the way it is in the world, between Jesus' coming and his coming again. As a final example, look at II Samuel 7:1-16. The story is framed on a reversal: David lives in a house, God lives in a tent, and David wants to build God a house. David's desire is worthy and commendable. However, God responds by saying that David will not build God a house; God will build David a house. The reversal from human effort to divine gift is the basic format by which both Testaments present the surprise of God's grace. The preacher can learn from the writer that sermons on this and similar texts should not describe and explain reversals but be themselves designed as reversals so that the listeners can again experience the surprise of grace.

Thus far we have considered the selection of sermon forms in terms of source: a stock of proven and standard patterns or biblical texts. There is, however, another factor that may be operative in the selection procedure: the pastor's sense of congregational need. The need which is in mind here is not that of a particular topic or issue or text but a need in respect to the congregation's general "situation in life" or mind-set toward themselves and their context. In other words, does the pastor feel the need to support or to subvert the parishioners' present attitude or behavior? A pastor knows when a single major event or a constellation of minor events within or without the church has been uprooting, has disoriented and dislodged with reference to relationships, faith, and values. In such a case, the pastor as preacher may wish to be supportive and affirming, creating a sense of "at homeness" in the world and in the love and providence of God. There are a number of ways in which this might be achieved. For instance, particular themes and texts which assure and encourage could be treated. But the reorientation of the unsettled can be accomplished in part by the choice of sermon form. One does not rearrange daily the furniture in the room of an elderly person who has recently been dislodged from home and removed to a nursing care unit. One does not address the bereaved at a funeral with the novel, the clever, the different, the surprise-ending sermon. Then neither does the preacher make heavy intellectual or emotional demands on listeners already disoriented. Under such circumstances, the message will be in a form that is familiar, predictable, natural, making little demand and with clear closure. The form need not be simply a caress but one that does evoke amen, not surprise or shock. It is difficult enough to move about in the dark without the pain and confusion of a new floor plan.

On the other hand, a pastor also knows if the parishioners have been lulled and dulled in an unquestioned, unconfronted, unchallenged, and perhaps uninformed life-style in which attitudes and actions have not heard the gospel. In such a case the pastor as preacher will no doubt seek to subvert the attitude or apathy or behavior, and the means for doing so are many. The prophets and Jesus provide content aplenty, but again, our present concern is only with the form of the sermon. If a preacher ordinarily uses a certain sermonic design now grown familiar to the listeners, any noticeable change in that pattern will tend to create the discomfort essential to a new and fresh hearing of the Word. All of us have our ways of defending ourselves against messages we do not want to hear, even while we seem to be listening. Some preachers, knowing this, choose to continue to say the same thing in the same way but hope to succeed in storming the barricade of the ear by increased volume, frequency, anger, and threat. To do so is usually to underestimate the intransigency of the willfully deaf. However, the same message in a different form can often slip past the guard, reach the ear, and take captive the heart. Many of Jesus' parables apparently did just that; in fact, they still do. The listener prepared to contribute no more than a yawn is drawn into the parable of the prodigal son or the vineyard workers or the talents. Once inside, the usual method of handling a sermon by agreeing or disagreeing with the preacher no longer works; extricating oneself from a parable exposes one's values, faith, commitments, and fears. However, the preacher who decides upon an altered form must beware lest that new form be overused and soon take its place among the ineffective. After all, even Jesus' parables are not all in the same form. Some have a closing surprise of grace, as in the story of the vineyard workers, but others are straight and move predictably to the inescapable conclusion, as in the story of the foolish maidens. The change in form keeps the listener alert.

Creating a Form

To this point we have assumed that the preacher has a message, the fruit of interpreting the listeners and the text, and that in order for the message to be heard it must be given a shape congenial to the content, the preacher's purpose, and the listeners' capacity. In the service of that communicative task, what has been offered thus far has been the suggestion of a procedure for selecting a sermon form along with sources for such forms. The merits and demerits of both the procedure and the sources have been briefly sketched. It remains now to speak of creating, rather than selecting, a form in the process of preparing the sermon.

Creating rather than selecting a form involves delaying that which is the concern of every preacher, acquiring a structure or outline for the sermon. More exactly, it involves subordinating the quest for a form to another interest, one more vital to lively and effective preaching. Instead of asking, What is a good outline I can use for this message? one asks, What is the major communicative burden of this sermon? In other words, What has to be done in order to get this message heard? To ask that is to ask, What does the listener bring in terms of knowledge, attitude, feeling, and prior experience to the text and message for the day? In the privacy of the study the preacher reads aloud the text of the sermon in preparation and imagines how that text strikes the mind, the emotions, the memory, the experience of the listeners. The preacher says aloud the theme or subject as though it were being announced to the congregation (announcing subjects in advance or at least in the order of service is a common practice) and images the faces as they receive the announcement. Do any eyes brighten, does any nerve twitch, does anyone lean forward in anticipation? Does hostility flash, are arms folded across the chest in defiance, or do spirits visibly sink into tolerance and resignation?

The effectiveness of the sermon soon to be preached will in large measure depend on two factors: (1) the preacher's capacity to anticipate that listener response, and (2) the preacher's capacity to shape the sermon to meet the challenge of that response. If the anticipated response is clearly positive, preparatory efforts will not be relaxed on the assumption that on subjects of general interest less effort need be expended. One could argue that when favorable interest is high, preparatory work must be greater because the possibility of disappointed expectations is greater. He or she who leaves the desk early saying, "They always like this kind," is already being presumptuous and unfair. Rather, the preacher will want to maximize the anticipated favorable interest and make every effort to fill the mind already receptive with the bounty of the subject matter. If, on the other hand, the preacher has reason to believe that the text or theme will enter a room of apathy, disinterest, or perhaps opposition, then the burden on the design is to meet, overcome, and possibly convert the initial reception. Please notice: we are speaking of the task of shaping the sermon, not of deciding *what* to say. Anticipated response is not a primary factor in choosing *what* to preach. The message has already been determined, prayerfully, pastorally, prophetically, and is biblically and theologically sound. However, anticipated response *is* a primary factor in determining how the minister will form that message so as to be heard.

We repeat, then, that the burden on the preacher with each message lies at the point where that message meets the listener. The particular name for that burden will differ not only with each audience but with each message. If, for example, the listeners are uninformed or misinformed about a certain message, the task is clear: to educate. The message will be formed in such a way as to teach. With this aim in mind, certain guidelines discipline the creation of the sermon design: information will be provided, but not an overload to overwhelm and depress; the method and mood of sharing the information will be a reminder to them of what they already know; the information will be made easy to remember through the use of repetition, alliteration, sharp contrasts, and numbered items (seldom more than three); the information will be brightened with analogies and concrete "for instances." The Gospels teach about Jesus by means of stories that tell what he said and did; not a bad model. By no means will ministers permit themselves to sound pedantic or condescending. After all, the goal is not to exhibit how much they know but to enable others to understand. As in all ministerial functions, here also the preacher-teacher is servant. We need especially to warn ourselves about being apologetic in word, tone, or manner ("I know this is not interesting but try to stay with me; I promise to be brief"). All of us have had dull teachers at some time but we still know learning can be interesting as well as life-changing. The sermon designed primarily to teach can be delivered with passion and enthusiasm because the preacher knows that in situations of no information or misinformation, knowing is redemptive and freeing. But this excitement of learning, this freedom in knowing, is not experienced by listeners to sermons which push to the front a pile of facts so that the main business of exhorting and fussing can get a full allotment of time. And an opening joke does not help either, except to telegraph ahead that the sermon itself will be taking them through dry and waterless places.

Consider an example. The text for Sunday's sermon is I Corinthians 11:23-34, Paul's account of what he calls "the Lord's supper" (verse 20). Let us suppose the theme is, "Not the lives of the participants but the manner of participating is to be worthy." Let us also suppose that this message will move into a congregation where a general misunderstanding prevails. The practice and conversation of that community reveal a confusion about this text and hence about the observance of the Lord's Supper. Local oral tradition has it that Paul warned the unworthy not to participate lest they suffer God's condemnation. An adverb (unworthily, verse 27) has been taken as an adjective (unworthy). The task for the preacher is clear: create understanding so that the Table can again be a proclamation of good news. That task and not the search for an outline is the governing consideration. To educate is to lead out. One does not begin, therefore, with an indictment ("There is a lot of misunderstanding about our text") or with a mini-lecture on history ("Paul established the church in Corinth, a city in what is today Greece, on his second missionary journey"). To lead someone out means to take him or her by the hand and then move. Why not, "Is there anyone here who has not at some time hesitated before the Lord's Table, wondering whether it would be right to receive the loaf and cup? Probably not. In fact, some of us have not only hesitated but felt compelled to say no to the invitation. And why? Because we have such high reverence for the sacred rite. Who am I that I should sit at the Lord's Table?" From such a beginning one can go on to point out that such an attitude is not private or isolated but has at times and places been supported by official church practice. Examples could be given here of moral examinations once used to determine who was and who was not to partake. And why not? Does not the Bible itself warn repeatedly against unworthy hands on sacred things? Again, some examples, here from the Old Testament. In fact, does not Paul so instruct us here? Now the minister can move to the text, indicating that if there ever was a church in need of such warning it was the one at Corinth. Here sketch briefly the flood of problems plaguing that group. And to them Paul says what? Not a single excluding word, as Jesus said no excluding word to John or James or Peter or Judas in that upper room. What unbelievably good news: there is a place for them, for us at the Table. What, then, so concerned Paul? Now one discusses the manner of observance that properly reminds, celebrates, and announces the Good News. In such a way one leads the listeners out, with experience, church history, the Old Testament, the Gospels, and one's sermon text serving in the process. That text and the Lord's Table will be new experiences for many, and those present who did not have the misunderstanding will be confirmed in their understanding. And did the sermon have an outline? Yes, of course; but not because it went looking for one.

All who preach or who anticipate preaching know that not all situations call for putting the sermon in educative form, although there is some teaching in all sermons. Sometimes the anticipated response to a text or message is apathy, nothing more. It may be that the apathy is built into the occasion. Consider, for instance, the traditional Thanksgiving service. In many places it hardly matters whether the service occurs on the evening before or on Thanksgiving Day; the relatively small assembly of the Body of Christ hardly shows a pulse. The service is ecumenical, which is most appropriate as a community witness but which adds little if any either to the attendance or to the excitement. The pastor whose turn it is to preach has prepared a message on Philippians 4:10-20, Paul's note of thanks to the church at Philippi. The theme is interestingly framed: "It may be more blessed to give than to receive, but it is also a whale of a lot easier." But never mind the preacher's own stir of interest; anticipating the occasion and the same dutifully faithful worshipers has a dulling effect. Everything about the occasion has for years been so thoroughly predictable. If there is any uncertainty at all, it lies in the question as to whether this year's preacher will serve the pilgrims' five grains of corn as a pre-Thanksgiving guilt trip or remind everyone that Jesus healed ten lepers but only one returned to express thanks. "Where are the nine?" may again be the burning question. The preacher does not wish merely to toss the sermon into their faces and be done with it; an important and appropriate message has been prepared and is worthy of being heard. Of first importance is the determination not to allow the prospect of apathy to become a self-fulfilling prophecy. How, then, shall that mind-set be met? Complaining about those not present is hardly helpful; neither is questioning the motives of those who *are* present ("Are we really grateful or creatures of habit?"). The text from Philippians is so striking that one might choose to begin there: "If you received a thank-you note which read: 'Thanks for the gift but I want you to know I didn't need it. In fact, I don't need anything. Sincerely yours,' how would you feel? Of course you would, and so probably did the church which received such a note from Paul." The minister could then walk through the passage, exploring the difficulty, the complex, awkward, beautiful difficulty in expressing gratitude. If beginning outside the text is preferred, he or she might say, "A grace common to many tables begins 'Lord, make us grateful.' Is that not strange? God must not only provide the gifts but also the gratitude. Can't one simply choose to be grateful? Can't children be taught to be grateful? Is it so difficult?" And then move soon to the text. Some who planned not to listen, will.

In the hypothetical case just described, the apathy had its roots in the occasion but the preacher could counter it with an extraordinary text. What if the text, when read, generates an "Oh, no, not that one again!"? Such might be the initial response to John 15:1-6, the vine and branches figure in the farewell discourses of Jesus. Most church people can recite it, or at least paraphrase it, having heard scores of sermons, which repeated the imagery, and probaby feel there is nothing more to be said. However, in many traditions of preaching, sermons spawn sermons while the originating text goes neglected. In such cases, the best cure for the yawns is a return to the text. In the example just cited, John 15:1-6, the most powerful, most difficult, most appropriate, and perhaps even most central statement to the writer's purpose, seldom receives sermonic treatment. Christ is the vine, true, and that image yields many comforting and encouraging thoughts. We are the branches, true, and that image provides both identity and assignment. But the entire passage begins by presenting God as the vinedresser, the one who comes into the vineyard with a sharp blade. Some branches are cut off, some are cut back. In the Greek text, the words for cutting off, for burning, and cutting back (pruning) for increased production are the same except for a prefix. At some time everyone experiences the knife, said by the writer to be in the hand of God, but is the experience one of punishment or pruning for new life? Those who suffer want to know, if it is possible to know, Am I being punished or being prepared for something better? And they will travel some distance to hear a sermon which seeks to unravel that text, which no longer lies dead among half-remembered sermons.

Very likely the reader's mind has by this time raced ahead to texts and themes that meet other responses in the listeners. There is, for example, an array of texts which arouse a feeling of resentment, of offense, of being treated unfairly. These are the texts that announce the radical grace of God. When God "repented" and spared Nineveh, Jonah charged God with being full of mercy and steadfast love. Matthew's Jesus declares God impartial, sending sun and rain on good and evil alike, and paying one-hour workers a full day's wage. "Do you begrudge my generosity?" asks the master in the parable. Luke's Jesus celebrates God's kindness toward the ungrateful and selfish and tells stories of peasants at the king's table and parties thrown for prodigals. John's Jesus heals the lame and blind before they even know who he is, much less have faith in him. Paul preaches grace, lest anyone should boast. For the preacher to deal with these texts is to deal with the listeners' sense of justice being abrogated, wrong being overlooked if not condoned, sound principles of hard work and self-determination being eroded, not to mention the blurring of one's clear sense of who the enemies are and finding oneself on the same pew with the very characters about whom our children have been warned. Most people want grace but not so amazing, and the preacher who truly wants to have the word of grace heard will not hit and run. The sermon will be designed so as to sit among the listeners, to express what they feel, then to let them hear what they are feeling as their own response to God's announcements of amnesty, freedom, and forgiveness. There will be pain, no doubt about it, as there always is when sin meets grace, but it will be the right pain located at the right place and not a distracting scuffle over the size of Noah's ark in an effort to forget what the real issue is.

When the preacher thinks in this fashion about the task of the pulpit, usually there is not any premature search for an outline or listing of "points." Questions such as, How many points should a sermon have? die from neglect because the preacher is not thinking as a speechmaker but as a pastor and prophet. Before the first word of the sermon is spoken, the preacher has a clear idea of the listeners' posture of mind and heart in relation to the message to be delivered. In order to shape that message into a sermon the task for the day is fixed in mind: today's text and message will meet with misunderstanding, apathy, lack of information, skillful avoidance, resentment, indifference, defiance, disagreement, total approval, too easy agreement, or countless other mind-sets. Beginning at that intersection of message and hearer, the sermon begins to unfold, moving from where they are, through the text, using analogies, examples, images, perhaps even pleasant interruptions in the form of asides or hints of roads not now to be taken, until preacher and congregation know the message has been said. Whether or not it is expressed in the pulpit in exactly the same words, the preacher can state the message in that single sentence which emerged as the fruit of study before the sermon itself was ever begun.

If at the close of this procedure of creating a sermon shape, what has emerged is a form similar to or even identical with one of the many available from which an earlier selection could have been made, that fact is not important. What is important is that the preparation has followed the contours of this particular communicative task with this particular group of hearers on this particular text or theme. The form of such a sermon is therefore a part of the warp and woof of the message itself and was not laid as a grid over the message, alien to it and rising from another source. And as we will notice when considering delivery, that congeniality between form and content is an extraordinary advantage to the memory that otherwise might complain of having difficulty with outlines and manuscripts.

It will be the case sometimes that the form thus created will not really be noticeably an outline as such and certainly not recalled by the listener. That probably is as it should be. Quite often a communicative design is like scaffolding which has no further function once the construction is done. Or, to change the analogy, a form may properly self-destruct once the message has reached its destination. For a listener, even another preacher, not to have discerned the outline may be a high compliment to the energy, interest, movement, and compelling force of the sermon. However, if the intent of the sermon is to have the hearers remember certain statements in a particular sequence, as may be the case in an educational sermon, then the structure will be properly visible and call attention to itself by repetition and summary.

Finally, let the preacher who follows this process, as uncharted as it may seem, as new every time as it may be, devote full energies to it and devote none to any nagging fear that some old homiletics textbook has been violated or that some revered old homiletics professor is disquieted in the grave. Of first importance is that someone has found a way to preach the gospel, and in that all should rejoice.

Putting the Form on Paper

We have not talked yet of writing anything, and deliberately so. It would be a mistake to think that the goal of all this work is to write a sermon; it is not. The goal is to preach, and writing is a servant, nothing more, nothing less, of that goal. Let a preacher begin thinking that the point is to get Sunday's sermon written, and a string of negative results follow. In the first place, the written sermon is a kind of closure which offers not only a sense of satisfaction—thank God, I'm finished with it!—but also a shutting down of germination and gestation, often prematurely. Being finished, being able to walk away and attend to other things, is so attractive a prospect that it can inch forward into the thinking, feeling, imagining, forming process and put periods where commas, dashes, and question marks are still at work.

Second, to make writing the sermon the goal of the process is to cause one to think writing, rather than speaking, throughout the preparation. Preaching is oral communication and to do it most effectively the minister needs to image himself or herself, talking with the parishioners as the sermon is being formed. Select from the congregation representative persons: elderly, young, active, inactive, educated, uneducated, conservative, and liberal, and with them in the mind's eye, say the words of portions of the sermon as they are being prepared. Will she understand this? Will he be interested in this? Will they follow the flow of this story? The vast difference between orality and textuality will become apparent as the minister prepares as speaker not as writer. In textuality, there is more often an overload of information while orality tends to adjust quantity to the brevity and fragility of the communicative moment. Oral presentations cluster ideas and images by association; written presentations arrange ideas and illustrative materials in a linear sequence like words on a page. Writing tends to be more abstract; after all, the reader can double-check and triple-check and pause for reflection. Speaking moves as vibrations across the ear with no second chance and therefore strives for clearer phrases and more concrete imagery. The writer will try to complete every sentence properly; the speaker may at times say the first few words and see clearly that the listeners will complete the thought. When writing, one also tends to describe or summarize conversations, thus avoiding the mechanics of frequent quotation marks, while when speaking, one can and more often does reconstruct the direct speech. Quoting direct speech is much more lively and present; describing a conversation distances the hearer from it and places it in the past. These differences between writing and speaking are sufficient to impress on us the importance of designing the sermon and preparing ourselves with the delivery of the sermon in mind throughout the process.

A third negative result of making the writing of the sermon one's preparatory goal is that this approach creates for the preacher the very difficult task of getting the message off the page again and into the air. Preparation that moves *toward* writing must soon thereafter make a radically different move: *from* writing to speaking. As we have just observed, the two modes of communicating are sufficiently different to prohibit ease of movement from one to the other. Some preachers who write the sermon and then lay it aside until Saturday night or Sunday morning never seem to return to it with comfort. They handle the manuscript in the pulpit as though it belonged to someone else. The very use of a manuscript is spoken of as one would speak of a weakness or of a rule broken, with the tones of confession. Some give the impression of uncertainty, as when some important decision has long been postponed. Shall I memorize it? Shall I read it but make every effort to disguise the reading? Or shall I come clean and simply read it without pretending otherwise? We are now ahead of ourselves and into the subject of delivery, soon to be discussed, but it needs to be said now that much of the awkwardness and discontinuity created by writing and then oralizing a text can be relieved by preparing orally from the outset.

However, many preachers—and some very effective ones, too—will protest: "I always write my sermons in full. I was so taught and would be a rambling babbler without it." Three responses are in order. First, the intent here is not to contrast the carefully prepared manuscript with the hastily and poorly prepared sermon delivered without notes. In such a contest the manuscript wins, hands down. Without question, some ministers have allowed the popular appetite for preaching without notes to seduce them into less not more preparation, into sloppy not disciplined patterns of work. Rather, what is intended here is to urge thorough preparation, but preparation that has orality in view, that makes every written word servant of the spoken word. Second, there is no denying the benefits of writing for one's ministry. Writing regularly tends to improve a person's grammar and syntax as well as clarity in the ordering of

191

ideas. More important, writing can extend one's ministry beyond the spoken word through correspondence and articles for the church paper, as well as for denominational journals and local newspapers. Writing as a form of communication has its own integrity, and skills in it should be cultivated. But writing is for reading, and speaking is for listening. Both are, of course, forms of communication, but that kinship is not sufficient ground to argue that one best prepares for the one by doing the other.

Finally, our discussion of putting the sermon form on paper does not concern at this point what one takes into the pulpit. There are many aids to effective delivery, as we shall discuss, but what one writes in the process of forming the sermon is to be distinguished from whatever papers, if any, one uses in the delivery. For example, some preachers write full manuscripts but never take them into the pulpit.

What, then, is put on paper if orality is the governing concern? The pen can serve the voice in the following five ways.

First, write and place front and center the text, the theme sentence, and the subject. In this way, writing helps the eye keep the mind in focus. A common and often justified criticism against unwritten sermons is their tendency to wander and lose their way.

Second, as you mentally talk through the message, list in phrases down the page the basic information and ideas. Most of these are transferred from the notes taken in the reading and study process by which you arrived at the message. Make no effort to be final. Be prepared to strike through and rearrange items on the list. The writing here is for only one purpose: to aid the ordering of material. In other words, attention here is on movement, and in oral presentations movement is of first importance.

Third, ask of each item of information or idea if it is clear; that is, does it need elaboration by an illustration, an analogy, a "for instance." Rephrasing an idea in concrete terms with familiar vocabulary is usually preferred over attaching to an opaque statement a clear illustration. Photographs relieve dull pages of textbooks but hardly atone for confused and unclear words.

Fourth, write in full sentences or even brief paragraphs those particular portions of the sermon in which the path of thought is narrow or difficult to follow or skirts near tension, strong feelings, or

192

misunderstanding. This does not apply to all parts of a sermon. In fact, some sermons do not require any careful and precise phrasing, but the air is too filled with variables for even the most gifted speaker to leave everything to spontaneity and the spirit of the moment. Writing at this point is simply calling in eye and hand to serve the voice. The name for this writing is scribbling as one talks to oneself until certain of the way to say it.

Finally, let the mind move through what now remains from the scribbling, striking through and rearranging, look again to the statement of the text, theme, and subject, and ask, Does this sermon treat that text, convey that theme, develop that subject?

All the writing done in this process, even if one chooses to continue until the sermon is written in full, is oriented toward and in the service of orality. The final product is remarkably different from that which is the fruit of an anxiety to get Sunday's sermon written. And as we shall see, the delivery itself is even more remarkably different.

Throughout this chapter we have used the words form, design, pattern, structure, and frame to discuss the process of developing the message into a sermon. Those words are admittedly too sparse and spare to characterize that which a listener experiences as preaching. We need now to give attention to those elements that enliven and enrich the form.

ten

Enriching the Form

It is important at the outset that the elements of the sermon which are here called "enriching" not be thought of as options, those luxury items that may or may not be added to a commodity such as an automobile. We will be considering qualities integral to the sermon and not decoration or embroidery. Lively language, clear description, and fitting illustrative materials *are* the sermon as surely as the form is the sermon. But there is a natural sequence in the sermon preparation process, and form precedes the elements now before us. Were matters of imaginative language and description not vital to preaching we could simply print the theme sentence of the message in the order of worship and eliminate the sermon. Preaching is not, however, merely saying it and being done with it. Preaching seeks to get listeners involved, to expose and to examine their own faith and values, to assume some responsibility for what they are hearing, to own the message, and to make decisions. Sermon outlines alone do not accomplish that.

Perhaps it is the case, however, that with many ministers priorities are the very reverse of what has been assumed above; that is, the enriching elements and not the form receive primary attention. If so, let it be emphasized again that we are concerned not with priorities in terms of what is more or less important but with sequence in the preparation process. The preacher who has a message will then move to the discovery or creation of a sermon design that can effect a hearing of that message. In a sense, the preacher and the listener are in a contract, and the form of the sermon will hold that in respect.

The same respect for a contract or covenant relationship will prevail as well in the choice and creation of all enriching materials. We are not, therefore, concerned solely with being interesting, but neither are we concerned solely with telling the truth. There is an ethic of the contract between preacher and listener which we will be careful not to violate. On the one hand, the preacher will not be cruel, creating false expectations of the sermon or leaving the message in such shadowy uncertainty that the hearers are frustrated and feel deceived. Of course, some ambiguity early in a sermon can be justified; after all, the aim of the sermon may be to bring the matter to clarity. However, to leave all ideas in an embryonic or confused state, even when supported by the conviction that all persons must take responsibility for their own conclusions, raises ethical as well as homiletical questions. It is true that some who sit before the pulpit are alert even to the point of being suspicious, but others, no less in need, sit quietly and naively submissive. Neither may represent what is most desirable, but both represent what is. Very likely the submissive ones are in the majority. In the course of time, when the preacher's way of weaving in the subtle, the implied, the incomplete has become familiar, perhaps even the submissive listeners will become more active, more participatory. In the meantime, they may need some homiletical help in handling their freedom and their responsibility as listeners. The question is pastoral and ethical, and will not go away.

On the other hand, the preacher will not want to violate the speaker-listener contract by insulting those who hear, not accepting them as partners in the sermon, not leaving any work for them to do, not permitting them alternative responses. Most listeners wish not only to get the preacher's point (amen) but also to make their own discoveries during the preaching (ah-ha). While it is true that natural sequence and some predictability are essential for every listener, being as obvious as high noon at every point is demeaning. Satisfying at every turn a supposed appetite for clarity and closure not only dulls the curiosity and closes a door to the seeking mind but it also means that much of the sermon will not even be heard, nor need it be.

We turn now to consider the enrichment of the sermon form

under three headings: the language of preaching, description, and illustration.

The Language of Preaching

Let us think about the language, the words and phrases, of the sermon, the whole sermon and not simply a story or a descriptive paragraph within it. The fact is, if consistent attention is given to the language, very little illustrative material is needed, while the hearers will very likely give the preacher credit for using helpful illustrations. What is clear does not need to be illustrated because it seems already to be full of light. The governing consideration in choosing words and phrases is that the goal is not to utter but to evoke, not to express anything about one's education, values, life, or views of a text, but to effect a hearing of a text, of a message. This principle focuses upon the listener's ear and upon the speaker's tongue only as servant of that goal. This perspective is important, even if it is perfectly obvious that it is the preacher who has to put the message into certain words.

The phrases which will be employed in the sermon are basically of two kinds: those that are designed primarily to convey information and those designed primarily to generate experience, feelings, memory.

The first type has its value and force in that to which the phrases refer, in that information borne by the words. For example, the sentence, "At five-thirty this afternoon a twin-engine Cessna enroute from Louisville to Shreveport crashed into Laurel Mountain, killing all six persons aboard," is an information sentence. It calls no attention to itself but is fulfilled in the freight it carries. Simple, accurate, and straightforward, it disappears after leaving its deposit at the listener's ear. The listener has the information to deal with and has no time or interest to devote to self-serving words and phrases. Some preachers have difficulty with this type of sentence. Perhaps the reason lies in the preacher's tendency to favor admonition and appeal. Perhaps the difficulty is a failure to appreciate the importance of information for a sermon, pure and simple, and the interest of listeners in that which is clear, accurate, and factual. Whatever the reason, the difficulty usually manifests itself in one of three ways: "preaching" the information by giving it the urgent importance of a news flash; "preaching" the information by confusing it, inserting phrases that moralize and make application; "preaching" the information by treating it as other than information, as sentences designed to evoke emotional response. The better newscasters and reporters can be of immense help to the minister in framing clear and crisp informational sentences.

The second type of phrasing, that which generates experience, feelings, or memory, has its value and force in doing just that: generating, evoking, creating. The proverbial, "a lie will take you far but will not take you home," and the poetic, "my life is in the yellow leaf," are both evocative, even if they are quite different thoughts and feelings. Neither of these examples contains an unnecessary word to distract or dissipate energy on peripheral ideas. Neither contains information to be sorted out or lays any demand on the hearer. Each expression has a center, in each case an image which serves as a magnet drawing a cluster of reflections and emotions. Preaching which is truly effective, which continues beyond the parking lot and reemerges in parish conversation, contains a sprinkling of such expressions. We should encourage one another in this regard, not only in the use of quoted lines, but in distilling our own thoughts and feelings into such phrases. However, generative language does not have to be quotable or memorable to be vital and effective. The primary requirements of the phrasing are that it not be hortatory and not be overlaid with excessive adjectives and adverbs. The primary requirement of the one who uses it is that the language be trusted to do its own work without the speaker's pushing. Generative language needs only to be turned loose in the room.

Trusting words to do their own work is not easy to do; in fact, for preachers it constitutes a real problem. The reasons are basically two, one being in the context of preaching and the other in language itself. Regarding the context, the regular and routinized repetition of preaching, and generally to the same people, is a strong force against maintaining a high respect for words and for what words can do. Unless the minister takes measures to counter this gradual erosion, the pulpit can fall victim to it without the minister being aware of how or when the pulpit dropped into insignificance. As for language

197

itself, the process of sedimentation goes on continuously, dulling the edge and sapping the vitality of words. Good words, rich and evocative, tend to be overused, losing their elasticity and eventually becoming the stock in trade of comedians who mimic the caricatured preacher. Some words simply wear out, some change their meanings, others become obsolete, while many fall victim to vulgarization.

This decay of language is not and has not been a concern for ministers alone; many writers have lamented it and some have taken initiative to delay if not halt the downward slide. For example, Gertrude Stein, writer and literary critic, sought to revitalize words by abandoning the usual and correct patterns of capitalization and punctuation. The reader was thereby forced to pay attention or get lost in the non-sentence sentences. The same concern lay back of her use of exaggerated repetition: "A rose is a rose is a rose is a rose." What measures, what steps, what exercises can aid the preacher in this constant battle to keep language fresh? The list that follows is offered to suggest and to stimulate. If none of these exercises seems particularly helpful, perhaps they will prompt the reader to find others more suited to need and circumstance.

1. Remind yourself of the importance and power of words by reading those writers whose expertise equips them to render this service. Among them are Max Picard, J. L. Austin, and Walter Ong. And one does not want to omit here the abundant testimony of Scripture (Isa. 50:4-6; 55:10-11; Matt. 12:33-37; Rom. 10:14-17 among many others).

2. In referring to one's work as preacher, think of and use expressions that are more imaginative and forceful than the usual "talking" or "speaking" or "preaching." For example, why not occasionally think of going into the pulpit to "give one's word" or to "break the silence"?

3. Read fifteen or twenty minutes each day (before breakfast or before retiring at night) from the essays, plays, short stories, poetry, and novels of those recognized as great writers. The intent here is not to imitate or to find useful material, but to sit among masters of the language and listen.

4. Write personal letters to friends or relatives. Of all the writing one can do, personal letters most nearly approximate orality.

5. Every five or six weeks, review your preaching in search of overused words and phrases. These do creep in, often undetected at the time. If any are discovered, put them on the shelf for awhile. Granted a sabbatical, words often revitalize themselves.

6. Listen to people talk with one another, not eavesdropping in any violation of privacy, but in the traffic of public life. Airports, buses, planes, park benches, ball parks, and restaurants offer such opportunity. These experiences can be especially helpful when they occur in regions of the country other than one's own. Different accents, dialects, and idioms quicken a person again to the rich range of ordinary speech.

7. Take the opportunity to converse with persons from other countries who are struggling to learn English. Hardly anyone anymore lives in an area so remote that there is no occasion to visit with someone for whom English is a second language. Such conversations force us both to listen to every word and to choose carefully our own vocabulary, often searching for synonyms and alternate phrases. Ironically, persons who hardly know English may give back to us our own language.

8. Talk with small children, preferably three to five years of age. Children this age are not simply repeating what they hear but are creating their own phrases and sentences. Delighted with themselves in this venture, they may wear out the listener with their endless talking. But for the preacher whose vocabulary has been worn slick to a slur, the value lies in hearing words pronounced for the first time and sentences framed in new patterns. The preacher might even recover some of the pleasure in words such as puppy, duck, zoo, jelly, Ashley, and Kevin.

9. As a regular practice, comb through your sermons for ideas and concepts that are vague and difficult for listeners to receive, much less experience. With each, or at least most, put the idea or concept into a phrase that appeals to one of the five senses. This is not to say that all truth and reality can be appropriated through the senses, but some can be. In other cases the senses can aid the faculties in understanding, sorting out, and experiencing. This exercise takes effort but listeners are grateful for the preacher who ponders the weight of a grudge, the touch of friendship, the odor of death, the sound of youth, the taste of remorse, the color of joy.

199

10. Play word games. If unfamiliar with word games, create some. It can be family fun and can help relieve the boredom of long trips. For example, say, "She is sleeping," and have others guess the context by the way the sentence is said—hospital room, classroom, theater, dinner table, party. The number of such sentences and possible contexts is endless. Or, start an original story, at a critical point pass it to the next person who continues it to a point and then passes it on. Or, repeat a phrase three times, changing only the prepositions, and ask, Which was the slowest? For example, which is slowest: out of the tree, down the tree, from the tree? Or, day to day, day after day, day by day? Enough of this; the point is that playfulness with tired words can often give them zest when they next appear in a sermon.

If during the reading of these suggestions, something potentially helpful has come to mind, try it. After all, most of us have miles of words to go before we retire, and if already our nouns have lost their dignity, our verbs are listless, and our participles are dangling, how dreary it will be for the parishioners who are our companions on the journey.

Description

It is difficult to conceive of a sermon that does not contain descriptions of persons, events, relationships, or places. But why description? What service to the proclamation of the gospel is rendered by a description of some scene from ancient or current life? Certainly the purpose is not to prove that the preacher has an imagination. It would be more correct to say the purpose is to activate the listener's imagination, but even that is not enough. Description has as its primary aim the creation in one's hearers of the experience of the subject matter. This purpose is grounded in the conviction that a sermon is not only to *say* something but to *do* something.

Let us suppose, for example, that one is preaching on the parable of the talents (Matt. 25:14-30), with special attention to the third servant who responded to the master, "Master, I knew you to be a hard man, reaping where you did not sow, and gathering where you did not winnow; so I was afraid, and I went and hid your talent in the ground. Here you have what is yours" (verses 24-25). Instead of whipping again this poor servant and exhorting the parishioners not to bury talent but rather to volunteer to teach, to sponsor, to join the choir, to pledge, or to attend to some other duty, the preacher needs to help the hearers stand in that servant's place. He knows the master, he is afraid, and he acts out of that fear. Moving the listeners inside that fear can be accomplished in part by description: What is it to be afraid? To be afraid of the person who has power over one's livelihood? To have to stand before that person and explain one's behavior? Only when one stands there and feels that fear can the master's word to the servant be heard. In such a case, to describe is to preach, and to describe with a clear grasp of the particulars of one situation is to enable those present to move directly to deal with their own situation.

Description provides images, and images are necessary for removing from the mind inadequate, erroneous, distorted attitudes and behavior. Along the hallways of the mind hang images, fixed and influential, hung there by experience, education, associations, stories heard or read, and by countless forces more subtle but no less effective. When the appropriate word is spoken, an image stands out vivid and clear: nun, minister, German, communist, messiah, African, schoolteacher, car salesperson, lawyer. If it is the case that certain images contradict the gospel and flaw the life of the one holding them, how can preaching make a difference? Ideas and concepts are of little effect against images, and scolding does even less. Images must be replaced, and this comes only gradually, by other images. In the ministry of preaching, much of this burden falls on description. In other words, we are not discussing how to decorate a sermon, but how to preach.

Description is difficult to manage in the sermon. On the one hand, there are the "no nonsense, let's get on with it" preachers who underestimate either the role of description or their capacity to employ it. Their preaching is therefore usually conspicuous in the use of general categories such as humanity, stewardship, responsibility, opportunity, and society today. Apparently these are offered in the safe confidence that they are broad enough not to miss any listener. The truth is, they miss most listeners. On the other hand, some ministers discover in themselves a skill, a flair for description, and in their sermons technique outruns substance. At times in the history of preaching elaborate descriptions have been popular, as was the case in America in the 1950s. Preachers of national renown lingered long over the banquet table of Belshazzar's feast, the straw in Bethlehem's manger, the donkey Jesus rode into Jerusalem, and the timbers for the old rugged cross. In retrospect, those grand, imaginative flights were, for the hungry and thirsty, similar to carrying water in a basket; it feels good passing through but one arrives home with nothing.

Again, the rule is, make description servant and not master of the message. Just as a toss pillow can bring out the color in carpet and drapery but not call attention to itself, so should description function in the sermon. One should also strive for balance of two kinds. One kind of balance has to do with the objects of description. In the course of one's preaching over a period of time, characters, actions, and settings should all receive attention. Such balance not only prevents development of a homiletical hobby, but all three ingredients are vital to lively and realistic communication. The other kind of balance has to do with two types of description: that which seeks to be an accurate representation, as with a photograph, and that which seeks to give an impression, as with a portrait. Which type to use will be dictated by one's message and purpose in each case, but both are appropriate to preaching as long as one does not deceive by offering portraits as photographs. If the preacher wishes to examine excellent models of description of different objects and of different types, he or she will find the novels of Thomas Hardy and James Agee's *A Death in the Family* and *Let Us Now Praise Famous Men* most helpful.

When preparing a description, it is important that one use an economy of words, adjectives appearing only when necessary. The reasons are three.

First, such descriptions correspond to reality. Overdrawn images are artificial in that they presume to see and hear more than can be seen and heard at any one time. No one experiences *all* of anything, whether it be tasting food, hearing an orchestra, or looking at a vase, so why describe so completely?

Second, a sketch of a few details is more evocative for the listener who will then complete the image than is a thorough description which overwhelms the listener who, because of the speaker's working overtime, is left unemployed.

And finally, unnecessary adjectives tend not to add to the image but rather to tell the listener how to respond. To say that a rose is "absolutely gorgeous, breathtakingly beautiful and unsurpassed" reveals nothing of color or size or scent but tells the listener how to regard the rose. It is better to describe it simply, and then perhaps the listener will say, "What a lovely rose." Most of us have countless ways to be imperialistic in our speaking, building into our sermons subtle instructions to those who hear us.

Ministers who say, "I'm not good at description," should not believe their words until it has been demonstrated over a period of time that they are, in fact, telling the truth. In order to know if anyone is "any good at it," three things are required. First, test one's sensitivity to the sights and sounds of the world around. Are persons and the flora and fauna of the neighborhood actually seen and heard? Could a stranger be directed to a certain address by description alone, using no numbers or street names? Expression begins with impression, and it may be that the problem lies not in lacking "a way with words" but in the inability to describe what has not been seen or heard. Second, practice orally and in written sketches descriptions that are unrelated to a particular sermon. Describe the huge and the minute, the loud and the quiet, the familiar and the strange, the comical and the tragic. If one's intent is serious, improvement is inevitable. Third, take the chance and risk description in a sermon. It takes courage, of course, just as it does to tell a joke, but if one has a message which is important and about which one has strong conviction, the energy from that will carry one through the effort at description. And if there is some disappointment at first, the freedom provided by confidence in the rightness of what one is doing in the ministry will encourage laughter and that shrug of the shoulders which does not say, "Who cares?" but, "Oh, well, maybe next time."

Illustration

In the proper sense of the term, an illustration refers to that which illumines or clarifies what has been said another way. Recall, for example, the pictures along with the text in public school books. The presence of an illustration assumes that for some, at least, the text alone may not be clear. However, a sermon may not need illustrations. If it possessed unity of thought, movement toward its goal, and language lively and imaginative, parishioners may speak of the sermon's illustrations when, in fact, there were none. The whole sermon was illumined and clear. Just as some very humorous people seldom if ever tell jokes, just as good storytellers do not have to tell stories all the time, so the preacher who leads the listeners down interesting and well-lighted streets does not have to load the sermons with illustrations.

Actually, in good preaching what is referred to as illustrations are, in fact, stories or anecdotes which do not illustrate the point; rather they *are* the point. In other words, a story may carry in its bosom the whole message rather than the illumination of a message which had already been related in another but less clear way. Removing the story is not just cutting the pictures from a history book, leaving only the text; it is removing the entire page. The story is the picture which is the text. Consider two examples. Nathan did not preach a sermon to David about taking something from another and then illustrate it with the story of a rich man taking a poor man's sheep. The story *was* his sermon. Jesus did not discuss the relation of forgiveness to righteousness and then illustrate his point with the parable of the loving father who had two sons. That parable *was* his sermon, that parable was his statement on righteousness and forgiveness. Those listeners who habitually think of stories or anecdotes as illustrative of something, and therefore expect discussion either to precede or to follow such material often find themselves left alone with their thoughts and decisions. The story is it.

It is frequently the case, however, that a preacher presents a matter of such complexity that some or all of its parts need the clarification that an illustration offers. "For instance?" is a question properly asked by the minister when preparing any sermon. The answer is best supplied not from books of sermon illustrations available in the bulk and wholesale, but by observation and experience, or by creating an analogy to fit the purpose. The guidelines for illustrating are simple but important. First, locate or create the familiar to introduce the unfamiliar. Second, the point of analogy between the thought and the illustration of the thought should be clear. Unlike stories such as parables that carry the freight of the sermon, illustrative material is to be single-minded and without distracting complexities. Multidimensional narratives tend to do many things other than what they are asked to do. Rather than working for the issue at hand they tend to create other issues and send listeners off in other pursuits. Third, illustrations, although they are rather simple, are not to be small and silly. Like all material in the sermon, they are to be worthy of their calling. Little "salt shaker and light bulb" oversimplifications do not illustrate an important point; they reduce it to insignificance. Fourth, illustrations are not to be exhorted or pushed upon the hearer in compelling tones. In fact, one of the benefits of such material is that it relaxes the speaker and hence, the listener. No doubt one reason illustrations are remembered after other parts of the sermon are forgotten is that they are presented conversationally, listener defenses are dropped, and genuine attention occurs. Probably nothing invites cartooning the preacher more than an intense, high-volumed telling of what was supposed to be an illustrative story. "Halloween night in the small town of my youth was a child's delight" is hardly the kind of sentence to be pressed on anyone; it should invite hearers to remember and enjoy. Fifth, once told, an illustration should be left alone; if it served its purpose, good, but if not, it cannot be repaired and redeemed. Since it is an illuminator, it needs no explanation; since it is not the point but is servant to the point, it needs no application. Like a joke, it lives or dies by its own merits. Sixth, and finally, illustrations, just like descriptions, are to be trusted and therefore presented without apology and without verbal scaffolding. The three most common of these violations are: "I have an illustration of this point" (translation: "do not take this seriously, it is only an illustration"); "we see" or "we find" (translation: "I am instructing you to see or find what I see or find"); "The story is often told" (translation: "I want you to know that I know that this is a tired and worn-out story").

A further word about stories in sermons, whether or not they function illustratively, is appropriate here as well as in the subsequent discussion of delivery. Stories are, on the whole, more emotionally charged than the sermon materials which constitute discussion, explanation, and description. By emotion we are referring to the full range from laughter and joy to grief and sorrow. The preacher has to be aware of the nature and amount of the emotional load of a story, for the sake of both the speaker and the listener. From the preacher's perspective, a judgment has to be made as to whether the emotion can be sustained through the telling. No one wants to get halfway into a narrative and be overcome by it. We have different capacities for emotional restraint and we must know ourselves. It would be better to decide against the use of an excellent story than to be overwhelmed by it. We will speak further about this matter in the next chapter. From the perspective of the listener, the emotional force of the material is welcomed, in fact desired, as long as there is no suspicion of an attempt to manipulate. This means that the emotion of the preacher must be experienced as restrained and that the story must be properly timed within the sermon. For example, material that dredges up deep feelings early in a sermon is awkward and ineffective, if not offensive. The relationship of trust and comfort between preacher and listeners must first be established and an appropriate context built in which to place such material. Otherwise, there is the general sense that matters usually reserved for talk among family and friends is being disrespectfully tossed out among strangers.

Consideration of materials having descriptive and illustrative functions in the sermon usually raises four questions which need to be addressed here.

1. In speaking how does one handle those materials which in writing would be footnoted? First of all, the basic principle is the same for speaking or writing: *Thou shalt not steal.* Listeners are to be made aware that what has been contributed by another (quotations, stories, and ideas peculiarly the property of one person) is not original with the preacher. In observance of that principle, three practical suggestions might be helpful. First, keep quotations to a minimum. Regardless of how a passage may impress the preacher, listeners are not usually as involved emotionally or intellectually with the words of another being read to them as they are with the minister's own words. Second, if the weight of the borrowed material really depends on the fame and authority of its author, then introduce it with the name and full credentials of the source.

Beware, however, of name dropping. Third, if the force of the material is in its content—and this is much preferred—then it is enough simply to tag it as another's. For example, "as one well-known historian has said," or, "as the historian Toynbee has said." Anyone wishing more details about the particular source can ask for it later.

2. Can ministers use in sermons events or conversations from their pastoral work? The temptation to do so is often strong since the appropriateness of such material will be very evident. However, private is private and confidence is confidence. No one will speak in confidence to a minister if there is a chance the conversation will make next Sunday's sermon. In fact, parishioners will be cautious if the preacher shares confidences from a previous parish since they know they will appear in sermons in the next parish. There are, however, events that occur in the church and the community that are not private and confidential, events that really belong to everyone. If there is no chance of pain or embarrassment, then these may shared. When in doubt, however, refrain. It will be the case, however, that preaching, which is concrete and particular rather than abstract and general, will often create in listeners the sense that "the minister is talking to me." Good; relevance is preferable to irrevelance. If someone says following a sermon that the message seemed to fit personally, the minister will have to resist the temptation to back away and apologize.

3. Is it ethical to create stories for a sermon? Yes; the parables of Jesus are created stories. Someone might have asked Jesus after his telling a parable, "Did that really happen?" but probably not, since such stories were familiar in that culture. In our culture, facticity has become of such concern that asking, "Did it happen or not?" is the only way some minds seem to function. However, in any culture, the ethical question is a proper one, and can best be handled by putting into a created story a signal to the listener that such is the nature of it. This is not to be a wide-screen, technicolor signal which pulls the teeth of the story: "What I am about to say is all made up, it did not happen, it is not factually true, but I imagined it in order to make a point." Rather, let the clue be less distracting, more on the order of those Jesus used. "There was a certain man" or, "Once upon a time," should be enough. An alternative method is to place within

the story an impossibility that will immediately tag the account as fiction but will not rob the story of its punch. "During a flight from St. Louis to Seattle, the passenger beside me became ill and went outside for a few minutes of fresh air." But be prepared, even after that, for the non-listener to ask, "That didn't really happen, did it?"

4. Are stories of self-disclosure appropriate in preaching? On this matter the practice of preachers and the advice of homileticians vary widely. Of course, through voice, face, gestures, and countless other ways the person of the preacher is revealed. However, with reference to intentional use of self-disclosure, textbooks and practice mention none, some, and too much. Self-disclosure does not mean those stories from a preacher's own observation or experience which do not really say anything about him or her. An account which begins, "When I was about ten years old, a man confined to a wheelchair moved next door," may focus entirely on the neighbor and make no further reference to the speaker.

Self-disclosure has a long and honorable history in the Scriptures. Accounts of being called of God were used by Jeremiah, Amos, Isaiah, and Paul to establish credentials for ministry where there was the lack of a strong supportive community. At least Hosea and Paul used their own experiences to proclaim the power and grace of God. And Paul, who insisted that "what we preach is not ourselves, but Jesus Christ as Lord" (II Cor. 4:5), did say to a church beset with conflicting messages and models of ministry, "Brethren, join in imitating me, and mark those who so live as you have an example in us" (Phil. 3:17). We can be reasonably guided by such cases of self-disclosure in the Bible without regarding them as a blanket endorsement of any and all references to oneself.

There are certainly times and situations in which the issues at stake call for putting oneself personally into the sermon ("as for me and my house"). There are also appropriate ways to concretize and personalize a matter by means of self-disclosure. In addition, the parishioners have a right to know that they and the minister belong to the same human family and faith family. However, the point of too much has been reached when the pulpit is turned into a confessional, when the preacher's experience is offered as normative, or when self-disclosure is a plea for sympathy or acceptance. Often efforts to prove how human one is, in fact, tend to

208

make being human an excuse rather than a reflection of the image of God.

On the conviction that self-disclosure in moderation is appropriate to preaching, these few guidelines may be helpful. In self-references, the straightforward "I" is preferred over the editorial and presumably self-effacing "we." The first person singular is not necessarily egotistical, any more than the first person plural is necessarily humble. It is important to avoid being trapped in poetic conceit; that is, attending more to how one feels about an event than to the event itself. John Milton aborted a poem on the crucifixion because he could not get past his own sorrow and tears to the account of Jesus' death. Knowing when to move the camera off oneself to the larger subject is vital. The "Magnificat" (Luke 1:46-55) is an excellent example of healthy self-disclosure. Opening with a few references to God's favor upon her life, Mary then moves from her own experience to the praise of the God of all persons and all generations. And finally, in selecting from one's life that which may be told from the pulpit, the choices should represent events or relationships with which the listeners can identify. If the preacher's experiences are always unusual and unique, set in exotic places with a remarkable cast of characters and ending in a surprising turn of events, the parishioners are merely audience, being or not being entertained, believing or not believing the accounts. If, however, the stories are within the present or remembered experiences of the listeners, the parishioners are a congregation, unconsciously changing the names and places in the story and claiming it as their own.

Delivering the Sermon

Perhaps it is a contradiction to *talk* about *assumptions;* after all, assumptions are to be assumed and discussing them tends to remove them from that category. However, some assumptions are of such importance that understanding is best served by stating them briefly before proceeding with the matter at hand. In that confidence, three preliminary comments are offered.

1. It is assumed that the slightest indication of a problem with the speech mechanism (vocal folds, lungs, larynx, nose, tongue, teeth) has already sent the preacher to the professionals at a speech and hearing clinic. Most seminaries have no one trained to detect, much less deal with, the physical complexities of public speaking.

2. It is assumed that the preacher has some routine of speech exercises. Going to the sanctuary early on Sunday to practice the sermon is not sufficient. Concert pianists continue to run the scales; tennis professionals who have already won the Wimbledon still take lessons. Can anyone think of a reason why a preacher should not work regularly with breathing, volume, tone, enunciation, and pronunciation, with all types of materials? A speech teacher, or for that matter, a speech textbook, will provide all that a person needs, except, of course, the motivation.

3. It is assumed that the Scripture texts have been read aloud. For all the noises ministers make about the centrality of the Bible in the church, the public reading of Scripture in many places does not support that conviction.

Let us turn now to the particular sermon soon to be delivered. What will be the listener's experience of this sermon? Or more precisely, what will be the listener's experience of this sermon delivered by this preacher on this occasion? Anticipate it for a few minutes. Think of this particular preaching event on the analogy of musical instruments: Is this one a violin, a drum, a trumpet, a flute, or a pipe organ? Or use the analogy of motion: Is this one a stroll, a race, a brisk walk, a parade, a march, or a dance? Or use the analogy of light: Is this one a candle, a flash, a neon, a reading lamp, a sunrise, or high noon? Sunday morning is fast approaching and a number of factors contributing to the nature of the listener's experience need attention.

Pre-delivery Considerations

There are at least four factors that bear significantly on the sermon and should receive attention prior to the preaching event.

1. *The place.* The preacher will be projecting a message into a certain kind of room with certain pieces of furniture. If that room is not a familiar one, it is most important to enter it before the sermon to get a sense of its size, atmosphere, and acoustics. The pulpit needs to be checked for height, ease of entrance, and relation to lectern and choir. Attention to such matters now removes later anxieties and the dissipation of energies more properly focused on the sermon itself. Even the pastor who is at home in this sanctuary and pulpit can well take a few moments in advance to be assured that all is in readiness. Preaching is too important to be carried out while doing battle with furniture and public address systems. For example, poor acoustics and room noise make impossible a nuanced sermon with pauses and voice variations. Under such conditions, the message has to be pushed with the steady force of a public announcement. Church committees which see to it that our gathering places are servants and witnesses of the Word render invaluable service.

2. *The liturgy.* The sermon is not the only event scheduled for Sunday; it will be set within a service of worship which in its entirety is an act of praise to God. The one who preaches may or may not also be the worship leader, but in either case, preparation for preaching

includes preparation for the whole act of worship. Therefore, sitting alone with the order of service for a while the evening before will be a very important time for the preacher. Moving quietly and prayerfully through the liturgy in this way is not practice or rehearsal; it is worship.

3. *Materials taken into the pulpit.* If attention to this seems small and insignificant, recall a time of being distracted to the point of disgust by a minister ensnared in a tangle of wires, trying to open a Bible without knocking to the floor a hymnal precariously balanced on a narrow ledge, while sermon notes slide off the steep incline of the pulpit. Some ministers are capable of giving the impression that they were informed only five minutes ago that it was Sunday. All one needs to do is decide what will be needed in the pulpit, place those materials together on the study desk, and be sure they are manageable. If the sermon contains quotations from books, typing the useful lines on cards or paper and leaving the books behind will be appreciated by all. This does not, however, apply to references from the Scriptures. The Bible is more than words on pages; it is a symbol of authority and inspiration. Passages of Scripture read from cards, even when accurately quoted, make an entirely different impression on the listener. (If anyone objects to honoring symbolism in favor of "the pure truth," try exchanging roller skates instead of rings at a wedding ceremony.) When ministers are reading the Bible it should be clear they are reading the Bible. Even if he or she can quote the sermon text in its entirety, reading it is preferred. Reading joins the text to the Bible, the very same source that every parishioner can read in the pew and at home; quoting joins the text to the preacher and subtly relocates the center of authority for the message.

4. *The preacher.* The message and the messenger are experienced together by the listeners. It goes without saying, therefore, that the person of the preacher can be an asset or a liability, even a contradiction, to the preaching event. Therefore, the person as well as the sermon is prepared. Mentally, the minister is prepared by knowing what is to be said and believing it to be important. Spiritually, the minister is prepared by the study and reflection that has gone into the sermon and by the prayer in which it has been bathed. The prayer is not simply that "I preach well" but that God

be sought and praised, that the Word come through the words, and that the parishioners receive that Word. The minister receives additional spiritual strength through listening to the sermon to be delivered. This is not to say the minister is being offered as a model of the message, but the minister certainly hears, embraces, and responds to the message. Being the voice of the sermon should not close the ears to the sermon. Emotionally, the minister is prepared by carving out some time to get distance and perspective on a vocation that is emotionally demanding. It is possible to be so involved in the emotional highs and lows of others that one is consumed, eventually drained of the capacity to laugh or cry anymore. One's own sails hang limp, and there is not even a breeze. The condition does not call for a sense of guilt but for a small retreat. At least Saturday afternoon and evening can be reserved to refresh oneself. Not absolutely reserved, of course; there is no parish rule that says crises will not occur on Saturday. Generally, however, that time can be claimed by the minister. Each person has to decide how best to spend the hours prior to Sunday. For example, recreation can be refreshing to some but not to others; being with friends for social occasions restores some but not others. Ministers must understand themselves and behave accordingly. If attending parties or sports events are times of such intense engagement that one is emotionally overextended, then perhaps Saturday evenings are best spent in quieter ways in preparation for Sunday's demands, expected and unexpected.

All these forms of preparation are tied, however, to physical condition. Very few ministers have a theologically or philosophically negative view of the human body, but many of them give the impression that they do. Not in practices of self-flagellation, of course, but by neglect. What is needed is not a fanatic plunge into some food or exercise fad, but a common sense appropriate to the understanding of the nature of the minister's life and routine. Poor physical condition directly affects both study and delivery, and while a state of continual weariness may evoke a sympathetic "poor preacher" here and there, generally the condition comes across as lack of preparation, lack of interest, or lack of conviction about the subject. Illnesses and occasions of unusual physical demands take their toll now and then, to be sure, but within the limits of one's general state of health, physical vigor is a proper condition for preaching. The body is the preacher's instrument for the proclamation of the gospel, not for display but for use. The violin left outside exposed to sun and rain, tossed carelessly in the corner, and used for storing contraband candy bars does not belong to a serious musician.

The Delivery Itself

Perhaps the most common concern among preachers relative to delivery has to do with what aids they take into the pulpit: manuscript, notes, or nothing. This is an appropriate concern but often it is wrongly approached and its importance exaggerated. Four suggestions on this subject may help confirm the experienced and guide the anticipations of the inexperienced.

1. Some writing is appropriate to every stage of sermon preparation but the writing has a different function at each stage. In the study to arrive at a message, properly there are many notes from research and reflection. These notes have an immediate yield in the message theme and a later yield in the sermon itself since there will be many thoughts and ideas directly transferable to the sermon. If these notes are preserved in a folder for a later time when this text, these readings from the lectionary, this subject will arise again, the minister will already have a start on the new occasion. As a rule one never uses all the fruit of research in the one sermon. In the next stage of processing the message into a sermon, writing assists in ordering ideas and determining as needed the exact phrasing to be used. At this point anticipated oralizing guides the nature and function of the writing done. In the final stage, the delivery, writing has an entirely different function. Up to this point, writing tended to hold and preserve the results of the germinating process; now whatever is written and taken into the pulpit is not result but cause, a releasing not a holding, a launching not a preserving. Whatever was written at stage two may be taken into the pulpit, but not necessarily. A manuscript may have served its purpose and can now be laid aside. Sermon notes for the pulpit may be a modification of the notes or manuscript at stage two. Some ministers lay aside all written materials and preach without notes. Many who preach in this way

speak of sitting alone with a note pad prior to the service, and as the sermon is spoken through in the mind, they make sketchy notes as a way of aiding the memory, notes that are then thrown away. If notes or manuscript are taken into the pulpit, they should be in a *form for an oral occasion.* This means in a form that facilitates ease of handling and ease of location at a glance and generally offers the least interference in the speaker-hearer relationship. Different sizes of type, different spacings and indentation, and color coding are all helpful servants of the process. The sole criterion is not what another may think of this material but what aids most effectively in the free, unhindered release of the message.

2. Making value judgments about the use or nonuse of manuscripts and notes can be more harmful than helpful. Consider, for example, the popular ranking of manuscript preaching at the bottom and preaching without notes at the top. With this diagram in mind, those who do use manuscripts, temporarily or regularly, tend to do so ineffectively and even apologetically, as if to say, "Please excuse my not being able to remember my sermon." In addition, excessive appetite for preaching without notes can cause a sacrifice of content in favor of the accolade. Rather than thinking in terms of better or worse in this matter, the preacher would do well to work at designing the most effective method for liberating self and listener.

3. It is wise not to be trapped into the invariable use of the same method for every sermon and on every occasion. Variety in the use and nonuse of a manuscript could, in and of itself, prove valuable in getting and sustaining interest. However, the greater truth is that the different methods may have their own appropriateness according to the occasion, purpose, and subject matter. It would be lamentable if a preacher, shifting on occasion from manuscript to few if any notes, were to be perceived by the parishioners as apparently having nothing prepared for the day. Equally lamentable would be the apology or explanation from a preacher who chose for clear reasons to move for this sermon to a manuscript. In this as in other matters, the minister should make decisions, not fall into stereotypes. For example, there are occasions and purposes best served by speaking without notes or manuscript, and the effectiveness of such a method could be increased if it were not always the habit of the preacher to do so. Likewise, the preacher usually associated with extemporane-

ous speaking might decide to come into the pulpit with a manuscript folder which would be opened in view of all and read with no attempt to pretend otherwise. Why do so? For surprise value? Hardly; the price of pulpit surprises is usually too high. Perhaps the subject is of such a complex or delicate nature that precision of expression takes precedence over freedom of expression. Or, perhaps in an emotional situation both speaker and listener need the distance which reading provides. After all, there is a time and place for a script and for reading; the message is on its own without the felt presence of either the listener or the speaker.

Of course, every method has its defenders and its detractors, and, in fact, every method pays a price for its advantages. Those who prefer the freedom and relationships available to the preacher without notes will not usually rate as high on careful phrasing and wealth of content. Those who prefer the tightly woven fabric of a manuscript must—a few extremely skilled are here excepted— accept the fact that a manuscript is less personal and its use less evocative of intense listener engagement.

4. In the final analysis, adequacy of preparation is not consistently evidenced by how much paper, if any, one carries into the pulpit. Rather, readiness to preach is demonstrated by certainty of theme and purpose and clear movement toward one's goal with serious delight. The listeners desire a sense that the message is important for them and for the preacher but not an impression from the pulpit of a super seriousness which is messianic in its manner and judgmental in its demands. The minister thoroughly prepared is free to preach with grace.

The preacher enters the pulpit undergirded by several funda- mental convictions about the experience of that moment. First and foremost is the belief that this message will make a difference. The effects may not be what the preacher defined as the purpose of the sermon, they may not be apparent or measurable, and they may not be immediate. Measuring the effectiveness of preaching has always been an uncertain, often discouraging, perhaps even useless business. Weary and discouraged ministers tend to pay excessive attention to the seeds that fall on the path, on rocky soil, and among the thorns, forgetting the promise of thirty, sixty, and one hundredfold yields. Unless the minister believes the Word will not return empty, the demons of self-pity, despair, and cynicism take over the pulpit and shout above the droning of the heartless sermon. A second conviction is that the listeners are *for* and not against the preacher. Once a minister becomes suspicious of the love and trust of the parishioners, a negative interpretation of every facial expression, every whisper, every motion appears. In such a frame of mind a preacher looks out upon frowns of disapproval not intense listeners, upon critical mumbling not soft amens, upon mutinous huddles not groups planning for the minister's fifth anniversary. When a person leaves the sanctuary during the sermon of one minister, it is assumed that he or she had to catch a plane or was suddenly ill. When a person leaves the sanctuary during the sermon of another minister, it is assumed the person is upset at something said, is angry, stomping out never to return. Those two scenes, worlds apart, are both creations of the preacher's attitude toward the listeners.

This line of thought leads us to a third conviction with which the preacher enters the pulpit: the sermon will neither be destroyed by nor dependent on uncertain variables in the service. Of course, there are extreme exceptions (earthquake, flood, a shotgun blast through a window) but ordinarily a well-prepared minister can be sensitive to, perhaps even pause to acknowledge, surprises and distractions without being victimized by them. Sooner or later, every minister has to deal with the stray dog, the sparrow on the chandelier, the rebellious organ, noisy teenagers in the balcony, and police radio interference in the public address system. Perhaps a greater difficulty lies with those preachers who *depend* on variables for launching the sermon. For some, there is dependence to the point of captivity to one's own feelings, as though the power of the gospel waited on the preacher's own visceral authentication of the message. It is a bonus, of course, to have all one's faculties of body, mind, and emotion saying amen during a sermon, but there are headaches, problems of digestion, disturbing phone calls, and sometimes domestic turmoil in the minister's own family. These are inescapable realities, and so the preacher needs always to remember that what is taking place during the sermon is vastly more important than how the preacher happens to feel that day.

For other ministers, there is an excessive dependence on the variables which the listeners provide. One preacher launches the sermon with informal and friendly chatter, but today, no response. Another warms up the listeners with a joke or two, but today, no laughter. Another has a favorite target group near the front; today they are absent. And yet another depends on organ music or the rheostat on the house lights to provide the right atmosphere, but today there is a substitute organist and the person controlling the lights is in a playful mood. Of course, all of us depend to some extent on the gifts of the occasions, but excessive dependence can turn preaching into a miserable chore.

It is important, therefore, to know exactly how one will begin and end the sermon. A clearly determined beginning liberates the preacher to respond or not to respond to unexpected events in the worship service. If it seems called for, a few opening remarks can clear the way for the sermon to begin as planned. If one is a guest in the pulpit, a few brief and carefully phrased remarks will not only take care of social amenities but will give a sense of the congregation and of the acoustics. These remarks are not, however, a substitute for the planned beginning of the sermon. And knowing exactly how the sermon will end has, in addition to achieving its own purpose, two other benefits. It gives confidence to the preacher throughout the sermon to have the end, the goal, clearly in view. Uncertain endings tend to infect the entire message with the tone of uncertainty. The second benefit is that the conclusion of the sermon is not sacrificed to that which follows in the service of worship. Whether a particular sermon is to be followed by an affirmation of faith, prayer, hymn, or invitation to discipleship, it should not be blurred into the other. The sermon, in order to have its own integrity, must have its own proper ending. Then, following silence, organ music, or transfer of leadership to a presider, the service continues.

As for the sermon itself, the most consistently effective delivery is by reexperiencing the message as it is being spoken. All who preach in this way acknowledge that the price paid for its power is the physical and emotional toll it takes. This not only means feeling drained afterward, but it also means that the transition to greeting worshipers at the door or to a coffee-conversation time is not easily made. The body moves out of the pulpit well in advance of the psyche. Family and parishioners usually understand and respect the need for a little recovery time.

If one has prepared for oral communication, this method of "unrolling" the message as it is delivered will seem quite natural. There is no unusual burden placed on the memory. On the contrary, the memory functions with uncanny ability even though there has been no memorizing at all. The experience is analogous to the easy recall of words to a song when the music is played, but the inability to remember a single stanza without the music. It is as though the memory rode along on the rhythm and melody of the song. Preaching in the fashion here described is getting in tune with the message. When that is achieved, the memory is no problem, and when someone asks, "How did you memorize all that?" the answer is, "I didn't." Storytellers can in this way tell a story exactly the same way scores of times without ever memorizing it. Some black preachers have tunes to their sermons and once "in tune," can preach ten-year-old sermons, never written down, with almost no variation. Congregations come to know these tunes and enter as full participants in the preaching event.

Those who have never preached this way, at least not an entire sermon, have probably communicated at some time by reexperiencing a message, and therefore understand some of the positive qualities. By trusting the message completely, the preacher is carried by the sermon, or, to put it another way, the sermon preaches itself through the minister. Entering into the message, one's gestures are congenial to content and are timed naturally. By reexperiencing the material, emotions appropriate to that material are genuine, not manufactured for purpose of persuasion or manipulation. Nor will the emotions be displayed, causing listeners to recoil, and being neither overstated nor understated by contrivance, they will be trusted by the hearers who can now give themselves fully to the message. And humor will be humor; not jokes, at best a risky business and at worst a violation of the sermon. Humor, properly joined to the matter of the sermon, feels at home and is thus free to frolic, laugh, and celebrate the grace of God. Humor is, after all, inevitable in truly good preaching because all the right ingredients are present: concrete and specific references, no one laughs at the general and abstract; concern for the significant

219

and sacred, why else are things funnier in classrooms and sanctuaries, at weddings and funerals; and a sense of freedom, only God is God, liberating us from postures and pretenses. Humor is, then, a genuine response to grace; grace works in us that most beautiful virtue, gratitude; and the grateful person acknowledges that there is usually a small party going on in the back of the mind. All this, of course, makes no sense to the humorless calculator who carefully inserts a joke here and there to break up the monotony of a sermon which, in its intense effort to be totally serious, generates smiles and muffled laughter.

A final positive quality of preaching by reexperiencing the message during delivery has to do with eye contact. Speech textbooks which enjoin eye contact are right in that looking at the people is better than looking at the ceiling or at one's shoelaces. However, eye contact which is indiscriminate is not only discourteous; it robs proper eye contact of its power. Reading calls for no eye contact. Furtive glances up from the sacred text every three seconds as though looking at the page were a breach of contract is unnatural. The mixture of reading and non-reading in lectures and in some preaching has some eye contact which is natural and personal. However, the preacher with only sketchy notes or no notes at all has the opportunity for total eye contact, but may feel total eye contact is too close to staring. Reexperiencing one's material during delivery offers immense help in this matter. The various textures and moods of the message will move the eyes naturally, unless one has already learned poor habits. For example, direct questions turn the eyes upon those being questioned; perplexity, doubt, searching, and frustration move the eyes quickly around the room; stories soften the eyes as they look at nothing while seeming to look out the window, at the floor, above the back wall; and admonition is eye to eye. The preacher's eyes can effectively serve the voice, underscore the Word, and enlist the hearers in various kinds of participation, but only the message itself is qualified to instruct the eyes as to their proper functions—what, when, and where.

The final word about delivery has to be "passion." It is difficult to believe that the message of the gospel, given by the Scriptures and for this occasion germinated in the compost of study, imagination, and prayer, could be preached as though nothing were at stake. When that seems to be the case, it could be just that: *seeming* to be a lack of passion. The fact is, some preachers have, for various reasons, rejected all demonstrations of passion. For some, the desire is to permit the sermon to have the autonomy of a work of art. Just as a painting in a gallery influences viewers even though the artist is unknown or absent, perhaps dead, so should the sermon do its own work without the burning of energy by the preacher. It is a pleasant thought to entertain: the gospel getting its deserved attention and making its own way in the world. Others regard passion as a kind of biological lag in the human race, a trait that will disappear when the species matures, but which, in the meantime, still remains in those frustrated by a lack of capacity. For such persons, high intensity serves as a substitute for the calm achievements of the skilled. Yet others have, through choice and training, adopted a counselor's mode for all acts of ministry, sensitive listening but cautious about attempting changes in society and persons. And in recent years, there is among ministers a widespread reaction against demagoguery, the rape of mind and emotions, the control of lives in the name of religion. Understandably, the passionate speech is suspect, especially if the passionate are fired by strong dislikes, antagonisms, and hatred. There are healthy signs, however, that hearers are developing skills to listen beyond the noise and discern that vigorous expressions of great convictions are not always accompanied by the convictions themselves. It is sometimes the case that a vehement embrace of one position and a sweeping intolerance of all others announce to the listeners the vastness of the speaker's own emptiness.

It seems only fair, then, to say that what appears as a lack of passion in a preacher may actually be a method of delivery deemed less fraught with dangers than the preachments of the passionate. On the other hand, it is also fair to point out the practical danger of a listless style. When preaching starves the sensibilities of listeners, driving underground their emotional life, they may be set up as easier prey for the vigorous propagandist. People cannot live by ideas alone; the whole being has to register the value of those ideas. We call this passion. A steady diet of evenly and objectively offered ideas can set listeners wishing for the once rejected enthusiast.

Those who stood on sticky cafe tables and volleyed against the cherished institutions of the sixties now seem more attractive than cold administrators of ideas who carefully grant equal time to pro and con.

All of this is not to call for fiery styles or a return to the ways of frantic evangelists. It is simply to say that there is a passion appropriate to the significance and urgency of the gospel, and there is no valid reason to conceal that passion. Restraint, yes; but to allow reaction to caricatured and exaggerated passion to determine our method is to permit the very thing to be avoided to be the primary shaper of preaching in our time. There is no thought here of manufacturing passion so that by a kind of imitative magic our listeners may catch it. There is no blindness here to the fact that one sometimes enters the pulpit with no heart aflutter, no pulse racing, no burning in the bones. But passion, even then, need not be absent. The fact is, the act of preaching is itself integral to our fuller embrace of the very message we speak. It is in teaching that we learn, and it is in telling the Good News that we hear and accept it ever anew. All of us know that it is in being kind that we become kind, in behaving as Christians that we become Christian. Is it unreasonable to believe, then, that it is in listening to our own sermons that we become more passionately convinced? If this is our conviction, then reexperiencing the message as we deliver it cannot fail to be a time of speaking from passion to passion.

And who can conceive of any greater motivation for preaching our very best than this: there is at least one person in the sanctuary listening, one person who, because of this sermon, may have a clearer vision, a brighter hope, a deeper faith, a fuller love. That person is the preacher.

Suggested Resources for the Preacher

The following suggestions have two preachers in mind: the one who is not near a good library and is concerned about the unavailability of resources, and the one who has access to resources but is overwhelmed by the quantity of them.

The task of preaching. To keep oneself fresh in the ministry of the pulpit and appreciative of its importance, there is hardly a better resource than R. E. C. Browne, *The Ministry of the Word* which continues to be reprinted (Philadelphia: Fortress Press, 1976). It bears rereading every three to four years.

Biblical study. Commentaries are so numerous, so expensive, and so uneven in quality, the preacher needs a second opinion before purchase. For the Old Testament, and on the assumption it will be updated, Brevard Childs' *Old Testament Books for Pastor and Teacher* (Philadelphia: Westminster Press, 1977) is of immense help. In 1984 the same publisher provided *New Testament Books for Pastor and Teacher* by Ralph Martin.

Interpreting Scripture for preaching. To help with the process of moving from text to sermon, the recent series entitled Interpreting Biblical Texts (Nashville: Abingdon Press, 1981-84) offers methods and examples in both Testaments. In 1982, John Knox Press (Atlanta) began publishing a new commentary for teaching and preaching entitled *Interpretation*. At this writing, the volumes on Genesis, Galatians, Mark, Romans, and Philippians were already available. Two excellent books for helping one think through the handling of Old Testament texts are: Elizabeth Achtemeier, *The Old Testament and the Proclamation of the Gospel* (Philadelphia: Westminster Press, 1973), and Donald Gowan, *Reclaiming the Old Testament for the Christian Pulpit* (Atlanta: John Knox Press, 1980).

History of preaching. For a rapid survey, one can trust Yngve Brilioth, *A Brief History of Preaching* (Philadelphia: Fortress Press, 1965) even though the appendix is specialized and not helpful to most. For actual sermons from ancient to modern times, there is Clyde Fant and William Pinson, *Twenty Centuries of Great Preaching,* 13 vols. (Waco, Tex.: Word, 1971).

Theology of preaching. Two small but very helpful volumes are: Richard Lischer, *A Theology of Preaching* (Nashville: Abingdon Press, 1981), and Karl Rahner, ed., *The Renewal of Preaching,* Vol. 23 Concilium (Ramsey, N.J.: Paulist Press, 1968).

Preaching and worship. To begin one's reading in this area along with suggestions for further study, William Skudlarek's *The Word in Worship* (Nashville: Abingdon Press, 1981) is worth exploring. For those following the lectionary or considering doing so, Fortress Press (Philadelphia) continues to publish the widely used series, Proclamation: Aids for Interpreting the Lessons of the Church Year. More recently, Abingdon Press (Nashville) began offering *Preaching the New Common Lectionary,* which will cover the three years of the lectionary in three volumes per year.

Preaching and pastoral care. In this area, many ministers have responded favorably to David Switzer, *Pastor, Preacher, Person: Developing a Pastoral Ministry in Depth* (Nashville: Abingdon Press, 1979), and Gary Stratman, *Pastoral Preaching* (Nashville: Abingdon Press, 1983).

Journals for keeping current. In addition to denominational and ecumenical news journals, two others are well worth the subscription cost. One is *Interpretation, A Journal of Bible and Theology* (Richmond: Union Theological Seminary), a quarterly which joins Bible, theology, and preaching in its major offerings in addition to excellent book reviews. The other, *Homiletic,* is published semiannually and reviews new books and articles related to preaching. This is a most helpful aid and is quite inexpensive. It is available from 3510 Woodley Road, N.W., Washington, D.C. 20016.

As a final suggestion, write to the offices of continuing education at several seminaries asking to be put on their mailing lists. Seminars and workshops on preaching are in abundance and occur throughout the year.